ALLIANCE GUIDE

TO

ANTIQUE & CRAFT MALLS

A TRAVELER'S COMPANION

JIM GOODRIDGE

ALLIANCE PUBLISHING, INC.

ISBN 1-887110-13-5

Design by Cynthia Dunne

Alliance Books are available at special discounts for bulk
purchases for sales and promotions, premiums,
fund raising, or educational use.
For details, contact:

Alliance Publishing, Inc.
P. O. Box 080377
Brooklyn, New York 11208-0002

Distributed to the trade by National Book Network, Inc.

10 9 8 7 6 5 4 3 2 1

Contents

From the Author

As with so many things in my life, my introduction to the world of antique malls was pretty much by accident. Maybe some people have these great plans that guide their lives, but not so with me.

I have been in the vending business for over 30 years, exhibiting and selling at the great state fairs, the small county ones, the large national wholesale trade shows, the small town apple festivals, not to mention the mega flea markets, all the way down to the out-of-the-way, wide-spot-in-the-road markets. You name it and my wife and I, to borrow a phrase "have been there, sold that."

Traveling the width and breadth of this great and beautiful country with a wife who is a confirmed shopaholic will take one into a lot of malls.

Over the years, my dear wife, who is not the world's greatest traveler, would study the billboards as we journeyed the highways, looking for the next retail mall. As for myself I have always had a strong dislike for large enclosed retail shopping centers. I find them very boring, store after store of same 'ol, same 'ol, new glittery foreign made junk with exorbitant price tags. The same stores, same brands, same franchises, one as much alike as the one 500 miles back down the road. Boring, uninteresting stores, with equally boring and uninteresting salespeople.

During a typical stop I would usually spend an hour or so on a bench, sitting, gawking, and smoking. (Now they don't let you smoke or gawk. What's a guy to do?)

Well, my salvation came in discovering the antique mall. My wife, who is an avid antiquer and devoted collector, is also a lover of crafts and a frustrated crafter who fell in love first with the concept of multidealer antique and craft malls.

For me, who was a little slower to catch on, it meant the end of stopping at the retail shopping malls. A place I have never felt safe in. I always feel that I am the one that the gangs are going to mug or steal or strip my van. To put it rather simply these shopping malls are just not my cup of tea. A lot of the big city malls have some pretty unsavory "customers" walking up and down the halls.

Now I'm bitten by the antique mall bug and wouldn't have it any other way. Here I can browse among the friends of my childhood: Roy Rogers, Gene Autry, Hopalong Cassidy. Admire and acquire beautiful pieces of Griswold cast iron, which I dearly love. And to top it off, the antique mall is a comfortable, safe, pleasant, and most enjoyable place to spend an idle hour or two looking for that perfect treasure to tote back home. I have never felt unsafe or worried at an antique mall.

Besides that, there are some very interesting people working in the antique malls. Individuals who possess great information about the items that are for sale in the mall. Plus treasure troves of info on the local area. It's always a great pleasure to visit with the mall personnel.

There are many items in our home that we purchased at different malls around the country, and each one has a little story of its own we treasure.

An added delight we have discovered in our antique mall travels is the fine cuisine that is available at many. Some have charming tearooms, others may offer a menu of desserts and liquid refreshments to die for. Still others may be found with wonderful local restaurants neighboring them, which are rich in local color and flavor. As you might guess, I don't like franchise restaurants any better than I do the retail mall/stores. If you are going to eat at franchise restaurants, you might as well stay home.

Until now I have shared my thoughts on the joys of

shopping at antique malls. But this book is also written for those who have discovered, as I have, the pleasures as well as the financial benefits of selling in them.

We have booths in a couple of malls and some of my most enjoyable days are taking a new batch of goodies to the booth. I enjoy stocking it and making it pleasant for those who will shop in it. I not only sell collectibles, I sell nostalgia. 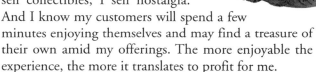 And I know my customers will spend a few minutes enjoying themselves and may find a treasure of their own amid my offerings. The more enjoyable the experience, the more it translates to profit for me.

It goes without saying that a great deal of time and effort are spent in looking for those special items for my booths that will give someone else great pleasure to own.

We hope that you will enjoying using this book whether you are a collector, a dealer, or like us, both, and that it will serve you well. We likewise hope you will find the antique mall experience as rewarding as we have.

Jim and Georgia Goodridge

Author's Notes

I'd like to say just a few words about using this guide and shopping in antique malls, in general. You may find the following information present elsewhere in this book but that is because I believe it is so important that it bears repeating.

About the Listings: A name, is a name, is a name… or so it's said. Except when it comes to antique malls. You may find a listing in this guide that has the words Flea Market or Swap Meet somehow tied to its name. If you are an antique shopping "purest" don't be turned off. It is only a name and it has to do with evolution. No, not of the Darwin type, but of the antique mall variety. Many antique malls started out as flea markets and their owners, changing as their own interests changed, are simply keeping pace with the times by converting their operations into full-fledged antique malls. Some may only permit true antiques. Others may allow new collector items in addition to antiques and collectibles. If they are listed in this book, however, regardless of the name of their business, you can be assured that they deal in antiques and/or collectibles.

Times of Operation: Most of the major antique malls are open daily, seven days a week. Many are open evenings. In the antique industry, a quirk of its nature, I suppose, things seem to start slowly. The majority of the malls I know of open sometime around 10 am. In this guide, then, where I have listed a mall as open daily, expect their doors to open in midmorning. Always play it safe and call ahead to verify times and days of operation to avoid disappointment. You will hear me say this over and over again in this guide. That is because there is nothing more frustrating than driving up to a place you've read about to find the doors locked for one reason or another. I know, too well, from my own experience how maddening it can be. It sure can put a crimp in your day's plans.

Seasonal Hours: This guide is as accurate and up-to-date as any guide can be. But, and this is a big "but," antique malls often change their hours and even days of operation during different seasons of the year. Some may extend their hours in the summer and cut back on them in the winter. If the mall is located in a warm weather tourist area, the opposite scenario may be true. There is no way I know of to predict antique mall operators' sudden policy changes. Some antique malls close for holidays. Others (rare) may even close for vacation. The information contained in this book is accurate to the best of my knowledge, and every effort has been made to verify it. However, the rule of thumb mentioned above can't be stressed too often. Call ahead to malls before driving long distances to reach them. That simple call can spare you a lot of grief.

Mall Shopping Policies: Antique malls value their customers. Most provide as many amenities as they can to keep you coming back. Most accept payment by credit card, traveler's checks, and good old American cash. A lot of malls will now take checks: these malls are almost always connected to some type of check verifying service. Identification will be needed. Some may be able to ship purchases home for you. Others may offer "layaway" for your convenience. Check at the front desk before you start shopping and ask questions if you don't see signs posted declaring these policies. A few malls may allow you to return merchandise. Ask the cashier if it makes a difference in your buying decision. Breakage—if you break something, plan to pay for it.

Most malls will expect you to, and it is the honorable thing to do, so antique malls are really not the best places for small children. Busy little fingers can cost you a pretty penny. Remember, when you are in an antique mall you are not at Wal-Mart, and you are expected to watch and also be responsible for your children.

Special-Needs Shoppers: Many antique malls are housed in old buildings that were constructed before consideration was given to the need to accommodate shoppers in wheelchairs and with other special needs. The aisles in many malls are extremely narrow with lots of bric-a-brac cluttering them. It can be very difficult in these older buildings to navigate from booth to booth and up and down the rows. Restroom facilities and parking can also be a problem with many old buildings that haven't been updated. So if these things might be a problem for you, call ahead to the mall you want to visit and ask questions. In this book, where I have been provided with the information, I have tried to let you know which malls are handicapped accessible. But doing your own homework could spare you a lot of frustration.

To Dealers Using This Guide: Same song…different verse. If you have purchased this guide to use on buying trips, *always* call ahead before you plan to visit a particular antique mall. I can't stress too often, hours change, days of operation change, etc. One thing I haven't mentioned that can be a problem is that malls may *move* or even *go out of business.* The old adage is alive and well…an ounce of prevention is worth a pound of cure. Make that telephone call. Time is money.

Your Suggestions: Did we miss a good antique mall? If so, I have provided a form within the pages of this book and ask that you fill it out and return it to us so that we can include it in our next edition. Also, if you have any suggestions or other information you would like to see included in future editions of this guide, let us know that as well. You may drop a line to me at Alliance Publishing, P.O. Box 080377, Brooklyn, NY 11208.

Here's to great shopping.

Jim Goodridge

The Antique Mall Explosion

by Georgia Goodridge

Antique malls as we know them today are one of the fastest-growing segment in the entire retail field in America. Statistically, there are more than 2,000 of them operating across the country. And new ones open their doors each day.

Housed under every imaginable type of roof, from restored train stations and rehabbed discount store buildings to shiny, newly built facilities, the antique mall explosion has reached a city or town near just about every American, today.

The origin of the antique mall began with the cultural renaissance that took place in the 1960's. It was a time when we were drawn, through art, music, and literature, to take a long look at ourselves as a society, to rediscover and in some ways revisit our roots.

It was during these years that more and more people began to take a serious interest in learning about their heritage. Genealogy became a huge pastime that consumed a society thirsting to get in touch with it's past.

The frantic pace of the world and the pressures that seemed to be turning us into faceless statistics drove us to search for reminders of slower, simpler times.

The nation's avid craving for collecting, a reflection of our continuing need for reminders of bygone times, began to accelerate in the 1980's. And, driven by the sheer volume of interest, more shops were joined by wonderful and exciting antique shows that brought yet more and more antiques out of attics and other dusty hiding places.

Pure antiques (items at least one hundred years old) were

joined with contemporary but equally nostalgic collectibles, becoming a passion for thousands of people. People discovered joy through them by seeing and touching bits and pieces of their youth and of bygone eras.

The concept of multidealer malls is nothing more than an exciting and wonderful outgrowth of the depth of commitment society has made to preserve our past and those reminders of days gone by for ourselves and for our children.

Like early explorers, malls began to spring up here and there during the 1980's. By the late years of the decade, the pioneers of the antique world who followed had begun to spread out and settle in larger numbers.

With the 1990's came the explosion that has brought the antique mall into mainstream American retailing.

The mall concept is a tremendous but simple one. A central cash register area provides the shopping convenience found in any department store or discount house. Combine that with booths rented by individual antique dealers and you have the variety of an antique show with the advantage of the daily accessibility you would find in any other retail business.

Shopping in an antique mall is treasure hunting at its finest. Week after week, dealers bring in new and different merchandise. The scene is one of constant change as antiques are continually being bought and sold. This constant flux adds to the "thrill of the hunt." There is sheer joy in not knowing what you might find just around the next corner in any antique mall in America. Every trip to a mall is an adventure to see "What's here today?"

By numbers, the Midwest leads the rest of the country, with the most multidealer malls. The South and West Coast aren't far behind, however. In the eastern U.S. where tradition generally rules over trend, more malls have sprung up in the past five years.

Any discussion of the East Coast and antiquing must

include a special word about the state of Pennsylvania. Rich in history and a long-time mecca for antique dealers and collectors, the state plays host to dozens of fantastic, nationally followed antique shows and has been, for some time, a haven for antique malls.

As more and more buyers hunger for these fabulous treasure centers, their increased growth is becoming stronger.

Is there a ceiling to their growth? Will they peak? Probably. For if we have learned anything from history it is that there is nothing so constant as change.

But today collecting has become big business. Some people invest in antiques and collectibles just as they would in stocks, bonds, or precious metals. Clubs and associations for enthusiastic collectors, in every imaginable field of interest, are flourishing. Many fine collecting-related periodicals are available that educate and keep the public up to date on the market. In addition, there are hundreds of price guides and books to feed an ever growing world of people with more than a passing interest in antiques and memorabilia.

One thing is certain. Shopping in an antique mall is always a unique experience and every shopper is sure to find something of interest. It doesn't matter if you are looking for something to decorate your home with, something to add to your particular collection, or simply looking for the enjoyment of finding an item that will touch a special cord in you. Antique malls are here to enjoy—and enjoy them we will!

Savvy Shopper—
Understanding How Antique
Malls Operate

by Georgia Goodridge

Antique malls do not operate like traditional antique stores. They can be likened to a cross between a store with multiple partners and a permanent antique show. Understanding them will help make shopping easier and much more fun.

Here are some things you should know that will make you a savvy shopper:

❧ First, unlike a single owner shop, it is important to know that all the antiques and collectible you see for sale in a mall belong to different dealers. A small mall may have as few as 25 individual sellers. A large one may have over 500!

❧ Dealers are not on the premises to sell their antiques as you would find in shop or at a show. Instead, there is a central cash register area where all business is transacted. When you find an item you wish to buy, you simply carry it to the front check-out and pay for it, just like you would in a department store or other retail establishment. If the item is too large, or in a locked case, someone from the front desk will need to help you, of course.

❧ The floor space in a mall is generally divided by some type of partitioning arrangement into individual "tiny" shops usually referred to as booths. The booths are assigned numbers, even though you may not see a sign posted reflecting that. The numbering system is the standard used by almost every mall in the country, having proved to be the best way to keep track of the location and sales of a particular dealer.

❧ Each item in a booth will have some kind of price tag attached. Somewhere on the front of the item, will be the cost of the item, as well as the booth's number. Generally, but not always, a tag will also include a description of the piece. Some tags will also include a dealer's inventory tracking number. Price tags are very important. Unlike a traditional retail store, they are the way a dealer gets paid for his merchandise.

❧ When you take an item you wish to purchase to the cashier, he or she will remove the tag before they wrap, bag or box it for you to take home. That is because the tags are kept and returned (in most but not all malls) to dealers at the end of each month or pay period along with a check for what they have sold during that time. So, if you want to know what you paid for an item, you will have to jot the information down on something before you leave the mall. Of course there are always exceptions. Some malls have a standardized two-part tag that they require all of their dealers to use. This perforated tag allows one part to stay with the item and one part for the mall to return at the end of the month. Dealers don't like this system very much because it creates twice the work in price marking each antique or collectible they display. Thus they are not popular and not widely found.

❧ Some malls have a Lay-Away program generally, but not always, reserved for big ticket items. If the option to put something in lay-away could sway your decision to purchase it, by all means ask at the desk. Remember, antique malls are in business to *sell* their dealers' merchandise so most try to accommodate their customers in every way possible.

❧ Many booths have their most valuable and/or

fragile antique and collectible items in some type of locked display case. If you wish to take a closer look at something in one, once again, ask for help from a mall floor worker or at the front desk, where individual case keys are usually kept. To save yourself time and aggravation, however, remember the mall staff will need to know the booth number so they can get the right key. If you don't see the booth's number posted somewhere, just take a quick look at a price tag attached to something in the same space and jot it down. It will save you valuable time by eliminating the need for a staff person to run back and forth trying to find the right booth and case key.

❧ With few exceptions, nearly all antique malls have a "You buy it, you own it, no return" policy. If you look the next time you shop at your favorite mall, you will probably see a sign, somewhere near the cash register, declaring this policy. This is necessary and fair to the dealers who have entrusted their goods to the antique mall to sell for them. You might wonder why. That certainly isn't the way you do business at Wal-Mart or any other typical retail store.

The simple reason is that unlike new, mass-produced products available at other types of stores, antiques and collectibles are unique unto themselves. The very nature of each piece's age, rarity, and fragility is the primary factor that determines its value.
Antique malls simply cannot, and in most cases, will not, assume the risk and liability that a returned item might have become damaged or devalued in some other way 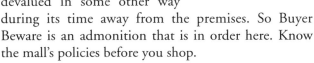 during its time away from the premises. So Buyer Beware is an admonition that is in order here. Know the mall's policies before you shop.

❧ Discounts…everybody likes them. Some booth

operators will attach *sale tags* to items they wish to discount. Others may have signs declaring a percentage off of every item in their booth or certain items marked in a special way. Occasionally you will even find a "going out of business" booth filled with marked down wares. In any case, if you are looking for a bargain, look for *sale* signs.

Antique mall management cannot negotiate or haggle with you over the price of an item because they are not the owners; the individual dealers are the only ones who can set prices.

But, what if you find an item and it doesn't have a sale tag. Does that mean the price is firm. The answer may surprise you but *no*, you may still be able to buy it for less than the tagged price. How? Unless a tag is actually marked with the words *firm* somewhere on it, it is acceptable to ask the person at the check-out if the dealer who owns the item has a discount policy. Some dealers will take off 10–15% on items as a standard (unadvertised) practice. Usually, however, this discounting is reserved for higher ticket pieces. But don't be afraid to ask.

On more expensive items, generally over 100 dollars, it is also acceptable at most malls to make the dealer a reasonable offer. The key here is *reasonable.* In such circumstances, the malls that offer this service will generally give the dealer a call at home and make the offer for you.

Now you know what antique dealers and mall operators know and that knowledge will make you a savvy shopper giving you the "insider's edge" the next time you visit an antique mall.

How to Shake Your Share Loose from the Antique Mall Money Tree

by Georgia Goodridge

A casual walk through any antique mall may lead many to believe that it's easy to become an antique dealer. Why, it looks like everybody is doing it, doesn't it? You probably just round up some things out of your attic and *voilà*, you're in business. No sweat. Right?

Wrong! Wrong! Wrong! It is true that there is still a lot of room for growth in the antiques and collectibles field. It is also possible to launch a fine business, with relatively little capital, from as humble a place as your kitchen table.

And make no mistake, there can be terrific profits in selling antiques and collectibles. For many professional antiques dealers, the antique mall has become a money tree of sorts: working for them even when they are not present.

But, please do not be misled. Going into business for yourself is no bed of roses. And it's the thorny parts that cause the majority of all small businesses to fail within the first five years.

If you have been flirting with the idea of starting an antique or collectible business, do your homework first. Lots of it. Consider all the angles.

Here are some things to ask yourself: A) What do I know about going into business for myself? Is it right for me and my family? Would it be a hobby or full-time endeavor? How many hours of work does the average dealer put into their antique mall business? B) How do I know what to sell and/or where to find more of it?

Where does pricing know-how come from? C) Where am I going to sell my antiques? Is there a mall nearby that you think you'd like to sell in? If so, check it out. How do they operate? Do they charge just a monthly rental fee? Do they take a percentage of each sale? Do you have to work in the mall in lieu of their sharing a percentage of your sales? How large are the spaces? Is there a waiting list for exhibit space? Find out how they attract business. Do they advertise? Where?

There are thousands of questions that must be answered before you can even make a sensible decision about going into any business.

Besides your local mall, where else can you learn what you need to know about going into business for yourself?

Your local library and bookstore are two good places. Read, read and read some more. Keep a notebook with all the questions and answers that come to mind.

On visits to antique shops, malls, and shows, pick up all the free trade papers you can get you hands on.

If collecting (anything) is already a hobby, you will stand a far greater chance for financial success than someone who tries to enter this field cold.

It is a well-documented fact that people who have a love, a real passion for their work, are more likely to be successful at it. And most collectors have that passion. One of the great side benefits of selling antiques and memorabilia is that you can so easily add to your own collections with an insider's edge you wouldn't otherwise have.

If you are a collector, subscribe to publications dealing with your area of interest. Become an expert by learning everything you can about your favorite subject.

You might want to join a collector club so you can make contacts with others who share the same interests as you. Clubs and associations often put out fine newsletters that give you information with which you can start to form a solid foundation for selling your wares.

If you don't think you want to specialize in one area but you have a love and appreciation of all kinds of heirlooms and nostalgic treasures, you can still join various clubs. Read those publications and books that will give you a good all-around working knowledge of the market. Knowing a little bit about a lot of fields is the category that the largest number of antique dealers seem to fall into.

Networking with other dealers is also helpful. Especially when you are just beginning. Strike up conversations with them at auctions, antique shows, etc., and become a sponge. Soak up and retain as much as you can from those who have already been down the road you are thinking of traveling.

If you are looking for instant gain, forget about selling antiques or collectibles. There's far too much to learn. And while it is certainly possible to learn much of it as you go, some lessons can turn into costly mistakes that could be avoided with better planning and less of the "ready-fire-aim" mentality that comes with people in too big a hurry. To grow a business slowly is to grow it on a solid footing. It isn't a sure-fire guarantee of success. There aren't any of those. But your chances for building a business that is a profitable one will certainly be greater.

If you are still convinced that you want your share of the antique mall "money tree" roll up your sleeves, prepare for a lot of hard work, shake away, and most of all…enjoy!

Some Helpful Tips
For Getting The Most From Your
Mall Shopping Experience

Shopping at multidealer antique malls can be a mind-boggling experience. Whether you're visiting one featuring the wares of fifty different antique dealers or five hundred—yes, there are malls with that many differnt sellers and more—even the most seasoned shopper can find it a challenge.

The row after row of nostalgic memorabilia—often packed floor to ceiling in booths ranging in size from mere cubbyholes to blocks of space that would make an interior decorator envious—can make for a wonderful or frustrating shopping adventure. And make no mistake, shopping at an antique mall is always an adventure!

Has this ever happened to you? You are shopping in a mall and you suddenly can't remember where you saw that "whatsit" that you thought would look so great next to your sofa at home.

How about this? You found an item you've fallen in love with. You shop a little further and find another one you think is almost identical. Now you can't find the first one to compare prices, condition, and so forth. Frustrating? You bet it is.

And what about specific wants? locked cases? a mall's special services?

Here are some tips that will help you get the most out of the time you spend searching for treasures.

SHOP LIKE A PRO

⚜ Keep A Notebook and Pencil Handy. It is not difficult to spend a couple of hours browsing in an antique mall. After a while, however, things can begin to look like one big blur because you have seen and inspected so many different pieces of memorabilia. It is no wonder, then, that it is easy to forget where you've been, a place you wanted to return to, an item price you wanted to remember, and so forth. Jotting down booth numbers, row numbers (if they have them) or other important things you want to remember, is the way seasoned antique mall shoppers get the most from their visit, with the least amount of frustration and wasted time.

⚜ Wear Comfortable Shoes. Be sure to wear comfortable shoes because even though you will be shopping in a nice climate-controlled building, you will undoubtedly do a lot of walking.

⚜ Searching for a Specific Item. If you are looking for something specific, make your first stop the front desk. There are two very good reasons. First, many mall operators are very familiar with their dealers' wares. Some dealers, for instance, specialize in one particular field: clocks, dolls, quilts, etc. They may be able to show you exactly what you are looking for. Secondly, some malls keep a "wants" book. If the one you are shopping in does, you will be able to leave a description of what you want and your name and phone number. Dealers check "want" books frequenty and if somebody has what you are looking for, they will contact you.

— A special note about "want" books. Antique malls get a percentage (usually) of every item sold in them. For that reason, the majority of them don't want to put buyers and sellers together for any kind of off-premises side-deal for which they won't get a cut. That's why you won't find this helpful service everywhere. To get around this problem and still offer the service, some malls may call you when the dealers has brought the item to them and you can come in and inspect it in their building. This way the sale still is rung through the cash register and the mall retains their share. You are *not* under any obligation to buy the item, even if dealers and malls go through the process of bringing it in for you to look at. It still has to meet your satisfaction as far as condition, etc.

OPENING DISPLAY CASES

It can be a bit inconvenient to have to seek help with a locked showcase. Just remember though, patience is all part of the game that can lead to some juicy rewards in the adventure of treasure hunting in an antique mall.

For the most part, you will find a dealer's most valuable and fragile antiques under lock and key. Besides the possibility of dam- age in leaving things out on shelves, theft has become a problem for antique malls, just as it is for other retail stores. Sometimes parts "go missing". Sometimes whole items. So locked cases are a sensible solution for certain pieces.

To speed the process along, be sure to give the mall worker the booth/case number so they can find the right key. The number may be posted on the case itself or on the wall in the booth. If you don't find it, then pick up any item in the booth and look at the price tag. Some- where on that tag should be a number identifying that booth. This will save everybody, especially you, time and effort in matching the right key with the right case.

TRAVELING? LOCAL? CONSIDER YOUR PERSONAL PURCHASING NEEDS

If you are traveling and space is a consideration, ask the management if the mall offers a shipping service. Many will box and send your treasures home for you via UPS, or some other domestic carrier for no more than the shipping costs.

If you are making a round trip and wish to purchase an item that is bulky, the mall may be able to store it for you, on site, until you return. This can be especially helpful to dealers on extended buying trips. It never hurts to ask. Most mall operators are eager to help their dealers make sales and to turn their shoppers into repeat customers.

Local shoppers are generally expected to take possession of their purchases at the time of sale, and to make their own arrangements for getting their treasures home. However, when buying furniture or other large or heavy items, some malls can refer you to an individual or business they know of that offers delivery services. Some malls (but very few) will make deliveries themselves. To be on the safe side, always ask before you buy if delivery is a consideration in your decision to take an item.

Tips for Safe Travel

- While you're away, ask a neighbor to take in your paper or mail.

- Take with you only the credit cards you plan to use.

- Dress comfortably and inconspicuously.

- Don't take more luggage than you can carry.

- If driving, make sure your car has been properly serviced and the tires are in good condition.

- Obtain specific directions to your destination, including expressway entrances and exits.

- If you get lost, drive to the nearest public place to check your map.

- Always keep your car doors and windows locked.

- If your car is bumped or flashed by oncoming headlights, do not stop. Drive to the nearest public area and dial 911 to report the incident to the police.

- At a stoplight, make sure you leave enough space in front of your car so you can pull away if you have to.

- If you have a flat tire in a remote location, drive slowly to a populated, well-lit area to fix it even if you ruin the tire.

- Day or night, do not park in a rest area to sleep.

- Never leave your luggage unattended.

- Make sure your bags are locked. For extra protection against pilferage, place a strap around each piece of luggage.

✤ At the airport, board a bus or taxi only at specified pickup points.

✤ Do not answer a knock on the door of your hotel or motel room without identifying who is there. If the person says she or he is an employee, call the front desk for verification of authorized access to your room. Never open the door to a stranger.

✤ Keep valuables in the hotel safe.

✤ If you witness anything suspicious, call the front desk. Do not try to take care of it yourself.

✤ While at the pool or beach, do not leave your wallet or keys unattended.

✤ If you lose your room key, report the loss to the front desk immediately.

IMPORTANT NOTICE

Although every effort has been made to ensure the accuracy of the information contained in this directory, conditions do change due to the volatile nature of this industry.

Information is subject to change. Malls close, hours change, new malls open. Please always call ahead before traveling long distances.

The publisher and the author assume no responsibility for errors or omissions in content or composition or for any changes that may occur.

Comments, questions or suggestions may be directed to the author at Alliance Publishing, P.O. Box 080377. Brooklyn, NY 11208.

Antique and Craft Malls

Antique malls, the multidealer markets that are booming in popularity, have revolutionized the way antiques are bought and sold. They are considered to be the fastest-growing segment in the retail field today. As we stand on the threshold of this new industry, the rapidly growing number of new malls opening across the country indicates that their future is bright. We have listed only multi-dealer marketplaces (no individual shops) in this book. If you have information about a mall that we missed, please let us know about it.

ALABAMA 🌿

ATHENS
Hickory House Gift Shoppe and Antique Mall. Highway 72E. (205) 232-9860. General line of antiques and collectibles.

BIRMINGHAM
Birmingham Antique Mall, Inc. Connie Holan. 2211 Magnolia Avenue. (205) 338-7761. Quality antiques and collectibles with 35+ dealers. Credit cards accepted. Restrooms, handicapped accessible, ample parking. Open Mon–Sat 10–5:30. Sundays 1–5:30.

Magic City Antique Gallery. 321 Valley Avenue. (205) 942-4466. Large, clean, friendly mall well-stocked with many booths of quality antiques and collectibles. Credit cards accepted. Restrooms, handicapped accessible, ample parking. Open Mon–Sat 11–6, Sundays 1–6.

Antique Mall East. 217 Oporto-Madrid Blvd. N. I-59 at 77th Street exit. (205) 836-1097.

Galleria Antique Mall. 3075 Highway 150. 35244. Across from Galleria. (205) 987-7351. 22,500 sq ft mall.

Peck & Hills Antique Mall. 2400 Seventh Avenue S. 35233. (205) 252-3179. 14,000 sq ft showroom. Open daily.

DAPHNE

The Gallery Antique Mall. 1302 Highway 98. (205) 626-0353. 25,000 sq. ft. showroom with 100 dealers featuring quality antiques and collectibles.

GUNTERSVILLE

Sand Mountain Antique Mall. Highway 43 between Albertville and Gunterville. Plenty of parking, restaurant. Located 7 miles from Boaz Outlet Center. Mall also conducts large flea market on Friday, Saturday, and Sunday. (205) 891-2790 and 582-0385. Open daily.

HANNA

Hanna Antique Mall. Bonny and Sandy Picard. 2424 - 7th Avenue S. (205) 323-6036. Large selection of quality American and European antiques and furniture. Credit cards accepted. Restrooms, handicapped accessible, ample parking. Open Mon–Sat 10–5. Sundays 1–5.

HAZEL GREEN

Hazel Green Antique Mall. 13685-A Highway 231. (205) 828-5766. General line of antiques and collectibles.

HOMEWOOD

Attic Treasures Antique Mall. 25 W. Oxmoor Road. (205) 942-1073. Antiques and collectibles. Credit cards accepted. Restrooms, handicapped accessible, ample parking. Open Mon–Sat 10–5.

Homewood Antique Mall. 2921 - 18th Street S. (205) 870-7106. Antiques, collectibles, gifts, decorator items, orientals. Credit cards accepted. Restrooms, handicapped accessible, ample parking. Open daily.

HOOVER

River Chase Antique Galleries. 3454 Lorna Road. (205) 823-6433. 36,000 sq ft showroom with 130+ dealers featuring quality antiques and collectibles. Credit cards accepted. Restrooms, handicapped accessible. Ample parking. Open Mon–Sat 11–6, Sundays 1–6.

HUNTSVILLE

Bulldog Antique Mall. 2338 Whitesburg Drive S. (205) 534-9893. Furniture, lamp restoration, antiques, collectibles.

Haysland Antique Mall. 11595 Memorial Parkway SW. (205) 883-0181. General line of antiques and collectibles.

Old Town Antique Mall. 820 Wellman Avenue NE. (205) 533-7002.

Pratt Avenue Antique Mall. 708 Pratt Avenue NE. (205) 536-3117. Twenty-five-dealer mall with antiques, books, fine art, furniture, quilts, collectibles, gifts.

Railroad Station Antique Mall. 315 Jefferson N. Take I-65, exit at Jefferson Street. Across from Railroad Depot Museum. (205) 533-6550. 23,500 sq ft showroom. Antiques, collectibles. Open daily.

Royal Antiques Mall, Inc. 601 Washington Street NW. (205) 533-1344.

Red Rooster Antique Mall. 12519 Memorial Parkway SW. (205) 881-6530. 10,000 sq ft showroom, 36 dealers, antiques and collectibles.

MADISON

Barr's Antique Mall. 7967 Highway 72W (University Drive). (205) 895-9277. 40+ dealers in one-story building featuring fine antiques and collectibles. Open daily.

Tally's Antique Mall. 7587 Highway 72W. (205) 722-7944. Antiques, collectibles, nice selection of antique furniture. Hours Tues–Sat 10am–5pm. Sun 1pm–5pm.

MILLBROOK

Sarah's Antique Mall. 2410 Wall Street. I-65 North, Exit 179. (334) 285-4888. Antiques, collectibles, furniture, country collectibles, kitchen collectibles, linen, silver, jewelry. Restroom, ample parking. Open daily.

MOBILE

Cotton City Antique Mall. 2012 Airport Blvd (at the Railroad tracks). (205) 479-9747. 90+ dealers, antiques and collectibles. Open daily.

Hogg Wilde Antique Mall. 3501 Cottage Hill Road. I-65 at Cottage Hill Road. (205) 660-7848. Forty-dealer mall with wide range of quality antiques and collectibles.

MONTGOMERY

Bodiford's Antique Mall. 919 Hampton. (334) 265-4220. One of the oldest and largest malls in the area. Large selection of quality antiques and collectibles. Mall features lamp and crystal repair. Credit cards accepted. Restrooms, handicapped accessible, ample parking.

PRATTVILLE
Linda's Antique Mall. 1120 S. Memorial Drive. (334) 361-9952. General line of antiques and collectibles. Restrooms, ample parking. Open daily.

SUMMERDALE
Highway 59 Flea Market and Antique Mall. Highway 59. Antique mall with furniture store. Open daily. Large flea market Fri–Sun. (205) 989-6642.

ALASKA ☙

ANCHORAGE
Antique & Specialty Center. 1036 E. 7th Avenue. (907) 276-8551. Furniture, specialty items, consignments.

Remember When Antiques Mall. 5441 Old Seward Highway. (907) 582-5441. General line of antiques and collectibles. Credit cards accepted. Hours Mon–Sat 10am–6pm, Sun 12pm–5pm.

ARIZONA ☙

APACHE JUNCTION
The Grand Antique Mall. 201 W. Apache Trail. Located in the Grand Hotel. (602) 982-1004. 200+ booths. Great selection of Western, ranch, and Indian items here. Restrooms, food available, ample parking, handicapped accessible. Open daily 10am–5:30pm.

BISBEE
Acorn Gift Shoppe. Highway 80, 1 mile east of tunnel. Five rooms with antiques, small collectibles, bric-a-brac. (602) 432-7314.

On Consignment in Bisbee. 100 Lowell Traffic Circle. (602) 432-4002. 10,000 sq ft building with lots of collectibles, jewelry, glassware. Open Tues–Sat and first Sunday of the month.

CLARKDALE

Clarkdale Antique Emporium & Soda Fountain. 907 Main Street. (520) 634-2828. Mall is located in an old bank and is decorated in a charming style, circa 1914. General line of antiques and collectibles. Ample parking, restrooms, handicapped accessible. Open daily.

COTTONWOOD

Home Sweet Home Antiques. 303 S. Main Street. (5620) 634-5461. One of the oldest and largest malls in the area. Well-stocked with antiques, collectibles, Western and Indian items. Mall features nice coffee house. Restrooms, ample parking, handicapped accessible. Open daily.

MESA

Mesa Antique Mart. Superstition Freeway and Stapley. (602) 813-1909. Eighty dealers. Quality line of antiques and collectibles here. Tearoom. Restrooms, ample parking, handicapped accessible. Open daily.

Treasures From The Past Antiques. 106 E. McKellips. (602) 655-0090. Large well-stocked 22,000 sq ft mall with 100+ dealers. Restrooms, ample parking, handicapped accessible. Restaurant on premises. Open daily.

PHOENIX

The Antique Gallery. 5037 N. Central. Corner Central and Camelback. Uptown Plaza. (520) 241-1174. Seventy-eight-dealer mall featuring wide selection of fine antiques and collectibles. Credit cards accepted. Restrooms, handicapped accessible, ample parking. Open Mon-Sat 10–5, Sundays 12–5.

Central Antiques. Corner Central and Camelback. (520) 241-1636. New mall with 60 dealers. Credit cards accepted. Restrooms, handicapped accessible, ample parking. Open Mon-Sat 10-5, Sundays 12-5.

Antique Outpost. 10012 N. Cave Creek Road. (520) 943-9594. Well-stocked mall with great selection of quality antiques and collectibles. Restroom, ample parking, handicapped accessible. Open daily.

Antique Gatherings. 3601 E. Indian School Road. (520) 956-8203. 95+ dealers with well-stocked booths of quality antiques and collectibles. Restroom, ample parking, handicapped accessible. Open daily.

Antique Center. 3801 E. Indian School Road. 18,000 sq ft building. Over 100 dealers. Lots of quality and unusual antiques. Open daily. (520) 957-3600.

Bradbury's Antiques Bazaar. 4238 N. 7th Avenue. (520) 279-7253. Open daily.

Bradbury's Antiques Bazaar. 6900 E. Camelback. (520) 946-3013. Open daily.

Brass Armadillo Antique Mall. I-17 and Cactus on 28th Drive. (520) 942-0030. Large 40,000 sq ft mall with 400+ dealers. If it can be pronounced, it is located in this giant mall. Restrooms, ample parking, snack bar, handicapped accessible. This is an all-day stop and well worth it. Open daily 9–9.

ALWAYS CALL AHEAD BEFORE TRAVELING LONG DISTANCES!

Antique Alley. Corner of Cactus and T-Bird Cave Creek Roads. (520) 867-4696. Open daily.

Historic District Antiques Mall. 539 W. McDowell Road. (520) 255-0212. Dolls, coins, jewelry, vintage clothing. Open Mon–Sat 10am–6pm, Sun 11am–6pm.

Big Easy Antique Mall. 9201 N. 29th Avenue. I-17 and Dunlap. (520) 943-1744. Open daily.

Unique Antiques. 5000 E. Speedway Blvd. (520) 323-0319. Open Mon–Sat 10am–6pm, Sun 11am–5pm.

SCOTTSDALE

Antique Centre. 2012 N. Scottsdale Road. (602) 675-9500. 130+ dealer mall with antiques, collectibles, furniture, Indian and Western items. Credit cards accepted. Restrooms, handicapped accessible, ample parking. Open daily 10–6.

Super Mall. 1900 N. Scottsdale Road. (602) 874-2900. New large 60,000 sq ft mall with over 200 dealers. Well-stocked mall with great selection of antique furniture. Nice restaurant on premises. Ample parking, restrooms, handicapped accessible. Full amenities here and great shopping. Open daily.

Antique Trove. 2020 N. Scottsdale Road. (602) 947-6074. 25,000 sq ft building. 100+ dealers. Lots of good quality antiques and collectibles. Furniture, bookstore. Hours, daily 10am–6pm, Thurs until 8pm.

SEDONA

Antique Center of West Sedona. 2679 W. Highway 89A. Large, well-stocked antique mall. Hours Mon–Sat 10am–5pm. (602) 282-9088.

TEMPE

Antique Center. 1290 N. Scottsdale Road. Corner of Scottsdale Rd. and Curry Street. 14,000 sq ft building, 100+ booths. Open daily. (602) 966-3550.

Arizona Antique Gallery. 1126 W. Scottsdale Road. (602) 921-3343. Junction of Scottsdale Rd. and Curry Street. 26,000 sq ft building. 125+ dealers. Large well-stocked mall with lots of antiques, collectibles, primitives, smalls. Credit cards accepted. Open daily 10am–6pm.

TUCSON

Antique Mall. Dwight and Christy Schannet. 3130 E. Grant Road. (520) 326-3070. Large 100+ dealer mall fully stocked with quality line of antiques, smalls, collectibles. Ample parking, restrooms, handicapped accessible. Open daily.

Arizona Mall. 3728 E. Grant Road. (520) 770-9840. Large mall well-stocked with antiques and collectibles. Great selection of antique furniture. Mall has special section featuring theatrical props. Credit cards accepted. Restrooms, handicapped accessible, ample parking. Open Mon–Sat 9–6, Sundays 11–4.

Firehouse Antiques Center. 6522 E. 22nd Street. (520) 571-1775.

90 Shop Antique Center. 5000 E. Speedway Mall. (520) 323-0319. Antiques and collectibles. Credit cards accepted. Restrooms, handicapped accessible, ample parking. Open Mon–Sat 10–6, Sun 11–5.

Antique Mini-Mall. 3408 E. Grant Road. (520) 326-6502. Ten dealers. Antiques and collectibles. Open Mon–Sat 10am–5pm.

WILLIAMS

Mothball Collectibles & Antiques. 111 S. 6th Street. Located behind Parker House Restaurant, off 5th Street. (602) 635-2757.

ARKANSAS 🌿

ALMA

Sisters 2-Too Antiques and Flea Market. I-40, Exit 13 on Highway 71 North. (501) 632-2292. General line of antiques, collectibles, country items, primitives, and gifts. Credit cards accepted. Restrooms, ample parking. Open daily.

ASHDOWN

Antique Mall of Ashdown. James Oden. 63 E. Main Street. 71822. (501) 898-6323. General line of antiques and collectibles. Hours Mon–Sat 9:30am–5pm.

BENTON

Benton Antique Mall. I-30, Exit 118, Congo Road. 45+ dealers. Open Mon–Sat 10am–5pm, Sun 1pm–5pm. (501) 778-9532.

EUREKA SPRINGS

Rock House Antique & Collectable Mall. Highway 62 East. 72632. (501) 253-5100. Approximately 75 dealers. 8,000+ sq ft. Many fine antique shops and bed and breakfasts are also located here, in what many consider to be America's most lovely little city.

FT. SMITH

Riverfront Antique Mall. 222 Garrison Avenue. (501) 785-5159. Roseville, Hull, Shawnee, crockery, depression, carnival, Fenton, Heisey. Clocks, jewelry, furniture, primitives, collectibles. Hours Mon–Sat 9am-5pm, Sun 1pm–5pm.

Ft. Smith Craft Mall. Carole Culpepper. 924 Garrison Avenue. (501) 783-1688. 115+ booths of country crafts. Hours Mon-Sat 10am–6pm, Sun 1pm–5pm.

HARRISON

Old Town Mall. Highway 65 North. Lots of antiques, collectibles, many rare/unusual items. (501) 741-7778 or 679-2832.

MENA

Mena Street Antique Mall. 822 Mena Street. (501) 394-3231. Open Tues–Sat 10am–5pm.

Storck Antiques & Country Crafts. Highway 883 (3 miles from town). (501) 394-3033. Open daily.

NORTH LITTLE ROCK

Argenta Antique Mall. 201 E. Broadway. (501) 372-7750. General line of antiques and collectibles. Restrooms, ample parking, handicapped accessible. Credit cards accepted. Mon–Sat 10am–5pm. Sun 1pm–5pm.

ROGERS

Tuck's Chapel Antique Mall. Highway 62 North (Avoca). (501) 631-3839. Antiques, furniture, collectibles, carnival glass, Hull, Roseville pieces. Hours Mon–Sat 9am–5pm, Sun 12pm–5pm.

Country House Flea Market. 1007 N. 2nd Street. (501) 631-9200. Crafts, antiques, collectibles, primitives, furniture. Restrooms, ample parking, handicapped accessible. Credit cards accepted. Open daily.

Bear Creek Flea Market & Antiques. 15790 E. Highway 12. (501) 925-BEAR. Antiques, glassware, dolls, crafts. Ample parking, restrooms, handicapped accessible. Credit cards accepted. Open daily.

SILOAM SPRINGS

Fantasy Land Flea Market. 1490 Highway 412 Bypass. (501) 524-6681. Antiques, collectibles, primitives, glassware, antique furniture, crafts. Restrooms, ample parking, snack bar, handicapped accessible. Credit cards accepted. Open daily.

SPRINGDALE

Famous Hardware Company Antique Mall. 113 W. Emma. 72764. (501) 756-6650. Eleven dealers with a variety of quality antiques and collectibles. Restrooms, ample parking, handicapped accessible. Credit cards accepted. Mon–Sat 10am–5pm. Sun 1pm–5pm.

Jennifer's Antiques, Crafts, Collectibles & Flea Market. 824 S. 48th Street. Springdale, AR 72762. Highway 412 W and Highway 71 Bypass. Next to Arkansas state police headquar-

THE ALLIANCE GUIDE TO

ters. (501) 750-4646. Over 200 booths, 15,000 square feet. Antiques, crafts, collectibles, flea market. Hours Mon–Sat 9am–6pm, Sun 1pm–6pm.

TONITOWN

Tonitown Flea Market & Antique Mall. Highway 412 (1 block W. of Highway 112). Jim and Kathy Miller. 10,000 sq ft facility with 120 booths. Antiques, collectibles, primitives, glassware and crafts. Restrooms, ample parking. Credit cards accepted. Open Mon–Sat 9–5, Sundays 12–5.

Historic Mercantile Flea Market. Highway 412 West. Jerry and Mary Childress, (501) 361-2003. Antiques, collectibles, glassware, furniture. Restrooms, ample parking. Credit cards accepted. Open Mon-Sat 9–5. Sundays 12–5.

CALIFORNIA ❦

AGOURA HILLS

Agoura Antique Mart. 28863 Roadside Drive. (818) 786-8366. Antiques, collectibles, furniture (including oak), primitives, dolls, jewelry, country gifts. Great selection of Western collectibles here. Credit cards accepted. Restrooms, handicapped accessible, ample parking. Open daily.

Showcase Antiques. 5021 Kanan Road. (818) 685-8268. Fifty-dealer mall featuring jewelry, art, and wide selection of rare and collector books. Restrooms, ample parking. Open daily.

Sandy Lane Antique Mall. 28826 Roadside Drive. (818) 991-8541. Large 300-dealer mall with wide range of merchandise. Open daily 10am–6pm.

ANAHEIM

Lincoln Avenue Antique Mall. 1811 W. Lincoln Avenue. 92801. (714) 778-2522. Approximately 160+ booths in a 15,000 sq ft facility. Some very fine antiques and collectibles here. Credit cards accepted. Restrooms, snack bar, ample parking, handicapped accessible. Open daily 10–6.

BAKERSFIELD

Central Park Antique Mall. 701 - 19th Street. (805) 633-1143. Large well-stocked mall with over 80 dealers displaying quality antiques and collectibles. Restroom, ample parking, handicapped accessible. Open daily 10–5.

➜ ➜ ➜ ➜ ➜ ➜ **38** ❦ ❦ ❦ ❦ ❦ ❦

Great American Antique Mall. 615 - 19th Street. 38,000+ sq ft building. Lots of small antiques and good selection of ornate furniture. (805) 322-1776. Open daily 10am–5pm.

BARSTOW

Old Town. Five antique malls located on one block. Exit Barstow Road from I-15 to Main Street (Old Route 66). Malls are open daily and full amenities are here.

> **SHOPPING SMART—**
> EXAMINE ITEMS CAREFULLY BEFORE YOU BUY, LOOKING FOR: CHIPS, SIGNS OF REPAIR, MISSING PARTS, ETC. MOST ANTIQUES CANNOT BE RETURNED TO ANTIQUE MALLS DUE TO THEIR AGE AND FRAGILE CONDITION. AN OUNCE OF PREVENTION BEFORE YOU BUY WILL SAVE YOU MONEY AND DISAPPOINTMENT WHEN YOU GET YOUR PURCHASE HOME!

BELLFLOWER

China Plate Antique Mall. 16512 S. Bellflower Blvd. (213) 866-2950. Antiques, collectibles, lots of collector plates, clocks, dolls, toys, jewelry, nice selection of glassware. Open Mon–Sat 11am–5:30pm.

BELMONT

Belmont Antique Centre. 700 Ralston Avenue. Highway 101, Ralston Exit. 20 miles south of San Francisco. (415) 593-8267. Sixty-five dealers. Quality American and European antiques and collectibles. Credit cards accepted. Restrooms, handicapped accessible, ample parking. Open Mon-Sat 10–5:30, Sundays 12–5.

BERKELEY

It's About Time Antiques. 1621 San Pablo Avenue. (510) 526-0626. Antiques, collectibles. Credit cards accepted. Restrooms, ample parking, handicapped accessible. Open daily.

BUENA PARK

Old Chicago Antiques Mall. 8960 Knott Avenue. (714) 527-0275. One hundred and ten individual shops located at this mall; well-stocked with many fine quality items. Credit cards accepted. Restrooms, handicapped accessible. Mall open daily 10am–6pm.

CARMICHAEL

Antiques Unlimited. 6328 Fair Oaks Blvd. (916) 482-6533. Large well-stocked mall with 96 dealers, quality antiques, collectibles, furniture, jewelry, glassware, toys, clocks. Credit cards accepted. Restrooms, handicapped accessible. Ample parking. Mall open daily 10am–6pm.

CARSON

Memory Lanes Antique Mall. 20740 S. Figueroa Street. (310) 538-4130. Two hundred dealers in large 20,000 sq ft facility. Antiques, collectibles, decorator items, nostalgia, memorabilia. Credit cards accepted. Ample parking, restrooms, snack bar, handicapped accessible. Hours Mon–Sat 10am–6pm, Sun 12pm–8pm.

CHOWCHILA

Frontier Towne Antique Mall. 521 Robertson Blvd., 93610. Well-stocked mall with antiques, collectibles, and an excellent selection of jewelry, both antique and fine. (209) 665-3900. Open daily.

CITRUS HEIGHTS

The Olive Factory Antiques. 6008 Auburn Blvd. (916) 723-5969. Fifty individual specialty and antique shops, mall is very quality oriented. Open daily 11am–5pm.

ENCINO

Encino Antique Center. 17287 Ventura Blvd. (818) 783-7107. Antiques and collectibles. Credit cards accepted. Restrooms, handicapped accessible, ample parking. Hours Mon–Sat 11am–6pm, Sun 12pm–5pm.

EL CAJON

Main Street Antique Mall. 237 E. Main Street. (619) 447-0800. 14,000 sq ft facility with 100 dealers. Open daily.

El Cajon Antique Mall. 143 E. Main Street. (619) 588-0616. Forty individual shops. Open daily.

FOLSOM

Folsom Mercantile Mall. 726 Sutter Street. (916) 985-2169. Forty-two dealers, antiques, collectibles, furniture, firearms, fishing gear. Restrooms, ample parking, handicapped accessible. Open daily 11–5.

FRESNO

Tower Antique Mall. 1040 N. Fulton. (209) 233-7224. 8,000 sq ft facility. Antiques, collectibles, furniture, books, china, jewelry, glassware, toys. Credit cards accepted. Hours Mon–Sat 10am–5:30pm, Sun 12pm–5:30pm.

GARDEN GROVE

Garden Grove Mercantile. 12941 Main Street. (714) 534-1857. Forty individual shops located here under one roof featuring antiques, collectibles, crafts, and California pottery. Credit cards accepted. Restrooms, handicapped accessible, ample parking. Open Mon–Sat 10–6, Sundays 12–5.

GLENDORA

The Orange Tree Antiques. 216 N. Glendora Avenue. (818) 335-3378. Forty shops of antiques and collectibles at this location.

HAYWARD

Hayward Faire Antiques. 926 B Street. (510) 537-7823. Forty dealers. Antiques, collectibles, furniture. Open Mon–Sat 10am–6pm, Sun 12pm–5pm.

LONG BEACH

Sleepy Hollow Antique Mall. 5689 Paramount Blvd. (714) 634-8370. One hundred dealers.

LOS ANGELES

Westchester Faire Antique Mall. 8655 S. Sepulveda Blvd. $1/2$ mile North of LA International Airport. 70 individual shops, open daily 10 am to 6 pm. Sundays 11 am to 6 pm. This mall also has four excellent food shops for the benefit of hungry shoppers.

The Antique Guild. 8800 Venice Blvd. 90034. (310) 838-3131. One of the country's largest antiquing establishments. The Antique Guild building covers over two acres and is completely filled with fine antiques, furniture and collectibles. Hours Mon–Fri 10am–7pm, Sat 10am–6pm, Sun 11am–6pm.

LOS GATOS

Main Street Antiques. 1250 W. Main Street. (408) 395-3035. Thirty dealers, quality small antiques and collectibles. Open daily.

MODESTO

Hutch Road Antique Mall. 2909 E. Hutch Road. (209) 538-0663.

MONROVIA

Kaleidoscope Antiques. 306 S. Myrtle Avenue. (818) 303-4042. Thirty-five dealers. Credit cards accepted. Hours Tues–Sat 10am–5:30pm, Sun 12pm–5pm.

Monrovia West Antique Mall. 925 W. Foothill Blvd. (818) 357-5235.

MONTEREY

Cannery Row Antique Mall. 471 Wave Street. (408) 655-0264. 150-dealer mall displaying general line of antiques and collectibles. Credit cards accepted. Restrooms, snack bar, ample parking, handicapped accessible. Open daily.

NEWPORT BEACH

Antiques 4U. 312 N. Newport Blvd. (714) 548-4123. Mall features quality European and American antiques and furniture. Credit cards accepted. Restrooms, handicapped accessible. Open daily.

ORANGE

Antique Annex. 109 S. Glassell. (714) 997-4320. Forty shops here featuring fine antiques and collectibles. Credit cards accepted. Restrooms, handicapped accessible. Open Mon-Sat 10–5, Sun 12–5.

Orange Circle Antique Mall. 118 S. Glassell. (714) 538-8160. One hundred individual shops located here with many fine and varied antiques and collectibles. Credit cards accepted. Restrooms, handicapped accessible. Open Mon-Sat 10-5, Sundays 12-6.

Old Towne Antique Mall. 122 N. Glassell. (714) 532-6255. Antiques, collectibles, teddy bears, large gift selection, primitives, jewelry, vintage clothes. Credit cards accepted. Restrooms, handicapped accessible. Open daily.

Old Towne Orange. Glassell and Chapman Avenues. 50 quality antique shops located here.

PALO ALTO

Antiques Unlimited. 201 Hamilton Street. (415) 328-3748.

PANORAMA CITY

Antique Palace Mall. 8044 Van Nuys Blvd. (818) 786-3441.

PASADENA

Pasadena Antique Center. 480 S. Fair Oaks Blvd. (818) 449-7706 or 578-9556. Large, beautiful, 2-story Spanish building. 80 shops with period antiques, furniture, quality collectibles. Open daily 10am–6pm.

Showcase Antiques Gallery. 440 S. Fair Oaks Blvd. (818) 577-9660. 100+ dealers with quality antiques, collectibles, furniture, glassware, fine art as well as a large selection of quality original Western art. Open daily.

PASO ROBLES

Antique Emporium Mall. 1307 Park Street. (805) 238-1078. 40+ dealer mall with general line of antiques and collectibles. Open daily 10–5.

PETALUMA

Antique Market Place. 304 Petaluma Blvd. Approximately 20 dealers, antiques, furniture, nice selection of books. (707) 765-1155.

POMONA

Pomona's Antique Row. 100–200 Blocks East 2nd Street. (909) 629-1121 or 623-9835. Over 400 individual shops located here in this two-block area, which cover the entire range of antiques, collectibles, art and crafts. Tour buses welcome.

RANCHO CORDOVA

Antique Plaza. 11395 Folsom Blvd. (916) 852-8517. 50,000 sq ft facility. Large well-stocked mall with 200+ dealers offering a wide range of antiques and collectibles. Clean, friendly mall. Credit cards accepted. Restrooms, handicapped accessible, ample parking. Open daily.

REDWOOD CITY

Antique Arcade. 1823 El Camino Real and Highway 84. (415) 368-8267. Sixty-five-dealer mall with full line of American and European antiques and collectibles. Restrooms, ample parking, handicapped accessible. Open daily.

Finders Keepers Antique Collective. 837 Main Street. (415) 365-1750. General line of antiques, collectibles, Victorian, Art Deco, memorabilia, consignments. Open daily.

RIVERSIDE

Trolley Stop Antique Guild. 3466 University Avenue. (909) 683-6646. 11,000 sq ft mall featuring quality antiques and collectibles. Credit cards accepted. Restrooms, handicapped accessible, ample parking. Open Mon–Sat 10–6.

Shirley's Unique Emporium. 8989 Mission Blvd. (909) 681-2477. Forty antique and specialty shops here. Hours Tues–Fri 10am–5pm, Sat and Sun 11am–5pm.

Crystal's Antiques. 4205 Main Street. (909) 781-9922. Fifty dealers in an 11,000 sq ft, tri-level building. Credit cards accepted. Handicapped accessible. Hours Mon–Sat 10am–5pm.

Cinnamon Lane Antique Malls. 6056 Magnolia Avenue. (909) 781-6625. Antiques, collectibles, china, glassware, jewelry, paintings. Credit cards accepted. Restrooms, handicapped accessible, ample parking. Open daily.

ROSEVILLE

Antique Trove. 238 Vernon Street. (916) 786-2777. 25,000 sq ft. Antiques, collectibles. Large section featuring books and paper goods. Clean, well-stocked mall. Credit cards accepted. Mall features a great coffee house. Restrooms, ample parking, handicapped accessible. Open daily 10–6.

Memories Past Antique Mall. 801 Vernon Street. (916) 786-2606. 40 dealers.

Roseville Antique Mall. 106 Judas Street. (916) 773-4003.

SACRAMENTO

Antique Plaza. 11395 Folsom Blvd. Highway 50, Sunrise Exit. Large mall with 50,000 sq ft of showroom area and over 200 dealers. (916) 852-8517.

River City Antique Mall. 10117 Mills Station Road. 23,000 sq ft facility. (916) 362-7778. 100+ exhibitors with quality antique and collector lines. Credit cards accepted. Restrooms, handicapped accessible, ample parking. Open daily 10:30am–6pm.

57th Street Antique Mall. 875 - 57th Street. (916) 451-3130. Antiques, collectibles, jewelry, postcards, china, glassware, furniture. Credit cards accepted. Restrooms, handicapped accessible. Hours Tues–Sun 10am–5pm.

Antique Promenade. 6011 Folsom Blvd. (916) 457-1447. Antiques, collectibles, glass, lots of unique items. Hours Mon–Sat 10am–6pm, Sunday 11am–5pm.

SALINAS

Hall Tree Antique Mall. 202 Main Street. (805) 757-6918. Twenty-six dealers. Quality line of antiques, collectibles, ceramics, toys, fine jewelry, gems. Hours Mon–Fri 10am–6pm, Sat 10:30am–6pm, Sun 10:30am–5pm.

Country Peddler Antiques Mall. 347 Monterey Street. (805) 424-2292. Antiques, collectibles, large selection of oak furniture, country and Victorian collectibles. Hours Mon–Sat 10am–5pm.

SAN BERNARDINO

Treasure Mart. 293 Redlands Blvd. (909) 825-7264. Large well-stocked mall with 90 open shops. Furniture, antiques, collectibles, clocks. Credit cards accepted. Handicapped accessible. Open daily.

Emma's Trunk. 1701 Orange Tree Lane. (909) 798-7865. 100-dealer mall featuring antiques and collectibles and full restoration services. Credit cards accepted. Restrooms, handicapped accessible, ample parking. Open daily.

SAN CARLOS

Antique Trove. 1119 Industrial Blvd. 30,000 sq ft building. 150 dealers. Antiques, collectibles, and misc. (415) 593-1300. One of the area's largest and finest malls. Credit cards accepted. Open daily 11am–6pm.

Collectors Market. 1128 El Camino Real. (415) 593-1645. Thirty-five individual shops here. Open Mon–Sat 10:30am–5:30pm, Sun 12pm–5pm.

INFORMATION IS SUBJECT TO CHANGE—ALWAYS CALL FIRST!

SAN DIEGO

Antique Alley Mall. 1911 San Diego Avenue. (619) 688-1911. Collectibles, furniture, credit cards accepted. Restrooms, handicapped accessible, ample parking. Open daily.

Broadway Antique Mall. 7945 Broadway. (619) 461-1399. Thirty dealers. Open Mon–Sat 10am–7pm, Sun 10am–5pm.

Main Street Antique Mall. 237 E. Main Street, El Cajon. (619) 447-0800. 100+ dealer mall with general line of antiques.

Newport Avenue Antique Center. 4864 Newport Avenue. (619) 222-8686. 18,000 sq ft quality oriented mall with great selection of high-grade merchandise. Credit cards accepted. Restrooms, ample parking, handicapped accessible. Open daily.

Newport Avenue Antiques. 4836 Newport Avenue. (619) 224-1994. Fifty dealers with quality line of antiques and collectibles. Credit cards accepted. Restrooms, handicapped accessible, ample parking. Open daily.

D & B Collectors Mall. 4847 Newport Avenue. (619) 523-1262.

59th & J Antique Mall. 5021 J Street. 92101. Downtown, gaslamp quarter. (800) 427-MALL or (619) 338-9559. Antiques, collectibles, furniture, pottery, dolls, military items, Indian items.

Antique Mall. 452 - 8th Avenue. 8th and Island Mall. (619) 239-MALL. Quality antique and specialty shops, restaurant, deli.

Unicorn Antique Mall. 714 J Street. (619) 232-1696. Three-story, 30,000 sq ft facility. Well-stocked mall with wide variety of antiques and collectibles. Credit cards accepted. Handicapped accessible, restrooms, ample parking. Open daily.

SAN FRANCISCO

Great American Collective. 1736 Lombard. (415) 922-2650. Forty-dealer antique and collectible mall. Open Mon–Sat 11–6, Sundays 12–6.

SAN JOSE

Antiques Colony. 1915 W. San Carolton. (408) 293-9844.

SAN MARCOS

Antique Village. 983 Grand Avenue. (619) 744-8718. Fifty dealers, 10,000 sq ft mall. Lots of furniture, mining, and

Western collectibles here. Credit cards accepted. Restrooms, handicapped accessible, ample parking. Open daily 10–5:30.

SANTA MONICA

Santa Monica Antique Market. 1607 Lincoln Blvd. Approximately 150 dealers. This is an outstanding mall, with many high-quality and unusual items. Open daily. Plan an all-day stop at this mall. Full amenities here. Mon–Sat 1pm–6pm, Sun 12pm–5pm. (310) 314-4899. Fax (310) 314-4894.

SAUGUS

Country Antique Fair Mall. 21546 Golden Triangle. I-5 Freeway, Valencia Blvd Exit. (805) 254-1474. Near Magic Mountain and the Saugus Swap Meet. Over 100 shops, antiques, collectibles, gifts. Hours daily 10am–5pm. Fri until 9.

SIMI VALLEY

Penny Pinchers. 4265 Valley Fair. (805) 527-2056. Seventy-dealer mall. Antiques, collectibles, jewelry, dolls, china, furniture, truly a collector's paradise. Credit cards accepted. Restrooms, handicapped accessible, ample parking. Open Mon–Sat 10–5, Sun 11–5.

SHERMAN OAKS

Sherman Oaks Antiques Mall. 14034 Ventura Blvd. (818) 906-0338. One hundred shops at this mall. Antiques, collectibles, great selection of antique and fine jewelry, including watches. Restrooms, ample parking, handicapped accessible. Near Magic Mountain and a great weekend flea market, the Saugus Swap Meet. Hours Mon–Sat 11am–6pm, Sun 12pm–5pm.

SOLANO BEACH

The Antique Warehouse. 212 S. Cedros Avenue. (619) 755-5156. 100+ individual shops here in 15,000 sq ft facility. Friendly well-stocked mall. Credit cards accepted. Restrooms, handicapped accessible, ample parking. Great beach town to spend the day in. Open daily 10–5. Closed Tuesdays.

VENTURA

Times Remembered. 467 E. Main Street. (805) 643-3137. 7,000 sq ft facility with antiques, collectibles, jewelry, linens, vintage fashions. Credit cards accepted. Restrooms, ample parking, handicapped accessible. Open daily 10:30–5:30.

Ventura Antique Market. 457 E. Thompson Blvd. (805) 653-0239. Twenty-dealer mall. Open daily 10:30–5, closed Tuesdays.

The Nicholby Antique Mall & Coffee House. 404 E. Main Street. (805) 653-1195. Fifty-dealer mall with antiques, collectibles, furniture. Credit cards accepted. Restrooms, ample parking, handicapped accessible. Great coffee house. Open daily.

WHITTIER
King Richard's Antique Mall. 12301 E. Whittier Blvd. (213) 698-5974. Antiques, collectibles, Three-level facility. Credit cards accepted. Mall open Wed–Fri 10–9, Sat, Mon, Tues 10–6, Sun 12–5.

WILMINGTON
Butterfields Antique Mall. 402 W. Anaheim Blvd. (213) 518-7008. Antiques, collectibles, glassware, books, excellent selection of furniture. Hours Mon–Sat 10–6.

COLORADO ✇

ARVADA
Stage Stop Antique Mall. 7340 W. 44th Ave. South of I-70 at 44th and Wadsworth. 93030. (719) 423-3630. 24,000 sq ft facility with 130 dealers. Good variety of antiques and collectibles. Restrooms, ample parking, handicapped accessible. Open daily.

BUENA VISTA
Banana Bel Emporium/Marketplace. E. Main Street. (719) 395-4005. Thirty-five dealers. Antiques, collectibles, primitives, Western art. Open 10–6 daily.

COLORADO SPRINGS
Adobe Walls Antique Mall. 2808 W. Colorado Avenue. (719) 635-3394. Antiques, collectibles. Open daily 9–6.

The Antique Gallery. 21 N. Nevada. 17,000 sq ft, 50+ dealers, featuring over 500 pieces of furniture, lamps, clocks, jewelry, fine china, sterling silver, books, postcards, toys, quilts, primitives, depression glass, Coke and Pepsi items, and nice selection of Black memorabilia. Credit cards accepted. Open daily at 10 am. (719) 633-6070.

Antique Mart. 829 N. Union Street. (719) 634-6038. Large selection of antiques and collectibles. Dolls, teddy bears, crystal, silver, china, primitives, tools, depression glass, jewelry, Roseville, Hummels, fine furniture, quilts, large selection of vintage clothing. Hours Tues–Sat 11am–5:30pm.

Consignment of Collectibles. 5681 N. Academy, in Erindale Centre. Exit 150A off I-25. (719) 528-5922. Great selection of antiques, furniture, books, quilts, toys, crystal, jewelry, and art. Some real bargains here. Hours Mon-Sat 10am–6pm.

Kit & Kaboodle Estate Sales & Consignment Center. 4110B N. Academy Blvd. (719) 593-1044. Antiques, collectibles, crafts, clothing, china, furniture, books. Open Mon–Sat.

Nevada Avenue Antiques & Collectibles. 405 S. Nevada Ave. 80903. (719) 473-3351. 8500 sq ft building with 35+ dealers. Antiques, furniture, glassware, primitives, linens, toys, jewelry, decorator items, consignments. Hours Mon–Fri 9–6, Sat 10–5, Sun 12–4.

DENVER

Antique Market & Guild. 1200 Block S. Broadway. (303) 744-0281. Over 250 dealers located within this block. Full amenities here. Open daily.

Collectors Corner. 10615 Melody Drive. 22,000 square feet. Antiques, collector lines including RR, dolls, paper, vintage jewelry. (303) 450-2875.

Stuff Collectors Market. 2796 S. Federal Blvd. 80236. (303) 761-6995. One hundred dealers, 10,000+ sq ft building. Antiques, collectibles, glassware, china, antique and country furniture, jewelry, Art Deco, toys, tools, good selection of Southwestern items. Credit cards accepted. Hours daily 10am–6pm.

FT. COLLINS

Front Range Antique Mall. 6108 S. College Avenue. (970) 282-1808. Forty-dealer mall with furniture, glassware, primitives, collectibles. Open daily 10–6.

Western Flea Mart. 6012 S. College, (Highway 287). Over 80 dealers. Indoor market. Furniture, country primitives, Victorian era items, glassware, coins, dolls. Open daily 10am–7pm.

FRISCO
Junk-Tique. 313 Main Street. (303) 668-3040. Antiques, gifts, and wide range of Western collectibles. Mall features an 1875 narrow gauge steam engine.

GREELEY
Antiques at Lincoln Park. 822 - 8th Street, downtown. (303) 351-6222. 22,000 sq ft building. Antiques, collectibles, consignments, quilts, china, pottery, cut glass, clocks, furniture, primitives, linens. Hours Mon-Sat 10am–5:30pm.

JULESBURG
Antiques & Artisans Store. 101 Cedar. I-76 Exit 180. Local artisan market with trendy art, crafts and antiques. Open June–August, Mon-Sat 9am–5pm, Sun 1pm–5pm.

LAKEWOOD
The Antique Mall of Lakewood. 9635 W. Colfax Avenue. 34,000 sq ft building with over 100 individual antique shops. Fine furniture, primitives, flow blue, decorative items, china, glass, advertising items, toys, Victorian items. This is probably the finest overall mall in the Rocky Mountain area. (303) 238-6940. Hours Mon–Fri 10–7, Sat 10–6, Sun 11–5.

SHOPPING SMART—IF YOU BUY AN ITEM THAT HAS BEEN REPAIRED, REFURBISHED, REPAINTED, RESTORED, ETC., REALIZE THAT YOU ARE BUYING SOMETHING THAT HAS LOST ALL OF ITS ANTIQUE VALUE. BUY IT FOR FUN, IF YOU WANT. BUY IT FOR DECORATION. BUT DON'T EXPECT IT TO HAVE THE SAME VALUE IT WOULD HAVE HAD BEFORE IT WAS "IMPROVED." ALSO, DON'T THINK THAT YOUR NEWLY RESTORED ITEM WILL NOW BE WORTH "BOOK PRICE" BECAUSE IT LOOKS LIKE IT DID WHEN IT WAS NEW. ANTIQUE AND COLLECTIBLE VALUES AREN'T DETERMINED LIKE THAT. SERIOUS COLLECTORS ONLY WANT THE REAL, AS-IT-CAME-EVEN-IF-IT-WAS- WELL-USED GOODS. THAT'S WHY TOP PRICES ARE PAID FOR THOSE PIECES THAT HAVE SOMEHOW WEATHERED TIME, KEEPING THEIR ORIGINAL, PRISTINE SHAPE. PIECES IN GOOD BUT *ORIGINAL* CONDITION, THEN, ARE YOUR WISEST CHOICE FOR LONG-TERM INVESTMENT.

Buckboard Antiques & Collectibles. 3265 Wadsworth Street. Behind Furrs Cafeteria. Lots of toys, furniture, brewery items. Open Mon–Sat 10–6, Sun 11–5. (303) 986-0221.

Something Different Antique Co-Op. Connie and Bob Palermo. 8427 W. Colfax. 80215. (303) 237-7228. Antiques, collectibles, jewelry, glass, decorator items, pottery, art, books, furniture, large selection of Czechoslovakian glass. Hours Mon–Sat 10–6, Sun 11–6.

LIMON

Treasures Unlimited. 571 Main Street. (719) 775-2057. Sixty dealers with antiques, collectibles, and crafts. Furniture, decorator items, vintage jewelry, glassware, pottery.

LITTLETON

Colorado Antique Gallery. 5501 S. Broadway. 50,000 sq ft building (one level). 150+ dealers. Great selection and prices on over 200,000 antiques and collectibles. Open daily, closes at 6 pm. (303) 794-8100.

LOVELAND

Rocky Mountain Antiques. 3816 W. Eisenhower Parkway. (Highway 34). One of the largest malls in northern Colorado. Country primitives, Victorian items, decorator pieces, dolls, china, glassware. Open daily 10am–6pm.

NIWOT

The Village Collective. 210 Franklin. Corner of 2nd and Franklin Streets. (303) 652-3636. Antiques, collectibles, country, primitives, Victorian, quilts, lots of small decorative items. Great cafe/tearoom. Open daily 10am–5pm.

PUEBLO

Tivolis Antique Gallery. 325 S. Union Avenue. Furniture, art, glassware, gifts. Open Mon–Sat 10am–5pm. (719) 545-1448 or (800) 545-1448.

Why Not Antiques. 1240 Berkeley. I-25, Exit Central Avenue. Lots of estate merchandise and nice antiques. Glassware, jewelry, pottery, china, silver, advertising and paper items, books. (719) 544-4104.

SPRINGFIELD

Treasure Chest Mall. Gary and Mary Hanna. 948 Main Street, downtown. (719) 523-6542. Collectibles, quilts, vintage clothing, furniture, jewelry, toys, glassware. Open daily.

CONNECTICUT ✧

DARIEN

Antiques of Darien. 1101 Boston Post Road. (203) 655-5133. Multidealer shop. Furniture, oriental collectibles, paintings, textiles. Credit cards accepted. Restrooms, handicapped accessible, ample parking. Open daily.

MYSTIC

Mystic River Antique Market. 14 Holmes Street. (203) 572-9775. 40+ dealers featuring quality antiques and collectibles. Great place to shop and just nose around. Credit cards accepted. Ample parking. Open daily.

NIANTIC

Between the Bridges. #65 Pennsylvania Avenue. (203) 691-0170. Exit 74 from turnpike, go right 3 miles. 50 dealers, antiques, collectibles, flea market items. Ample parking, restrooms. Open Thurs–Tues 10–5, closed Wednesdays.

WOODBRIDGE

Red Barn of Woodbridge Antiques & Collectibles. 378 Amity Road. (Route 63). (203) 389-4536. Multidealer co-op featuring a general line of antiques and collectibles. Quilts, linens, china, glassware, jewelry. Credit cards accepted. Restrooms, handicapped accessible, ample parking. Open daily.

DELAWARE ✧

CAMDEN

Camden Antiques Mall. Camden and Wyoming Avenue. (Route 10). Mall open Saturday and Sunday. Great array of quality antiques and collectibles. Glassware, china, quilts, country primitives, jewelry, furniture. Credit cards accepted. Restroom, handicapped accessible, ample parking. Open daily.

DOVER

Dover Antique Mart. Route 13 South. (302) 629-4393. Hours Mon-Sat 10–7, Sun 12–7. Thirty dealers. Furniture, glassware, jewelry, glassware, collectibles, decoys, dolls, clocks, military items, and trunks. Credit cards accepted. Restroom, handicapped accessible, ample parking. Open daily.

LAUREL

O'Neal's Antiques. Route 13, at stoplight. (302) 875-3391. Multidealer shop. Large selection of estate jewelry and diamonds. Furniture, glassware, china, country primitives, Victorian items, decorator pieces, collectibles. Credit cards accepted. Restrooms, handicapped accessible, ample parking. Open Mon–Sat 10–5.

LEWES

Garage Sale Antiques. 1416 Highway One. (302) 645-1205. Antiques, used furniture, architectural pieces, collectibles, jewelry, bric-a-brac. Restroom, ample parking. Open daily.

MILLSBORO

Antique Alley. 225 Main Street. Route 24. (302) 920-4001. Multidealer shop featuring, furniture, books, glass advertising items, tools. Credit cards accepted. Ample parking. Open daily.

Millsboro Antique Mall. 401 W. Dupont Highway. (Route 113). (302) 924-1203. Antique furniture, vintage clothing and jewelry, glassware. Credit cards accepted. Restrooms, handicapped accessible, ample parking. Open Mon–Fri 10–5, Sat and Sun 10–7.

SEAFORD

Seaford Antique Mall. Route 13 North. (302) 629-4393. Hours Mon–Sat 10–7, Sun 12–7. Thirty dealers featuring furniture, glassware, jewelry, books, and collectibles. Credit cards accepted. Restrooms, handicapped accessible, ample parking. Open daily.

ST. GEORGE

Antique Station. Route 13 South. (302) 836-5160. Hours daily 10am–5pm. Twenty-one shops with furniture, postcards, glass, primitives, nautical items, pottery, ephemera, and kitchenware. Credit cards accepted. Restrooms, handicapped accessible, ample parking. Open daily.

DISTRICT OF COLUMBIA ✽

WASHINGTON

Chevy Chase Antique Center. 5215 Wisconsin Avenue NW. (202) 364-4600. Large, very prestigious mall with high-quality museum and investment quality pieces. Credit cards accepted. handicapped accessible. Restrooms. Tea served daily at 4pm. Ample parking. Open Mon–Fri.

(NOTE: When visiting our nation's capital, there are many fine malls in the neighboring states, Virginia, Maryland, etc. Please check those state listings for malls in the suburbs of Washington, D.C.)

FLORIDA ❧

ALTAMONTE SPRINGS
Slade's Antique Mall. 1460 E. SR 436. West of 17-92. (407) 331-3337. 5,300 sq ft facility with antiques and collectibles. Glassware, coins, dolls, toys, country primitives, vintage jewelry.

BRADENTON
The Old Feed Store Antique Mall. 4407 U.S. Highway 301. (813) 729-1379. One mile west of I-75. 6,000 sq ft showroom with 35 dealers. Antique furniture, glassware, quilts, Victorian items, toys. Hours Mon–Sat 10am–5pm.

DANIA
Antique Galleries Mall. 60 N. Federal Highway. Furniture, china, coins, dolls, vintage clothing and jewelry, country primitives. (305) 920-2801.

DAYTONA BEACH
Riverfront Antique Mall. 140 N. Beach Street. (800) 749-0688. Great assortment of fine quality antiques. Mall conducts antique auction on Monday nights. Restrooms, ample parking, handicapped accessible. Snack bar, credit cards accepted. Open daily.

The House of Gamble Antique Mall. 1102 State Avenue. Holly Hill. 13,000+ sq ft. Antique furniture, quilts, linens, Victorian and country items, glassware, collectibles. Open Mon–Sat 10am–6pm, Sunday 12pm–5pm. (904) 258-2889.

DELAND
Rivertown Antique Mall. 114 S. Woodland Blvd. Mall is located in a national historic district. (904) 738-5111. General line of antiques and collectibles. Credit cards accepted. Ample parking, restrooms, handicapped accessible. Open Mon–Sat 9–5.

DELRAY BEACH

Delray Antique Mall. 2145 N. Federal Highway. Collectibles, antique furniture, linens, china, silver, glassware, small decorator items. (305) 368-8877.

FT. LAUDERDALE

Nostalgia Mall. 2097 Wildon Drive. (888) 394-7233 or (954) 537-5533. 9,000 sq ft facility. Fine antiques and collectibles. Mall has been newly remodeled. Credit cards accepted. Restrooms, ample parking, handicapped accessible. Open daily.

FT. MYERS

Myers Antique Mall. 924 Ortiz Avenue. (813) 693-0500. Quality antiques and collectibles with 15 dealers. Located one mile north of the flea market. Furniture, country primitives, quilts, vintage jewelry, collectibles, glassware.

FT. PIERCE

Red Barn Antiques #1. 2001 N. Kings Highway. (407) 468-1901. 50+ dealers, antiques and collectibles. Furniture, collectibles, glassware, books, glassware, pottery. Open daily 10am–5pm. Closed Wednesdays.

Red Barn Antiques #2. 5135 N. U.S. Highway #1. (407) 778-9860. 100+ dealers, antiques and collectibles. Credit cards accepted, restrooms, ample parking. Open daily 10–5, closed Wednesdays.

GAINESVILLE

Smiley's Antique Mall. Barbara Collins. I-75, Exit 74. Seven miles south of town. New mall. 175 dealers. Antiques and collectibles. Restaurant next door. Restrooms, ample parking. c/p Christie Collins, Box 129, 32603. (904) 335-2821 or 486-0707. Open daily 10am–6pm.

HIGH SPRINGS

Wisteria Corner Antique Mall. 225 N. Main Street. I-75, Exit Highway 441, 5 miles west. (904) 454-3555 Glassware, china, quilts, linens, silver, dolls, coins, pottery, books, vintage clothing.

HOLIDAY

Lyon's Head Antique Center. 1824 U.S. Highway 19 N. Pappas Plaza. (813) 943-0021. Three miles north of Tarpon Springs. Hours Sun–Thurs 10am–6pm, Fri–Sat 10am–9pm.

150+ dealers. Furniture, glassware, china, collectibles. Air-conditioned.

JACKSONVILLE

Beyard Country Store Antique Mall. 12525 Phillips Highway. Three miles south of I-295 on Highway #1. Three-floor building with approximately 25 dealers. The building that houses this mall is a very old, restored hotel. (904) 262-2548.

Lovejoy's Antique Mall. 5107 San Jose Blvd. Furniture, glassware, china, coins, dolls, books, collectibles in every line. (904) 730-8083.

Avondale Antique Mall. 3960 Oak Street. Glassware, china, quilts, linens, country primitives, Victorian items, books, collectibles. (904) 384-9810.

Southside Antique Mall. 11000 Beach Blvd. (904) 645-0806. 50,000 sq ft showroom with over 190 dealers. Very large well-stocked mall with many fine antiques and collectibles. Excellent tearoom. Open daily.

ANTIQUE MALL INFORMATION IS SUBJECT TO CHANGE!

Frontier Antique Mall. 3637 Phillips Highway. (904) 398-6055. 15,000 sq ft facility. Mall conducts regular monthly antique and collectibles auctions.

JACKSONVILLE BEACH

Beachs Antique Gallery. 1210 Beach Blvd. Glassware, china, silver, pottery, dolls, toys, dolls, coins, military items, collectibles. (904) 246-3149.

LAKE CITY

Grandpa's Farmer's and Flea Market. Highway 41. I-75, Exit 80. Open daily 9am–6pm. Market conducts large flea market with approximately 600 dealers outdoors on weekends. (904) 758-5564 or 755-7011.

LAKE PARK

MJ'S The Antique Mall. 1412 - 10th Street. (407) 844-1887. 3,000 sq ft facility. Glassware, some furniture but mostly small collector items. Quilts, linens, country primitives, Victorian era items, glassware, china, silver, advertising and paper, books.

LAKE WORTH

Ada's Olde Towne Antique Mall. 25 South J Street. New mall, antiques and collectibles. Vintage clothing and jewelry, glassware, china, pottery, books, quilts, toys. Open daily 9am–5pm. (407) 547-1700.

Carousel Antique Center. 815 Lake Ave. 33460. (407) 533-0678. Mall has wide variety of merchandise at good prices. Open 10 am to 5 pm daily. Furniture, paper and advertising items, glassware, dolls, toys, collectibles.

Heritage Antiques. 621 Lake Avenue. (407) 588-4755. Multi-dealer mall. Furniture, glassware, china, quilts, linens, books, collectibles, vintage jewelry, Victorian and Art Deco items. Open daily.

Tiffany's Antique Galleria. 620 Lake Avenue (407) 588-6700. Eighty-five dealers. Antiques and collectibles. Quilts, china, glassware, toys, banks, paper and advertising items, vintage jewelry.

Yesterday's Antique Mall. 716 Lake Street. Collectibles, glassware, china, silver, linens, quilts, vintage clothing, Victorian items, country primitives. (407) 547-3816.

MAITLAND

Halley's Antiques Mall. 473 S. Orlando Avenue. Fine quality antiques and collectibles in all categories. Glassware, china, silver, jewelry. (407) 539-1066.

MELBOURNE

Flea Mall. 915 S. Babcock Street. 32901. Booths full of unique antique treasures and collector finds of all kinds make this a great stop for casual or serious shoppers. (407) 951-2240. Open daily.

MIAMI

Only Yesterday Antique Market. 6576 SW 40th Street. (305) 666-2585. Twenty dealers. Very quality-oriented mall. Credit cards accepted. Open daily.

MT. DORA

Wild Rose Antique Mini Mall. 140 E. 4th Avenue. Quality antiques and collectibles. Quilts, china, silver, toys, banks, dolls, paper and advertising items, vintage jewelry. (904) 383-6664.

NAPLES

Yahl Street Antiques. 5430 Yahl Street N. (813) 591-8182. Over 65 dealers. One of the area's largest malls. Furniture, glassware, china, silver, coins, toys, books, vintage clothing, country and Victorian items, decorator finds. Credit cards accepted. Restrooms, ample parking. Open Mon–Sat 10–4, closed Sundays.

Antique Guild. 183 - 10th Street S. (813) 649-0323. Over 20 dealers. Antiques and collectibles of all descriptions. Glassware, silver, linens, quilts, Victorian items, Art Deco pieces, china, pottery, advertising and paper finds. Credit cards accepted. Restrooms, ample parking. Open daily.

NEW SMYRNA BEACH

Antique Mall. 419 Canal Street. Downtown. (904) 426-7825. Twenty dealers. Open Mon–Sat 9–5.

OCALA

Ocala Antique Mall. 3700 S. Pine Avenue. (941) 622-4468. Fifty dealers, 10,000 sq ft facility. Antiques, collectibles. Credit cards accepted. Restrooms, ample parking. Mall conducts antique auctions bimonthly. Open daily 10–5.

Remembering You Antique Mall. 3970 S. Pine Avenue. (941) 690-6988. Antiques, collectibles, furniture, china, glassware, orientals, art work. Credit cards accepted. Restrooms, ample parking. Open Mon–Sat 10–5, Sundays 12–5.

ORLANDO

Antique Mall of Central Florida. 1101 Virginia Drive. (407) 896-0031. One of the area's larger malls. Collectibles, glassware, china, silver, pottery, dolls, toys, country nostalgia items, vintage jewelry.

Olivia's Heirlooms. 1219 N. Orange Avenue. (407) 898-5400. Multidealer and consignment mall featuring fine furniture, china, artwork, clocks, collectibles.

PALMETTO

Midway Antique Mall and Flea Market. Main Street, Downtown. Mall is open daily. Flea market is held Wednesday, Saturday, and Sunday. (813) 723-9093 or 723-6000.

PENSACOLA

American Antiques Mall. 2019 North T Street. (904) 432-

7659. 5,000 sq ft facility. Antiques, collectibles, furniture, lamps, linens, quilts, old bottles, silver, china.

Antique 9th Avenue Mall. 380 N. 9th Avenue. (904) 438-3961. Fifty individual shops, 10,000 sq ft facility. Antique furniture, china, silver, quilts, linens, dolls, toys, pottery, glassware, collectibles. Open daily.

Ragtime Antique Mall. 3113 Mobile Highway. (904) 438-1232. Antiques, collectibles, jazz age, Art Deco, glassware, vintage jewelry, books, paper and advertising items.

PINELLAS PARK

Tri-City Antique Mall. 8010 U.S. Highway 19N. Quality collector items in all descriptions: dolls, toys, vintage clothing and jewelry, lamps, bottles, RR items, coins, china, pottery. (813) 546-3531.

SARASOTA

Creative Collections Antique & Collectible Mall. 527 Pineapple Ave S. (813) 951-0477. Booths full of great collectibles, glassware, china, pottery, furniture, Victorian era finds, country nostalgia, quilts, linens.

ST. CLOUD

Heritage Antiques & Mall. 1136 New York Avenue. (407) 892-9663. Collectibles, antique furniture, glassware, books, toys, jewelry.

ST. PETERSBURG

Antique Exchange of St. Petersburg. 2535 Central Avenue. (813) 321-6621. This is a full city block with over 100 dealers offering a wide range of items from museum quality to decorator items. This is a great antique shopping experience. Full amenities here. Open daily 10–5.

Gas Plant Antique Arcade. 1246 Central Avenue. (813) 895-0568. 32,000 sq ft showroom with over 70 dealers. Well-stocked mall with fine antiques, collectibles, and memorabilia. This is a good, all-around mall with a wide selection of merchandise. Open daily.

Patty & Friends Antique Mall. 1225 - 9th Street North. (813) 821-2106 or 367-6550. Open daily 10am–4pm. 80+ dealers in three large, old, remodeled houses. Silver, primitives, oriental items, furniture, advertising, banks, clocks, toys, movie memorabilia.

Park Street Antique Center. 9401 Bay Pines Blvd. (813) 392-2198. 10,000 sq ft facility with over 80 dealers. Good selection of oak and wicker furniture, glassware, clocks, collectibles. This mall also has a weekend flea market on premises.

4th Street Antique Alley. John and Laura McNeal. 1535 - 4th Street N. (813) 823-5700. Over 35 dealers. Booths full of small desirables. Collectibles, glassware, china, silver, country and Victorian items. Open daily.

Person's Antiques Too. 1250 - 9th Street N. Antique furniture, glassware, collectibles, lamps, clocks, coins, vintage jewelry, pottery, toys, dolls, advertising items. (813) 898-1232.

SILVER SPRINGS

Della's Depot. 5361 E. Silver Springs Blvd. (Highway 40). Open daily. (904) 236-0036. Collectibles, glassware, advertising items, decorator finds, vintage jewelry. Open daily.

TAMPA

Antique Mall of Tampa. 1102 E. Busch Blvd. I-275, exit 33. (813) 933-5829. Large well-stocked mall with 70+ dealers. Glassware, china, silver, paper and advertising items, coins, dolls, lamps, clocks.

Forever Yours Antique Mall. 110 Montclair Ave. N. (813) 684-3339. Multidealer mall with 2,000 sq ft of collectibles and antiques. Glassware, china, collectibles, china, books, paper and advertising, country primitives, small desirables.

South Macdill Antique Mall. 4004 MacDill Avenue S. (813) 832-7366. 60+ dealers. Antiques, collectibles, vintage clothing, American primitives, oriental items, quilts, china, glassware. Open daily, 10am–6pm.

TARPON SPRINGS

Taylor Arcade Antique Mall. 118 Tarpon Ave. Collectibles, jewelry, glassware, pottery, art, dolls, toys, coins, paper and advertising items. (813) 942-4046. Note: This mall is located in a very quaint Greek fishing community. Papa's, a wonderful Greek restaurant, is located here. A visit to this eating establishment makes visiting the town a distinctly memorable experience.

WEST PALM BEACH

Palm Beach Flea Market and Antique Mall. 8011 S. Dixie Highway. c/p Orville Rodberg. Collectibles, china, furniture, small desirables and decorator items, glassware. (305) 586-4002.

Old Timer's Antique Mall. 3717 S. Dixie Highway. Antiques and collectibles of all descriptions. There are some treasures to be found here if you are an observant shopper. Collectibles, glassware, china, silver, country primitives, Victorian items, Art Deco pieces.

Palm Beach Antique & Art Exchange. 1907 S. Dixie Highway. (407) 832-9325. Multidealer emporium. Antiques, collectibles, furniture, paintings, prints, toys, dolls, silver, coins. Credit cards accepted. Restrooms, ample parking. Open daily.

WILTON MANORS

Antique Liquidation Gallery. 2205 Wildon Drive. (305) 568-9005. Antiques, collectibles, furniture, art. Credit cards accepted. Snack bar, restrooms, ample parking. Mall conducts retail antique auctions. Open daily.

WINTER PARK

Orange Tree Antique Mall. 853 S. Orlando Avenue. (Highway 17-92) South of Fairbanks. (407) 644-4547. An 85-dealer mall with antiques, art, collectibles, and furniture. Credit cards accepted. Ample parking, restrooms, handicapped accessible. Open Mon–Sat 10–6, Sundays 1–5.

Antique 'N Country Nancy's. 1965 Aloma Avenue. (407) 657-1863. Thirty dealers with a general line of antiques and collectibles. Glassware, china, silver, linens, quilts, vintage clothing and jewelry.

Our Antiques Market. Hardy Hudson. 5453 Lake Howell Road. (407) 657-2100. 5,000 sq ft facility with 40 dealers. Antiques and collectibles of all descriptions. Glassware, china, silver, advertising items, country primitives, furniture, small desirables. Open Mon–Sat.

Antique Mall. 3170 U.S. Highway 17 N. (813) 293-5618. 4,500 sq ft of quality antique shopping. 20 dealers under one roof. Glassware, china, silver, coins, toys, dolls, collectibles,

GEORGIA ❧

ACWORTH
Beverly's Antique Mall & Flea Market. 4853 N. Main Street NW. Collectibles, antique furniture, glassware, books, advertising items. (404) 974-8275. Open daily.

ALPHARETTA
A Flea Ant'tiques. 225 S. Main Street. Quality antique and collectible of all kinds. Glassware, small desirables, pottery, china, silver, country items, vintage jewelry. (404) 442-8991.

ASHEVILLE
Smiley's Antique Mall. I-26, Exit 13, Highway 25, ½ mile north. Open Mon–Fri 10–5, Sat and Sun 9–5. c/p Polly Hickling, (704) 684-3515.

ATLANTA
Broad Street Antique Mall. 3550 Broad Street. (404) 458-6316. Thirty dealers. Antiques and collectibles of all kinds. Open daily.

AUGUSTA
Antiques Marketplace. 3179 Washington Road. Village West Shopping Center. One mile north of I-20. Sixty dealers. Quality line of antiques and collectibles. Good place for dealers to shop, lots of nice items at good prices. Open Mon–Sat 10–7, Sun 12–6. (706) 860-7909.

Broad Street Antique Mall. Mary Cape. 1224 Broad Street. (706) 722-4333. General line of antiques and collectibles. Hours Mon–Sat 10–6, Sun 2–6.

Downtown Antique Mall. 1243 Broad Street. (706) 722-3571. Fifteen individual antique shops located here. Hours Mon–Sat 10am–5:30pm, closed Sundays.

MACON
Smiley's Antique Mall. Highways 129 and 247, 4 miles south of town. Large well-stocked mall with a quality line of antiques and collectibles. Open Mon–Fri 10–5, Sat and Sun 9–5. c/p Charles or Phylis Reagan, (912) 788-1330.

MADISON

Madison Antique Mall & Flea Market. 1291 Eaton Road. Collectibles, glassware, small bric-a-brac, china, books, paper and advertising items. (404) 342-3753.

MARIETTA

Abe's Antiques. 1951 Canton Road NE. (404) 424-0587. Multidealer co-op featuring general line of antiques and collectibles. Glassware, china, art, pottery, vintage clothing, clocks, lamps, RR items.

The Antiquity Mall. 815 Pine Manor NE. (404) 428-8238. Multiple dealer mall with antiques and collectibles of all kinds. Clock repair a specialty.

PINE MOUNTAIN

Pine Mountain Antique Mall. Highway 27. Callaway Gardens area. New antique mall with 75+ dealer booths on monthly rental of $100 to $250 per month. No crafts or flea market items allowed. Restaurant with good home cooking. This is a great place to spend the day. Lovely market, grounds, and area. Large auction center located on the grounds conducting antique and estate auctions. C/p Chuck Beam, Box 64. 31822. (404) 663-4071. Hours Mon–Sat 10am–6pm, Sun 1pm–6pm.

SAVANNAH

Memory Lane Antiques Mall. 230 W. Bay Street. 8,000 sq ft showroom with 25 dealers. Lot of unusual items here including many German antiques. Good stop for dealers. Hours Mon–Sat 10-5, Sun 11–4. C/p Jim and Bev Weredy, (912) 232-0975 or 232-6010.

Antique Mall - Seventh Heaven. 3104 Skidaway Road. (912) 355-0835. Twenty-six dealers. Antique wicker, furniture, glassware, collectibles.

Waters Avenue Antique Mall. 3405 Waters Avenue. (912) 351-9313. Twenty-seven dealers, furniture, collectibles, glassware, antiques. Hours Mon–Sat 10:30am–5:30pm, closed Sundays.

SMYRNA

Village Mall Antiques & Crafts. 762 Concord Road SE. Collectibles, glassware, china, pottery, art, silver. (404) 438-0090.

TUCKER

Annalisa's Antiques & Flea Market. 4373 Hugh Howard Road. (404) 493-7348. Antiques, furniture, glassware, china, silver, collectibles. Hours Mon–Sat 11am–6pm.

WOODSTOCK

Samson's Mall of Antiquity. #6 South Main Street. (404) 516-4000. General line of antiques and collectibles. Open daily.

HAWAII ☙

HONOLULU

Downtown Unique Collections. 1121 Nuanu Ave. (808) 536-1890. Collectibles, glassware, china, silver, small desirables, vintage jewelry, books, quilts, linens. Credit cards accepted. Restrooms, handicapped accessible. Open Mon–Sat 10am–6pm.

KAILUA

The Hunter Antiques & Collectibles. 764 Kailua Road.(808) 262-4868. Quality antiques and collectibles makes this mall a delightful shopping experience. Many unique and unusual finds. Glassware, china, small desirables. Credit cards accepted. Restrooms, handicapped accessible, ample parking. Open Mon–Sat 10am–5pm.

MAUI

Upcountry Maui Antiques. Paia Town. Booths full of great antique and collectible items. Glassware, china, vintage jewelry, toys, paper and advertising items, Hawaiian collector items. Credit cards accepted. Restrooms, handicapped accessible, ample parking. Open daily, 10am–5pm.

IDAHO ☙

BOISE

Collectors Choice. Corner of Franklin and Orchard Streets. 60+ dealers in two shops. Glassware, china, silver, collectibles, country and Victorian era items. Open daily. (800) 992-8936.

Antiques Etc. Co-Op. (208) 343-2905. General lines of antiques and collectibles. Glassware, furniture, china, pottery, art, dolls, toys. Specializing in Fenton glass.

COEUR D'ALENE

Coeur D'Alene Antique Mall. This company has two malls in town; one at 3650 Government Way, (208) 667-0246, and the other at Haycraft and Highway 95, (208) 664-0579. Both malls have a general variety of collectibles and antiques. Glassware, furniture, small desirables and decorator items. Credit cards accepted. Restrooms, ample parking, handicapped accessible. Open daily.

Lake City Antique Mall. 401 N. 2nd Street. (208) 664-6883. Antiques, collectibles, farm and ranch items. Indian and Western collectibles and jewelry. Credit cards accepted. Restrooms, handicapped accessible, ample parking. Open daily.

Wigget Mall. 119 N. 4th Street. (208) 664-1524. Mall is located in a four-story building. Antiques, collectibles, gifts, new merchandise. Credit cards accepted. Restrooms, ample parking. Open daily.

JEROME

Rose Antique Mall. 130 E. Main Street. (208) 324-2918. 8,500 sq ft. Glassware, pottery, china, coins, paper and advertising items, country primitives. Credit cards accepted. Restrooms, ample parking. Open Tues–Sat 10am–5pm.

LEWISTON

Bargain Hunter Mall. 1209 Main Street. (208) 746-6808. Forty booths full of great finds in antiques and collectibles.

> **SHOPPING SMART**—IF YOU WEAR EYEGLASSES, DON'T FORGET TO TAKE THEM ALONG WITH YOU ON YOUR ANTIQUE SHOPPING MALL ADVENTURE. THEY WILL BE INVALUABLE FOR LOOKING ITEMS OVER FOR THEIR "HALLMARKS" THOSE MARKS/STAMPS ON THE BOTTOM OF CHINA, POTTERY, TOYS, ETC., THAT IDENTIFY THEIR MANUFACTURERS OR COUNTRIES OF ORIGIN. DON'T WEAR GLASSES? A MAGNIFYING GLASS IS A HANDY GADGET THAT WORKS GREAT FOR EVERYBODY WHO IS REALLY INTO THE "THRILL OF THE HUNT" FOR ANTIQUE AND COLLECTIBLE TREASURE.

Unique collector items, glassware, pottery, art, small furniture, vintage jewelry. Credit cards accepted. Restrooms, handicapped accessible, ample parking. Open daily.

ILLINOIS ❦

ALBANY
Albany Antique Mart. Great River Road. 61230. (Highway 84.) I-80, Exit 1, then 18 miles north. (309) 887-4850. Antiques, collectibles, furniture, glassware, china, primitives, postcards and nice selection of vintage Christmas collectibles. Open Mon–Sat 10–5, Sun 12–5.

ALTON
Alton Exchange. 510 W. Delmar Avenue. (618) 467-0820. 16,000 sq ft facility. One level with 150+ dealers. Antiques, crafts, collectibles. Many neighboring antique shops. Handicapped accessible, restrooms, parking can be difficult. Credit cards accepted. Open Mon-Sat 10–8, Sundays 10–5.

ARCOLA
Emporium Antiques. 201 E. Main Street. 61910. (217) 268-4523. Antiques, collectibles. Glassware, china, silver, pottery, paper and advertising items. Restrooms, ample parking, multilevel building. Open Mon–Sat 9am–5pm, Sunday 12pm–5pm.

ATLANTA
Route 66 Antique Mall. I-55, exit 140, west 4 blocks Quality antiques and collectibles in all categories. From furniture to small desirables. (217) 648-2321. Open Mon–Sat 10–5, Sun 12–5.

AVON
Avon Antique Mall. Main Street. Glassware, china, linens, quilts, dolls, toys. Good selection of antiques and collectibles in all categories. (309) 465-7387. Open daily.

BEARDSTOWN
Beardstown Antique Mall. Route 125 East (east end of town). (217) 323-4569. 7,000 sq ft building. Antiques, collectibles, quilts, glassware, nice selection of antique furniture. Ample parking, restrooms, handicapped accessible. Good food nearby. Open Mon–Sat 10–5, Sun 12–5.

BEATHANY

Beathany Antique Mart. 402 W. Route 121. (217) 665-3978. Twenty-five dealers. Mall has tremendous selection of fine glassware. No reproductions allowed. Restrooms. Open Mon-Fri 9-6. Sat 10-8. Sun 12–5.

BELLEVILLE

Antique Gallery Mall. 201 W. Main Street. Vintage clothing and jewelry, china, silver, glassware, lamps, kitchen collectibles. Open daily 10–5. (618) 233-0700.

The Belleville Antique Mall. 208 E. Main Street. (618) 234-MALL. Fine antiques and collectibles, Victorian specialties, art pottery, estate and vintage jewelry, glassware, large selection of antique furniture. Restrooms, handicapped accessible, difficult parking. Open Mon 11–4, Tues–Sat 10–5, Sundays 12–4.

BLOOMFIELD

Memory Lane Antique Mall. 208 E. Franklin Street. (515) 664-1714. Sixty dealers. Antiques and collectibles. Mon-Sat 8–5, Sun 1–5.

BLOOMINGTON

Antique Mall. 102 N. Center Street. Front & Center Building. 61701. (309) 828-1211. Over 40 dealers. Quilts, country primitives, Victorian items, glassware, pottery, advertising items. Open Mon 10–7. Tues–Sat 10–5.

Mid-America Antique Mall. I-74 and Route 51. $^1/_2$ mile south of town. Donald and Nancy Geiselman. (309) 828-5697. Large well-stocked mall with quality antiques, crafts, and collectibles. Restrooms, handicapped accessible, ample parking. Hours Mon–Sat 10–6, Sundays 12–5.

BOURBONNAIS

Indian Oaks Antique Mall. North Highway 50 and Larry Power Road. 60914. 150+ dealers. Antiques, collectibles, gift items, and crafts. Credit cards accepted. Open 10–5:30 Sat–Wed. Thurs–Fri 10–8.

BROOKFIELD

Antique World Annex. 3100 Grand Blvd. Antiques and collectibles in all categories. From furniture to small desirables. (708) 387-2040. Open Mon-Wed 11–6, Thurs 11–5, Fri–Sat 11–6, Sun 11–5.

CENTERVILLE
Gingerbread Corner and Mini Mall. 141 S. Division Street. Marie Bruns. (618) 985-4550. Antiques, collectibles, dolls, glassware. Restrooms, ample parking, handicapped accessible. Open Wed–Sat 12–5 and sometimes on Sunday 1–5.

CHAMPAIGN
Vintage Antiques. 117 N. Walnut. Downtown. Ten dealers, two floors. Nice selection of antiques and collectibles. Glassware, china, primitives, Victorian and Art Deco items. Open Mon–Sat 10–5. (217) 359-8747.

CHENOA
The Antique Mall. I-55, Chenoa exit. Nancy Callis. (815) 945-7594. 9,000 sq ft mall with 32 dealers. Great selection of quality glassware, advertising items, toys, kitchenware, quilts, children's china and dolls. Credit cards accepted. Open Mon–Sat 10–6, Sun 1–5. Several additional interesting shops are located in the vicinity, making this a terrific stop.

CHICAGO
Armitage Antique Gallery. 1529 W. Armitage. 60600. (312) 227-7727. Forty-dealer mall. Lots of fine quality antiques and collectibles here. Glassware, china, pottery, country primitives, kitchenware, dolls, toys, banks. Open 11am–6pm daily.

Wrigleyville Antique Mall. 3336 N. Clark Street. Good variety of antiques and collectibles in all categories. (312) 868-0285. Twenty-five dealers. Open Mon-Sat 11–6:30, Sun 12–6.

CHILLICOTHE
The Heartland Craft Mall. Route 29. (800) 418-6410 or (309) 274-2283. Large 23,000 sq ft facility with wide variety of locally produced crafts. One of the largest craft malls in the Midwest. Restrooms, snack bar, ample parking, handicapped accessible. Hours daily 9am to 5 pm.

CLINTON
Clinton Antique Mall. Junction Highways 51 and 54. (217) 935-8846. 100+ dealers with a general line of antiques and collectibles. Restrooms, snack bar, ample parking, handicapped accessible, mall is one level. Open Mon–Sat 10–5, Sun 12–5.

Country Junction Mall. Junction Routes 51 and 54. (217) 935-5363. 75+ dealers in attractive room design settings. Mall specializes in country collectibles and antiques, primitives, folk art. Restrooms, snack bar, ample parking. Handicapped accessible. Hours Mon–Sat 10–5, Sundays 12–5.

DECATUR

Nellie's Attic Antique Mall. East of Decatur on Highway 121. One mile South of Junction Route 36 and Route 121. (217) 864-3363. Antiques, collectibles. Mall has nice restaurant, Uncle John's Chicken House. Restrooms, ample parking. Hours Tues–Sat 10–5, Sundays 12–5.

Franklin Mall Antiques & Travel Treasures. 304 S. Franklin. Ralph Owen, (217) 422-3456. Mall features stained glass, Lincoln items, bronze and marble statues, toys, international painting section. Restrooms, snack bar, ample parking. Credit cards accepted. Open Thurs–Sat, 10–3.

DIVERNON

Lisa's Antique Mall. I-55, Exit 82, (Highway 104). Twelve miles south of Springfield. (217) 628-1111 or 628-3333. Two large buildings, 40,000 sq ft total space. 150 dealers. Credit cards accepted. Glassware, quilts, linens, lamps, paper and advertising items. Open daily 10–6.

Nickorbobs Craft Mall. Route 104. At Exit 82 from I-55. Over 100 crafters in 15,000 sq ft setting. Great selection of locally produced crafts. Credit cards accepted. Restrooms, ample parking, handicapped accessible. Open daily, 10–6.

The Country Place Antique Mall. Exit 80 from I-55, on Frontage Road (old Route 66). (217) 628-3699. Large, clean, pleasant mall with great selection of glassware. Restrooms, ample parking, good food nearby. Credit cards accepted. Handicapped accessible. Open daily 9–5.

DIXON

Brinton Avenue Antique Mall. 725 N. Brinton Avenue. 61021. (815) 284-4643. Antiques, collectibles, art glass, lamps, toys, furniture, antique dolls, pottery. Open daily 10am–5pm.

DUNDEE

The Antique Emporium. Route 25. ¹/₂ mile north of I-90 at the Milk Pail. (847) 468-9667. 30+ dealers featuring a general line of antiques, collectibles, and unusual items. Restroom, ample parking, handicapped accessible. Open Tue–Sun 10–5.

DWIGHT

Home Spun Craft Mall. 136 E. Main Street. (815) 584-2171. Quality handmade crafts, custom wood designs, art, quilts, needlework, and jewelry. Restrooms. Open Mon-Sat 10–4. Closed Wednesdays and Sundays.

EAST MOLINE

Antique & Treasure Trove. 611 - 15th Avenue. 61244. (309) 755-2525. New mall, 2,400 sq ft, antiques, collectibles, gifts. Credit cards accepted. Open Mon–Fri 10–5, Sat 10–3.

EAST PEORIA

Pleasant Hill Antique Mall and Tea Room. 315 S. Pleasant Hill Road. 61611. (309) 694-4040. Large well-stocked mall 30,000 sq ft with a full line of antiques and collectibles. Tearoom and full family restaurant. Open Mon and Tues 7–7, Wed–Sat 7–10, Sun 7–5.

ELDORADO

Eldorado Antique Mall. 935 Fourth Street. John and Carol Oglesby (618) 273-6466. 5,000 sq ft facility with antiques and collectibles. Custom frame shop on premises. Restrooms, ample parking, handicapped accessible. Credit cards accepted. Open Mon–Sat 10–5, Sundays 1–5.

EL PASO

Old Fashioned Things Antique Mall. 27 W. Front Street. (309) 527-5740. Glassware, depression glass, costume jewelry, Hull and other pottery, Russel Wright items. Restrooms. Open Tue–Sat 10–5, Sundays 1–5, closed Mondays.

El Paso Antique Mall. I-39 and Route 24. New mall with over 200 dealers. Mall features quality antiques only. No crafts or reproductions. Restrooms, snack bar, ample parking. Credit cards accepted. Open Tues–Sat 10–6.

ELK GROVE VILLAGE

Antiques Mart. 1170 W. Devon Avenue. Approx. 125 dealers here. Booths full of antiques and collectibles of every description. Glassware, china, silver, coins, advertising items, country and Victorian pieces, vintage jewelry. Open Mon–Fri 11–7, Sat and Sun 10–5. (708) 894-8900.

Landmark Antiques. 1110 Nerge Road. (708) 924-5220. Thirty-five dealers, quality antiques. Quilts, furniture, dolls, glassware, toys, lamps, art glass, pottery. Open Mon-Fri 11-7, Sat and Sun 10–5.

ELWIN

Elwin Antique Mall. Route 151. Four miles south of Decatur. (217) 865-3292. Antiques, primitives, linens, glassware, crafts. Restrooms, ample parking. Handicapped accessible. Great tearoom. Open Mon–Sat 10–5, Sundays 11–5.

EUREKA

Courthouse Coffee Shop & Antiques. 122 N. Main Street. (309) 467-6923. Antiques, crafts, collectibles. Restrooms, ample parking. Cafe. Handicapped accessible. Open daily 7–7.

FAIRVIEW HEIGHTS

St. Clair Antique Mall. Junction Highway 159 and I-64. (618) 628-1650. Clean, attractive 140-booth mall with large 100 showcase section. Great selection of quality items here. No crafts or secondhand merchandise. Restrooms, handicapped accessible, ample parking. Open Mon–Sat 10–8, Sundays 12–6.

FINDLAY

The Arches Antique Marketplace. 200 Main Street. Quality antiques and collectibles of all descriptions. Books, glassware, decorator items, and plenty of small desirable collector finds. (217) 756-8243. 20+ dealers. Open Sun–Thurs 11–5, Fri and Sat 11–9.

FOREST

Old Hatchery Antique Mall. Route 47, three miles south of town. (815) 657-7070. 20,000 sq ft facility of very pleasurable shopping. Glassware, primitives, dried flowers, nice selection of crocks, Victorian and primitive furniture, flow blue china, rugs. Excellent tearoom with great desserts. Credit cards accepted. Restrooms, ample parking, handicapped accessible. Mall is open daily 10–5 and is closed on major holidays.

FOX LAKE

Antique Alley Mall. 415 S. Washington Street. (708) 587-0091. 3,000 sq ft mall located in a former bowling alley. Antiques and collectibles. Collector finds including: depression and pattern glass, pottery, lamps, vintage clothing and lamps, trunks, kitchenware, Victorian era items. Open Mon–Fri 11–5, Sat and Sun 11–4.

DAYS AND TIMES OF OPERATION ARE SUBJECT TO CHANGE!

GALENA

Galena Antique Mall. $1^1/_2$ miles east of town on Route 20. (815) 777-3440. Forty-five-dealer mall with general line of antiques and collectibles. Credit cards accepted. Restroom, ample parking, handicapped accessible. Open daily 10–5.

GENEVA

Geneva Antiques Market. 227 S. Third Street. 60134. (708) 208-1150. Antiques, collectibles. Open Mon–Sat 10–5, Sun 11–4.

GENESEO

Geneseo Antique Mall. 117 E. Exchange Avenue. 61254. I-80, exit 19 downtown. Good selection of antiques and collectibles for every taste and budget. (309) 944-3777. Credit cards accepted. Open Mon–Sat 9–5.

Heartland Antique Mall. Pam Ropp. 4169 S. Oakwood Avenue. 61254. A bit of everything at this mall. Antique furniture, lots of small desirables. (309) 944-3373. Open 9am–5pm daily.

GIRARD

Wagon Wheel Antique Mall. 108 W. Center Street. Downtown square. (217) 627-3051. Eighteen dealers. Glassware, furniture, collectibles, crafts. Restroom. Open Mon–Sat 10–5, Sundays 1–5. Closed Thursday.

GODFREY

Tri-County Auction & Mini Mall. Routes 67 and 111, halfway between Godfrey and Brighton. (217) 466-1469. Great out of the way place. Primitives, collectibles, used tools, crafts, used furniture, gifts. Restrooms, ample parking, snack bar, handicapped accessible. Open Mon–Fri 9–4, Sat–Sun 10–3.

GRAYSLAKE

Antique Warehouse. #2 S. Lake Street. 65-dealer mall with lots of quality antiques and collectibles. No reproductions. Open Mon–Sat 10–5, Sun 12–4. (708) 223-9554.

GREENFIELD

Countryside Mercantile. 409 Chestnut Street. (217) 368-2531. Mall features the work of 30 local artists. Restrooms, ample parking, handicapped accessible. Credit cards accepted. Open Thurs–Sat 10–5.

GREENUP

Western Style Town Antique Mall. I-70 and Route 130. (217) 923-3009. New 6,000 sq ft mall with antiques and crafts. Restrooms, ample parking, handicapped accessible. Open daily.

County Seat Mall. 105 N. 3rd Street. Downtown courthouse square. Gene and Sandy Daum. (618) 664-8955. New antique mall. Antiques, collectibles, gifts, crafts. Restrooms, ample parking, handicapped accessible. Open Mon–Sat 10–5, Sundays 12–5.

GREENVILLE

County Seat Mall. 105 N. 3rd Street. Downtown courthouse square. Gene and Sandy Daum. (618) 664-8955. New antique mall. Antiques, collectibles, gifts, crafts. Restrooms, ample parking, handicapped accessible. Open Mon–Sat 10–6. Sundays 12–6.

HAMILTON

Antique Mini Mall & Flea Market. Route 136. Collectibles of every description and great antique finds for every taste and budget.

HENNEPIN

J & S Antiques Mall. Jim and Sandy Boender. Junction of State Highway 88 and I-80. (Exit 45). (815) 454-2066. 8,000 sq ft building loaded with quality antiques and collectibles. Open Mon–Sat 9–5, Sun 12–4.

HERRIN

Forgotten Treasures Antique Mall. #4 N. Park Street. Marty Franklin, (618) 988-1285. General line of antiques and gifts. Antique furniture, glassware. Open Mon–Sat 10–5.

JACKSONVILLE

Jacksonville Antique Mall. Corner Lafayette and Pine Streets. (217) 243-3219. Twenty-five dealers. Glassware, china, quilts, linens, antique furniture. Open Mon–Sat 10–5, Sun 12–5.

South Jacksonville Antique Mall. 1852 S. Main Street. Good selection of antiques and collectibles. Nice decorator items. Open daily 10am–5pm.

R. B. Craft Mall. 228 W. Morton Avenue. Robyn, (217) 243-2427. Crafts, floral arrangements, wood items, hand-sewn items. Restrooms, ample parking, handicapped accessible. Open Wed–Sat 10–5.

KANKAKEE

Kankakee Antique Mall. 145 S. Schuyler. Downtown. I-57, exit 312, west 1.5 miles to Schuyler Avenue. (815) 937-4957. Large mall housed in a 65,000 sq ft building. 225 individual dealer booths. Well-stocked mall with a virtually unlimited range of items for the antiquer or collector. Open daily 10am–6pm.

Bull Dog Antiques. 440 N. 5th Avenue. (815) 936-1701. Twelve dealer mall with antiques and collectibles. Open Mon–Sat 10–5, Sun 12–4.

River Valley Antique Mall. Route 45/52. I-57, Exit 308 south 4 miles. A nice variety of good antiques and plenty of collector items in all categories. Open daily 10am–5pm. (815) 697-3040.

KEITHSBURG

Commercial House Antiques. Gail and Rupert Wenzel. 413 Main Street. 61442. (309) 374-2330. Ten dealers, antiques, furniture, decorator items, lots of fine jewelry, sheet music, primitives. Open Mon–Sat 10–5, Sun 12–4, closed Tuesdays.

LA GRANGE

Antique World. 1005 E. 31st Street. Five miles west of Brookfield Zoo. Open Mon-Wed 11–6, Thurs 11–8, Sat 11–6, Sun 11–5.

LEBANON

General Store Antique Mall. 112 E. St. Louis Street, downtown. (618) 537-8494. Five-room facility with antiques, collectibles, furniture, glassware, nice selection of pottery, primitives, brewriana, paper goods. Restrooms, ample parking, handicapped accessible. Open Tues–Sat 10–5, Most Sundays 11–4. Closed Mondays.

LEROY
On the Park Antiques. 104 E. Center Street. (800) 543-8073 or (309) 962-2618. Twenty dealers. Antiques, collectibles, primitives, glassware. Open Mon–Sat 10–5, Sun 12–5.

LINCOLN
Route 66 Antique Mall. 1409 Short 11th Street. 62656. I-55 exit #126, use fairgrounds Frontage Road. (217) 732-RT66. Antiques, collectibles, books, small antiquarian items of all kinds. Open Mon–Sat 10–5, Sun 12–5

LITCHFIELD
The Furniture Doctor Antique Mall. 120 W. Union. (Route 16). (217) 324-6015. Glassware, furniture, collectibles, Two-story building. Restrooms, ample parking. Open Mon–Sat 9–5, Sundays 1–5.

LOMBARD
Village Green Antique & Gift Mall. 404 E. North Avenue. (708) 268-0086. 60+ dealers with nice line of antiques, collectibles, gift items, repair service. Open daily.

MAHOMET
Second Story Antique Mall. 408 E. Main Street. 61853. (217) 586-5902. Upstairs location, 5,000 sq ft. Twenty individual shops featuring country, oak and walnut furniture, china, collectibles, and books. Open daily. Many fine shops located adjacent.

MARION
Peddler Pete's Emporium. 503 N. Madison. (618) 993-9652. Antiques and collectibles. Buffet restaurant and ice cream parlor. Restrooms, ample parking, handicapped accessible. Open daily.

MARYVILLE
Maryville Antique Mall. Highway 159. 1 mile north of I-55/70. (618) 345-5533. Thirty-five dealers. Mall has good selection of quality antiques and collectibles, glassware, toys. Mon–Sat 10–6, Sun 12–5.

MATTOON

Mattoon Antique Mart. 908 Charleston Avenue. 61938. (Highway 16). (217) 234-9707. Twenty dealers. Glassware, books, vintage jewelry, china. Open Mon–Sat 10–5, Sun 1–5.

MCLEANSBORO

Southfork Antique Mall. 105 E. Broadway. 62859. (618) 643-4458. 12,000 sq ft building, antiques, collectibles, gifts, imports. Restroom, ample parking, handicapped accessible. Open Mon–Sat 10–5. Closed Sunday and Monday. J. R. no longer works here.

METROPOLIS

Ferry Street Mall. 212 Ferry Street. 62960. (618) 524-4805. Antiques, collectibles, crafts, 60+ booths. This town is the home of Superman, of comic book fame. They host an annual Superman Festival here that is a don't miss event. Mall is open daily 10am–5pm.

MOMENCE

Cal-Jean Shops. 127 E. Washington Street. (815) 472-2667. Antiques and collectibles. Open Mon–Sat 9–5, Sun 12–5.

MONTICELLO

Sisters Etc. Crafts Mall. 208 S. Market Street. (217) 762-2364. Features locally produced crafts. Restrooms, ample parking, handicapped accessible. Open Tues–Fri-9–6, Sat 9–5 and Sundays 12–5.

MT. VERNON

My Favorite Pastime Antique & Craft Mall. Three miles north of city on Route 37. (618) 246-0275. McCoy, Hull, USA, Roseville, Moon & Star, Fenton, Royal Copley, Fiesta planters, dolls, quilts, furniture, jewelry, coins, books. Restrooms, ample parking, handicapped accessible. Mall operates an outdoor flea market on the second Saturday of the month in warm months. Open daily.

MURPHYSBORO

As Time Goes By. 1329 Walnut Street. (618) 687-3288. Antiques, collectibles, depression glass, railroad collectibles, books, plates. Restrooms, handicapped accessible. Difficult parking. Open Mon–Sat 10–5, Sundays 12–5, closed Tuesdays.

NEWTON

Country Seed House Antique Mall. 604 E. Jourdan Street. 62448. (800) 642-0390. Antiques, collectibles, primitives, Victorian. No crafts. Open Wed–Sat 10–5, Sun 12–5.

OREGON

Silo Antiques. Highway 2 North. (815) 732-4042. 5,000 sq ft building. Good selection of furniture, walnut, cherry, pine, and oak. Also, glassware and smalls of every description. Open 10am–5pm daily.

OSWEGO

Oswego Antique Shops. Route 34 and Main Street. Seven shops, 50+ dealers. Glassware, toys, dolls, kitchen collectibles, decorator items. Open daily. (708) 554-3131.

PANA

Karla's Kollectibles and Antique Mall. Route 16 and Route 51 East. (217) 562-2344. The Dutch Mill Flea Market is located next door. Mall features quilts, glassware, comics, furniture, musical instruments, jewelry, and books. Credit cards accepted. Restrooms, ample parking. Open Wed–Sun 10–5.

PEORIA

Illinois Antique Center. 100 Walnut Street. 61602. (309) 673-3354. 35,000 sq ft, two story. Over 170 booths with more than 100 showcases displaying quality antiques and collectibles. Good selection of architectural items. No crafts or reproductions. Very nice sandwich shop. Very clean and high-quality operation here. Credit cards accepted, restrooms. Hours Mon-Sat 9–5, Sundays 12–5.

PETERSBURG

Petersburg Peddlers. Town Square, west side. (217) 632-2628. Two-story building with antiques, collectibles, country, primitives, furniture, quilts. Mall has an excellent tearoom. Hours Tues–Sun 10–5.

Heart's Home Craft Mall & Cafe. 502 S. 6th Street. (217) 632-3816. Restrooms, ample parking, handicapped accessible. Open daily 5:30–5. Yes that's 5:30 am. You can have crafts with your biscuits and gravy.

PLAINFIELD

Plainfield Antique Mart. 502 W. Lockport Street. 60544.

Downtown. Good selection of antiques and collectibles in all categories. (815) 436-1342. Open Mon–Sat 10–6, Sun 11–5.

POCAHONTAS

TG's Antique Mall. I-70, Exit 36. (618) 669-2969. Forty-five-dealer mall, antiques, collectibles. From glassware to books, perfumes to banks. Open daily 10am–5pm.

PRINCETON

Sherwood Antique Mall. 1661 N. Main Street. 61356. I-80, exit Route 26. (815) 872-2580. New mall, 40,000 sq ft facility. Furniture, glassware, small desirables in all categories. Open daily 10am–9pm.

RAMSEY

Ramsey Creek Antique Mall. 315 S. Superior (Route 51), downtown. (618) 423-2929. Twenty-four booths of quality antiques, collectibles, crafts, and gifts. Restrooms, ample parking. Open daily 10–5, Sundays 1–5, closed Wed and Thurs.

RICHMOND

1905 Emporium Mall. Downtown. Corner of 12th Street and Broadway. (815) 678-4414. Three-story, 7,500 sq ft building. Lots of antiques and great collectibles. Soda fountain and general store located on premises. Credit cards accepted. Restrooms, ample parking, handicapped accessible. Open 10:30–5 daily. Over 25 antique shops located in this town. It is very easy and enjoyable to spend the entire day shopping in this pleasant town.

ROCKFORD

East State Street Malls. 5411 and 5301 E. State Street. Approximately 250 dealers at both malls. These malls cover 60,000 square feet. Over 500 showcases filled with quality items. Antique furniture, china, pottery, art glass, vintage clothing and jewelry, advertising items, country primitives. Shopping here can turn into a vacation itself. Sandwich shop with ample parking. Credit cards accepted. Restrooms, handicapped accessible. Hours 10 am to 9 pm daily.

Eastwood Farm Antiques & Collectibles. 10255 Shaw Road. Quality antiques and collectibles of all kinds. Glass, wood, metal, and paper. (815) 885-3389.

SANDWICH

Sandwich Antiques Mall. 108 N. Main Street. Downtown. 30 dealers. Quality oriented mall with no used or secondhand items. Open Mon–Sat 10–5, Sun 1–5. (815) 786-7000.

SAVANNA

Pulford Opera House Antique Mall. Great River Road. (Highway 84). (815) 273-2661. One hundred and twenty dealers, 27,500 sq ft building, antiques, collectibles. Open Mon–Thurs 10:30–5:30. Fri–Sat 10:30–8.

SHELBYVILLE

The Ugly Duckling Mall. 250 E. Main Street. Downtown square. Crafts, collectibles, antiques.

SPARTA

The Olde Country School Antique and Craft Mall. Downtown, one block west of Route 4 and two blocks north of Route 154. (618) 443-3087. New mall located in large old one-level school building. Lots of collectibles, some antiques, large selection of locally made crafts including quilts. Restrooms, ample parking, handicapped accessible. Mall conducts a general consignment auction every Monday night at 6:30 pm. Mall is open daily.

Old Broadway Hotel Antique, Crafts & Flea Market. Routes 4 and 154 on corner of Broadway and St Louis Street, Downtown. 62286. (618) 443-2195. Antiques, collectibles, lots of good miscellaneous "stuff" here. Mall also holds special events during nice weather. Call for dates. This mall is located in an historic hotel.

SPRINGFIELD

Old Georgian Antique Mall. 830 S. Grand Avenue East. Quality antiques and collector items of all kinds. Glassware, china, pottery, paper and advertising items, country primitives, Victorian era finds. 62700. (217) 753-8110. Open Mon–Sat 10–4, Sun 12–3.

Springfield Mall. 3031 Reilly Drive. 62700. I-55, Exit Stevenson Ave, north at light onto Dirksen, then 1 mile. General line of antiques and collectibles. 50+ dealers. (217) 522-3031. Open daily 10am–6pm.

Peddlers Craft Mini-Mall. 1001 N. First. One block north of Memorial Hospital. (217) 525-6310. Restrooms, ample parking, handicapped accessible. Open Mon–Fri 11–5, Saturdays 10–4.

Country Lace Craft Mall. I-55 at Exit 82. Ten miles south of Springfield. (217) 628-1122. 15,000 sq ft facility with large selection of locally produced crafts. Restrooms, ample parking, handicapped accessible. Credit cards accepted. Open daily 10–6.

ST. CHARLES

Antique Markets. Three separate malls with over 75 dealers. 11 N. Third Street, (708) 377-1868, 303 W. Main Street, (708) 377-5818 or 377-5798, and 413 W. Main Street, (708) 377-5599. There is an unusually large amount of high-quality antiques here. Credit cards accepted. Restrooms, ample parking, handicapped accessible, food available. Each open daily 10am–5pm.

Consigntiques. 201 E. Cedar Ave. Antiques, collectibles, curios, furniture. (708) 584-7535.

ST. JOSEPH

I-74 Antique Mall. 302 Northgate. (217) 469-7464. Forty dealers featuring antiques and collectibles. Restrooms, ample parking. Open Mon–Sat 10–5, Sundays 12–5.

STAUNTON

Heartland Square Mini Mall & Tea Room. 121 S. Edwardsville Street. $1^1/_2$ miles west of I-55 Exit 41. (618) 635-8453. Handmade toys, florals, furniture, china, stained glass, dolls, quilts, original artwork, wooden items. Restrooms, tearoom, ample parking. Handicapped accessible. Credit cards accepted. Open Mon–Sat 10:30–5.

VOLO

Volo Antique Mall. Jan Voss. 27640 W. Route 120. 60073. (815) 344-6002. 150+ booths, quality antiques, collectibles, lots of nice quality smalls. Mall features over 200 classic autos that are on display and for sale. Very enjoyable stop. Credit cards accepted. Restrooms, snack bar, ample parking, handicapped accessible. Hours 10am–5pm daily, open until 8 pm on Fridays.

QUINCY

Broadway Antique Mall. 1857 Broadway. 62301. (217) 222-

8617. Primitives, collectibles, and antiques. Mon–Sat 9:30–5:30. Sun 12–5.

Yesteryear Antique Mall. 615 Maine Street. (217) 224-1871. One hundred Booths. Antiques and collectibles. Mon–Sat 10–6, Sun 12–5.

WASHINGTON
Country Mile Craft Mall. 109 Washington Square, downtown. Larry and Jacquie Maloney. (309) 444-2137. Craft patterns, fabric, supplies.

WEST FRANKFORT
West Frankfort Antique Mall. 117 W. Main Street. 62896. Glassware, furniture, silver, china, linens, dolls, toys.

WHEELING
Antiques Center of Illinois. 1920 S. Wolf Road. 60090. Wolf-point Shopping Center. (708) 215-9418. Great selection of merchandise here. This stop covers the entire spectrum of antiques and collecting. 50 shops of antiques, collectibles, and specialty items all located in one building. This is one of the Chicago area's leading malls. Credit cards accepted. Restrooms, ample parking, handicapped accessible. Open daily 10am–5pm.

WYANET
Wyanet Antique Mall. 320 W. Main Street. 61379. Junction of Highways 6 and 34. (815) 699-7256. Antiques, collectibles, crafts. Open 9am–5pm daily.

WILMINGTON
Antiques. Water Street and Route 53, downtown. (815) 476-7660. Glassware, furniture, clocks, china, books, advertising. Credit cards accepted. Restrooms, handicapped accessible, ample parking. Open daily.

INDIANA 🖎

ANDERSON
Anderson Antique Mall. 1407 Main Street. 46001. (800) 427-4121 or (317) 622-9517. New mall, 30,000 sq ft, four-story building. Glassware, collectibles, furniture, books. Open Mon–Fri 10–5, Sun 12–5.

ANGOLA

Conklin's Olde Towne Mall. 101 W. Maumee. 46703. (219) 833-1740. Antiques, collectibles, toys, glassware, gifts, furniture, country, Victorian. Open Mon–Sat 10–5, Sun 12–5.

ARCADIA

Arcadia Antique Mall. 101 W. Main Street. 46030. (371) 984-7107. Antiques, collectibles, 30+ dealers. Mall housed in a two-story building that has been recently remodeled. Very attractive mall. Open Mon–Sat 10–6, Sun 10–4.

BLOOMINGTON

Bloomington Antique Mall. 311 W. 7th Street. 47401. (812) 332-2290. 120+ booths laden with antiques and collectibles. Credit cards accepted. Hours 10–5 Mon–Sat, Fri 10–8, 12–5 Sun.

BOSWELL

Antique Mall of Boswell. Highway 41. (317) 869-5525. Forty dealers. Antiques, collectibles, art, jewelry, vintage clothing, furniture. Hours 10–5 Mon–Sat, Sun 12–5.

BRAZIL

Brazil Antique Mall. 105 E. National Avenue. 47834 Antiques and collectibles for every interest and budget. (812) 448-3275. Hours 10–5 Mon–Sat, 1–5 Sun.

E-Z City Super Mall. 240 N. Depot Street. 47834. Glassware, furniture, paper and advertising items, china. (812) 448-8988. Open 9am–5pm daily.

Treasure Chest Antiques Mall. 115 W. National Avenue. 47834. A wide variety of antiques and collectibles, even for the most discerning collector. (812) 446-0505. Hours 10–5 Mon–Sat, Sun 1–5.

BROOKSTON

Brookston Antiques. Highway 43. Seven miles north of I-65. (317) 563-3505. 4,500 sq ft building. Antiques, collectibles, furniture, quilts, primitives. Hours Mon–Sat 10–5, Sun 1–5.

CARMEL

Antique Mall of Carmel. 622 Rangeline Road. Mohawk Plaza Shopping Center. 46032. (317) 848-1280. Antiques, collectibles, furniture, nice selection of wicker, jewelry, glassware. Hours Mon–Sat 10–5, Sun 12–5.

CENTERVILLE

Tom's Antique Mall. 117 E. Main Street. 47330. Highway 40. (317) 855-3296. Thirty-five booths with antiques, collectibles, nice selection of fine antique furniture, glassware, toys, quilts, banks, carousel horses. A complete stained glass studio is located in the mall. Hours 10–5 Mon–Sat, Sun 1–5.

Little Creek Antique Mall. Highway 46 West. $1/2$ mile from I-65. (812) 342-9289. Antiques, collectibles, quilts, primitives, dolls, linens, postcards, pottery. Open Mon–Sat 9–5, Sun 12–5.

Webb's Antique Mall. 200 W. Union Street. Two miles south of I-70, exit 145. (317) 855-5542. 70,000 sq ft one-story facility with over 400 booths. Mall features high-quality dealers selling fine furniture, collectibles, glassware, and quality items of all descriptions. No junk. Nice restaurant in the mall. Credit cards accepted. Hours daily 9am–6pm.

CHESTERTON

Yesterday's Treasures Antique Mall. 700 W. Broadway. 46304. (219) 926-2268. Two-story building with 90+ dealers. Antiques, collectibles, art. Open Mon-Fri 10–5:30, Sat 10–5, Sun 12–5.

COLUMBIA CITY

The Hayloft Antique Mall. 224 W. Van Buren Street. Antiques, collectibles. Mall specializes in primitives. Open Mon–Sat 10–6, Sun 12–5.

CORYDON

Griffin Building Antiques Mall. 113 E. Beaver Street. 47112. Town square. Glassware, china, vintage clothing and jewelry, small desirables. (812) 738-3302. Hours 10–5 Mon–Sat, 1–5 Sun.

Red Barn Antique Mall. 215 Highway 62 West. 47112. Unique treasures of all kinds to be found at this market. Antiques and collectibles in all categories. (812) 738-2276. Open 10–5 Mon–Sat, Sun 1–5.

CRAWFORDSVILLE

Cabbages and Kings Antique Mall. 124 S. Washington Street. (317) 362-2577. Open Mon–Sat 10–5, Sun 1–5.

CROWNPOINT

Old Town Square Antique Mall. 103 W. Joliet Street. 46307. (219) 662-1219. Antiques, collectibles, Christmas room. Open 10–5 Mon–Sat, Sun 12–5.

DECATUR

Yvonne Marie's Antique Mall. 152 S. 2nd Street. (219) 724-2001. Three-story building with 75+ dealers. Well-stocked mall. Open Mon–Sat 10–5, Sun 1–5.

Memories Past Antique Mall. 111 W. Jefferson Street. (219) 728-2643. Antiques, collectibles, decorator items, nice selection of furniture. Open Mon–Sat 9–5, Sun 12–4.

DELPHI

Delphi Antique Mall. 117 S. Washington Street. 46923. (317) 546-3990. Antiques and collectibles. Open Mon–Sat 11–5, Sun 1–5.

Town Square Mall. 110 W. Main Street. 46923. (317) 564-6317. Antiques, collectibles, crafts. A beauty shop and tanning salon are also located in the mall. Open Mon–Sat 9:30am–5pm.

EDINBURGH

Back In Time Antique Mall. 126 E. Main Cross. 46124. I-65, exit 80. (812) 526-5409. Antiques, collectibles. Open 10am–5pm Mon–Sat.

ELKHART

Elkhart Antique Mall. 51722 Route 19N. Wayne and Kay Hostetler. (219) 262-8763 or 262-3030. Hours Mon–Sat 10–5, Sun 12–5.

The Caverns of Elkhart. 111 Prairie Court. Antiques and collectibles for every budget and taste. Glassware, country primitives, Victorian and Art Deco, oriental. (219) 293-1484. Hours Mon–Sat 10–6, Sun 12–5.

ELLETTSVILLE

Ellettsville Antique Mall. Highway 46, downtown. (812) 876-4527. Quality booths of fine antiques and collector items. Hours 10–6 Wed–Sat, 12–5 Sun.

EVANSVILLE

Old Evansville Antique Mall. 1419 W. Lloyd Expressway. 47732. (812) 422-1986. Large three-story historic building.

24,000 sq ft, air-conditioned and fully handicapped accessible. 135 dealers. Antiques, collectibles, furniture, quilts, jewelry, arts and crafts. Mall has many special promotions. Credit cards accepted. Open Tues–Sat 10–5, Sun 12–5.

Treasures Antiques & Collectibles. 800 N. Green River Road. Eastland Mall. 47715. (800) 479-1363. Large new mall located in nice modern shopping mall. A prototype of things to come in this business. Hours Mon–Sat 10–9, Sun 12–5.

FT. BRANCH

Windmill Antique Mall. Highway 41, $^1/_2$ mile north of town. Fine antiques and sought after collectibles. (812) 753-3053. Open Mon–Sat 9–5.

FT. WAYNE

Anna's Antique Mall. 1121 Taylor. Corner Taylor and Broadway. (219) 426-4197. 18,000 sq ft building. Antiques, collectibles, jewelry, postcards, rugs, Art Deco, classic used furniture. Open Thurs–Sat 11–5, Sun 10–2.

Antique Mall. 1510 Fairfield. (219) 422-4030. 18,000 sq ft two-story building. 60+ dealers. Antiques, collectibles, year-around Christmas shop. Specialty gift shop. This mall is the home of the Farnsworth TV Museum. Credit cards accepted. Hours 10–6 Mon–Sat, Sun 1–5.

FRANKFORT

County Seat Antique Mall. 306 N. Jackson Street. 46041. (317) 659-5490. Twenty dealers with antiques, collectibles, crafts. Open Wed–Fri 10–4, Sat 10–5, Sun 1–4.

FRANKLIN

Lighthouse Antique Mall. 62 W. Jefferson Street. 46131. (317) 738-3344. I-65 at the 90-mile marker. Mall features antique lighting, lots of collectible Christmas items, glassware, primitives, nice selection of furniture. Hours Mon–Sat 10–5, Sun 12–5.

GENEVA

Jemea's Antique Mall. Highway 27 North. (219) 368-9411. Antiques and collectibles. Open 10–5 Tues–Sat, Sun 12–4.

GOSHEN

Goshen Antique Mall. 107 S. Main Street. 46526. (219) 534-6141. Forty dealers. Antiques, collectibles, furniture, butter churns, linens, toys, jewelry, glassware, pottery. Hours 10–5 Mon–Sat.

GREENFIELD

Sugar Creek Antique Mall. 22244 Highway 40. Four miles West of town. (317) 467-4938. Antiques, collectibles. Mall features a rough and "as found" furniture building. No crafts. Hours 9am–6pm daily.

HUNTINGTON

Antiques & Not Mall. 515 N. Jefferson Street. Downstairs Penny Mall Building. (219) 359-9824. Open Sun–Thurs 11–5, Fri and Sat 11–7.

Flint Creek Antique Mall. 3050 W. Park Drive. (219) 359-9824. Antiques and collectibles. Open 10–5 Mon–Sat, 1–5 Sun.

INDIANAPOLIS

Diner & Antique Mall. 1105 Prospect. (317) 686-6018. New mall, in downtown historic Fountain Square. I-65, exit 110. Mall is located in an old bowling alley. Hours Mon–Sat 10–5, Sun 12–5.

Downtown Antique Mall. 1044 Virginia Avenue. (317) 635-5336. Forty dealers, antiques, collectibles, glassware, toys, furniture, primitives. Credit cards accepted. Open Mon–Sat 10–6, Sun 12–5.

Fountain Square Antique Mall. 1056 Virginia Avenue. (317) 636-1056. Large two-story mall with 70+ dealers. Well-stocked mall. It also features a wonderful tearoom. Open Mon–Sat 10–5, Sun 12–5.

ALWAYS CALL AHEAD BEFORE TRAVELING LONG DISTANCES!

Shadeland Antique Mall. 3444 N. Shadeland. I-70, exit Shadeland Street. (317) 542-7283. One hundred-dealer mall featuring antiques and collectibles. Open daily 10am–6pm.

JASPER

Treasure Chest Antique Mall. 321 U.S. Highway 231 South. Southgate Shopping Center. (812) 634-2986. New mall with 30 dealers. Antiques, collectibles, primitives, quilts.

Nice selection of Uhl pottery. Open Mon–Fri 10–6, Sat 10–4, Sun 12–4, closed Wednesdays.

KENTLAND

Kentland Antiques Mall. Bill and Pat Denham. 206 N. Third Street. 47951. (219) 474-3221. Open Mon–Sat 10–5, Sun 12–5.

KNIGHTSTOWN

Knightstown Antique Mall. 136 W. Carey Street. 46148. (317) 345-5665. Antiques, advertising items, glassware, toys, primitives, jewelry, furniture. This is a very large well-stocked mall. Open Mon–Sat 10–5, Sun 1–5.

Lindon's Antique Mall. 32 E. Main Street. 46148. (317) 345-2545. Credit cards accepted. Open Mon–Sat 10–5, Sun 1–5.

Heartland Antique Mall. 121 E. Main Street. 46148. (317) 345-5555. Open daily 10–5. Credit cards accepted.

KOONTZ LAKE

Keepsake Mall. Highway 23. Over 25 dealers. Antiques, collectibles, no crafts. Wed-Sat 10–5, Sun 12–5.

LAFAYETTE

Antique Mall. 800 Main Street. Jeff Shearer. (317) 742-2469. Antiques, collectibles, jewelry, furniture, art glass, primitives. Open Mon–Sat 10am–5pm.

LA PORTE

Antique Junction Mall. 711 Lincoln Way. Downtown. 10,000 sq ft building. Open daily. (219) 324-0363.

Coachman Antique Mall. 500 Lincoln Way. (219) 326-5933. 23,000 sq ft building, 100+ dealers. Antiques, collectibles, country, Victorian. A unique feature of this mall is their Carriage Shop. Open 9–5 Mon–Sat, Sun 12–5.

LEBANON

Cedars of Lebanon Antiques. 126 W. Washington Street 46052. Downtown. New mall. Open Mon–Sat 10–5, Sun 12–5.

Uncle Dudley's Antique Mall. Frank Woodruff. 2040 Indianapolis Avenue. 46052. (317) 482-7007. Open daily 10am–6pm.

LEO

Cellar Antique Mall. State Route #1, 1 block North of four-way stop. Rear entrance and parking. (219) 627-6565. Antiques, collectibles, jewelry, glassware, nice selection of furniture. Open Tues–Sat 10–5, Sun 12–4.

LINTON

Linton Antique Mall. Highway 54, downtown. (812) 847-8373. Two buildings full of antiques, collectibles, furniture. Open Mon–Fri 9–5, Sat 10–5.

The Country Store Antique Mall. Highway 54, Four miles west of town. (812) 847-9023. Antiques, collectibles, glassware, gifts, and nice selection of quality made crafts. Open Mon–Sat 10–5, Sun 1–5.

LOGANSPORT

Two Rivers Antique Mall. 412 E. Broadway. 46947. (219) 735-2119. Open Mon–Sat 10–5, Sun 12–5.

MADISON

Note: This town is an antiquer's paradise. Besides the malls there are numerous antique and specialty shops, some wonderful restaurants, bed and breakfast inns, art galleries, museums. This town is a true Americana vacation in itself. For a complete package of information about Madison, you can contact the Convention and Visitors Bureau, 301 E. Main Street, Madison, IN 47250. Telephone (800) 559-2956.

Broadway Antique Mall. Corner 5th and Broadway Streets. (812) 265-6606. Sixty dealers, quality antiques and collectibles. Open daily 10–5, Sun 12–5.

Lumbermill Antique Mall. 721 W. First Street. (812) 273-3040. Two-story facility with quality antiques and collectibles. Open Mon–Sat 10–5, Sun 12–6.

Madison Antique Mall. 401 E. 2nd Street. (812) 265-6399. Three-story facility with large selection of furniture. Antiques and excellent selection of collectibles and smalls. Open 9–6 Mon–Sat, Sun 1–5.

Miracle Antique Mall. 301 Jefferson Street. Antiques, collectibles, and crafts.

Wallace's Antique Mall. 125 E. Main Street. (812) 265-2473. Two-story facility, antiques, collectibles, secondhand items, bric-a-brac. Open 11–5 daily.

MICHIGAN CITY

Mona's Treasure Chest and Waterford Flea Market. 4496 N. Wozniak. (219) 874-5475. Open Sat and Sun 9–5.

Antique Market. Junction I-94 and Highway 421. (219) 879-4084. Seventy-five dealers. Open Mon–Sat 10–5, Sun 12–5.

MISHAWAKA

Antiques Etc. 110 Lincoln Way East. Downtown. (219) 258-5722. Thirty dealers and gallery of antique and boutique shops. Open 10–5 Tues–Sat, 12–5 Sun.

MITCHELL

Mitchell Antique Mall. Corner of 7th and Main Streets. (812) 849-4497. Open Mon–Sat 10–5, Sun 12–5. Several antique shops and nice restaurants located adjacent to mall.

MORGANTOWN

Gaslight Antique Mall. 79 W. Washington Street. (812) 597-2117.

MUNCIE

Off Broadway Antique Mall. Jack and Peggy Shafer. 2404 N. Broadway. 47303. (317) 747-5000. Open daily.

NAPPANEE

Amishland Antique Mall. 106 W. Market Street. 46550. (219) 773-4795. Open Mon–Sat 10–5.

NASHVILLE

Albert's Mall. Keith and Patti Alberts. Star Route 46W. (812) 988-2397. 4,000 sq ft building. Antiques, collectibles, glassware, primitives, furniture, coins, clocks, china. Open 10–5 Mon–Sat, Sun 1–5. Closed Tuesdays.

Brown County Antique Mall. State Route 46E. Three miles from town. (812) 988-1025. Antiques, collectibles, and mall specializes in furniture. Open Mon–Sat 10–5, Sun 12–5.

Frontier Antique Mall. 82 E. Gould Street. (812) 988-0800. Open 10–5 daily.

NEW ALBANY

Old New Albany Antique Mall. 225 State Street. 47150.

(812) 948-1890. Three-story building with antiques and collectibles. Open daily.

Seller Antique Mall. 128 W. Main Street. 47150. Over 80 dealers. Antiques, collectibles, glassware, country, primitives, furniture. Open 10–4 Mon–Sat.

NEW HARMONY
New Harmony Antique Mall. Church and Main Streets. 5,000 sq ft facility with antiques, collectibles, depression glass, kitchen collectibles, primitives, Fostoria and Heisey glass, books. Restrooms, ample parking, handicapped accessible. Several neighboring antique shops, nice all-day stop here. Open Mon–Sat 10–5, Sun 1–5.

NOBLESVILLE
Noblesville Antique Mall. Larry and Jan Smith. 20 N. 9th Street. 46060. Downtown courthouse square. (317) 773-5095. Mall is located in a beautifully restored three-story 1880's building. Antiques, collectibles, furniture, books, Art Deco, nice selection of Black memorabilia, glass. Open Mon–Sat 9–5, Sun 12–5.

PERU
Peru Antique Mall. 21 E. Main Street. 46970. (219) 473-8179. Antiques and collectibles. Open 10–5 Mon–Sat, Sun 1–5, closed Wednesdays.

PENDLETON
Pendleton Antique Mall. 123 W. State Street. (317) 778-2303. 30 dealers, antiques and collectibles. Hours 10–5 Mon–Sat, 1–5 Sun.

PLAINFIELD
Gilley's Antique Mall. 1209 W. Main Street. (Highway 40). (317) 839-8779. Two buildings with 300+ booths. Mall open 10am–5pm daily. It holds an outdoor flea market on weekends during the summer months.

PORTLAND
Portland Antique Emporium. 105 N. Meridian Street. 47371. (219) 726-2712. Over 80 dealers, antiques and collectibles. Well-stocked mall with many fine quality items and an excellent array of collectibles. Hours 10–6 Mon–Sat, Sun 12–5.

ROCKVILLE

Rockville Antique Mall. 411 E. Ohio Street. 47872. (Highway 36). (800) 585-9264 or (317) 569-6873. Twenty dealers. Antiques, collectibles, glassware, primitives, excellent selection of quality furniture. Open Mon–Sat 10–5, Sun 1–5, closed Thursdays.

Covered Bridge Mall. Downtown, east side of courthouse square. 47872. 5,000 sq ft mall with antiques, collectibles, and nice selection of crafts.

ROSSVILLE

Back Through Time Antique Mall. #9 W. Main Street. 46065. Antiques and collectibles in every imaginable category. From furniture to miniatures. (317) 379-3299. Open Mon–Sat 10–5.

RUSHVILLE

Rush County Mall. 700 block of W. 5th Street. (317) 932-5227. Antiques, collectibles. Hours 9–6 Mon–Sat. 12–6 Sun.

SCOTTSBURG

Scottsburg Antique Mall. #4 Main Street. 47170. I-65, exit 29, east 1 mile. (812) 752-4645. 10,000 sq ft two-story facility. Well-stocked mall with quality antiques, collectibles and lots of smalls. Open Mon–Sat 9–5, Sun 12–5.

SEYMOUR

Crossroads Antique Mall. Highway 50 West. Behind Holiday Inn. Junction I-65 and U.S. Highway 50. (812) 522-5675. 10,000 sq ft facility, 125 dealers. Two case rooms of quality smalls. Well-stocked mall with unique and original items in all collector fields. Open daily 9am–5pm.

SHIPSHEWANA

Amish Country Antique Mall. Highway 5. $^1/_2$ mile north of the flea market. (219) 768-4060. Open 10–5 Mon–Sat.

SOUTH BEND

Unique Antique Mall. 50981 Highway 33 North. (219) 271-1799. Over 100 dealers. Antiques, collectibles, jewelry, fine jewelry, dolls, bears, toys, furniture (oak, walnut, cherry), glassware. Credit cards accepted. Restrooms, ample parking, handicapped accessible. Open daily 10–5.

SWAYZEE

Swayzee Antique Mall. Route 13, downtown. (317) 922-7903. Open Mon, Wed, and Thurs 10–5, Fri and Sat 10–6, Sun 12–6, closed Tuesdays.

TERRE HAUTE

Ancient Thymes Mall. 1600 S. Third Street. (Highway 41). (812) 238-2178. Open daily.

Granny's Daughter Mall. 11750 S. Highway 41. Seven miles south of I-70. (812) 299-8277. Open 10–6 Mon–Sat, 10–5 Sun.

Nancy's Downtown Mall. 600 Wabash Avenue. (812) 238-1129. Open Mon–Sat 10–5, Sun 12–6.

Antiques, Crafts & Things Mall. Honey Creek Square South. (812) 232-8959. Open Mon–Sat 10–8, Sun 12–5.

Shady Lane Antique Mall. 9247 S. Highway 41. Six miles south of I-70. (812) 299-1625. Hours 10–5 Tues–Sat, Sun 1–5.

THORNTOWN

Countryside Antique Mall & Indian Trading Post. Highway 52. (317) 436-7200. 10,000 sq ft building. Antiques, collectibles, nice selection of furniture. Large section of collector books. The trading post features an excellent selection of Indian arts, crafts, and jewelry. Credit cards accepted. Restrooms, handicapped accessible, ample parking. Open 10am–5pm daily.

TIPTON

Dezerland Antique World. Sweetland Avenue, North. (765) 675-8999. 50,000 sq ft facility with over 100 dealers. Quality antiques and collectibles, furniture, rough room, lots of showcases. This is a quality mall, almost a city block in size. Fifties diner. Classic cars for sale. Full amenities here. Open Tues–Sat 10–6, 10–5 Sun, closed Mon.

Timeless Treasures Antique Mall. 116 S. Main Street. (317) 675-4537. Antiques and collectibles. Tues–Thurs, Sun 12–5, Fri and Sat 10–5. Closed Mon.

WINCHESTER

Winchester Antique Mall. 115 W. Franklin Street. Town Square. 47394. (765) 855-2489. Antiques, collectibles, Civil

War items, glassware, jewelry, furniture, credit cards accepted. Hours Mon–Sat 10–5, Sun 12–5.

WOLCOTTVILLE

Wolcottville Antique Mall. 106 N. Main Street. Ted Strawser (219) 854-3111. 10,000 sq ft building. Antiques, collectibles, bric-a-brac, crafts. Credit cards accepted. Restroom, ample parking, handicapped accessible. Open 9–5 Mon–Sat.

IOWA 🦢

AMANA

Smokehouse Square Antique Mall. 4503 F Street. (319) 622-3539. 30+ dealer mall with quality antiques and collectibles. Restrooms, ample parking, handicapped accessible. Credit cards accepted. Open daily. This is a great town to stop and spend a day. The Amana Colony has a very interesting history, quite similar to spending a day in an Amish village.

AMES

Memories of Main Antique Mall. 203 Main Street. 11,000 sq ft building, 75+ dealers. Lots of fine antiques and collector items of all kinds. Open daily. (515) 233-2519.

BLOOMFIELD

Memory Lane Antique Mall. 208 E. Franklin Street. (515) 664-1714. Sixty booths. Glassware, china, books, toys, banks, dolls, RR items, country primitives, kitchenware, pottery, crocks and bottles, china and silver. Open Mon–Sat 8–5, Sun 1–5.

CASEY

Pieces of Olde Antique Mall. Downtown. (515) 746-2853. Glassware, china, silver, dolls, toys, linens, quilts, country items, decorator finds. Open daily 9am–6pm.

SHOPPING SMART—CARRY A PENCIL AND PAD ALONG ON YOUR SHOPPING TRIP TO JOT DOWN BOOTH NUMBERS OR OTHER IMPORTANT BITS OF INFORMATION.

CEDAR RAPIDS

L Street Antiques. 1436 L Street SW. (319) 368-6640. Mall dealers carry a quality line of antiques and collectibles. No new or reproduction items. Credit cards accepted. Restroom, ample parking, handicapped accessible. Open daily 9–5:30.

CENTERVILLE

Country Heart Antiques & Uniques. Downtown, north side of the town square. 52544. (515) 437-1687. Antique furniture, primitives, collectibles, and crafts by local artisans.

CLARINDA

Gabby's Treasurers Antique Mall. 417 S. 8th Street. (712) 542-4380. Quality antiques and collectibles for every taste and budget. Ample parking, restrooms, handicapped accessible. Credit cards accepted. Mon–Sat 9am–5pm.

CRESTON

Timeless Treasures Antique Mall. 902 N. Summer. Paula Miller (515) 782-6517. General line of antiques and collectibles. Credit cards accepted. Ample parking, restroom, handicapped accessible. Open Mon–Sat 10–5, Sun 1–5.

DAVENPORT

Antique America Mall. 702 W. 76th Street. I-80, Exit 295A. Next to the Steeplegate Inn. 150+ dealer mall featuring a quality line of antiques and collectibles. No new, crafts or reproduction items. Credit cards accepted. Restrooms, ample parking, handicapped accessible.

DES MOINES

The Brass Armadillo Antique Mall. Mall has two locations with over 400 dealers in both malls. Located at SE 14th Street and Indianola Road, (515) 244-2140. Second mall at 2206 SW Third St. (515) 964-2003 or (800) 398-0105. Great variety of quality antiques and collectibles. Glassware, furniture, quilts, crocks, pottery, china. Credit cards accepted. Restrooms, ample parking, handicapped accessible. Open daily.

FT. MADISON

Memory Lane Antique Mall. 820 Ave G. Antiques and collectibles. Open Mon–Sat 10–5, Sun 1–5.

GLENWOOD

Antique Junction Mall. I-29, Exit 35. Fourteen miles south of

Council Bluffs. (712) 622-3532. Over 90 dealers. Antiques and collector items. A treasure hunter's paradise. Credit cards accepted. Restrooms, ample parking, handicapped accessible. Open daily.

HAMBURG

Hamburg Antique Mall. Main Street. Exit 1 from I-29. (712) 382-1368. General line of antiques and collectibles.

IOWA CITY

The Antique Mall. 507 S. Gilbert. I-80, exit 244. (319) 354-1822. Mall features a full line of quality antiques and collectibles. Credit cards accepted. Restrooms, ample parking, handicapped accessible. Open daily 10–5.

INDIANOLA

Golden Age Mall. Highway 92 West. Fifty-dealer mall with antiques, antique furniture, pottery, toys, tools, collectibles, extensive selection of high-quality glassware. Restrooms, ample parking, handicapped accessible. Credit cards accepted. Open Mon–Sat 10–6, Sun 1–5.

KEOKUK

Showcase Antique Mall. 800 Main Street. Antiques and collectibles. Furniture, glassware, art, lots of Roseville pottery, quilts. Mon–Sat 10–5, Sun 11–4. (319) 354-1822.

LOGAN

Logan Antique Mall. Highway 30. Forty dealers. Vintage jewelry and clothing, glassware, art glass, pottery, decorator finds. Open daily. (712) 844-2781.

MAQUOKETA

Banowetz Antiques & Uniques. Junction of Highways 61 and 64. (319) 652-2359. 155+ dealer mall. Quality antiques, collectibles, and gifts. Ample parking, restrooms, handicapped accessible. Credit cards accepted. Mall conducts many special events; call for dates. Open Mon–Sat 8–6, Sun 10–5.

MARSHALLTOWN

Main Street Antique Mall. 105 W. Main St. (515) 752-3077. Open Mon–Sat 10–5. Closed on major holidays.

MASON CITY

North Federal Antique Mall. 524 N. Federal Street. Forty dealers. Good variety of items. Open daily. (515) 423-0841.

Olde Central Antique Mall. 317 S. Delaware. 50401. (515) 423-7315. Forty dealers, two levels, 8,000 square feet. Restroom, ample parking. Mon–Sat 10–5, Sun 1–5.

MINERAL SPRINGS

Antique Mall. I-80 and Highway 177, Exit 155. General line of antiques and collectibles, good variety and selection of stock. Restroom, ample parking, handicapped accessible. Open daily.

MISSOURI VALLEY

Antique, Arts & Crafts Mall. $^1/_2$ mile west of I-29 on Highway 30. Sixty antique dealers, 45 crafters. Vintage soda fountain. Mon–Sat 9:30–5:30, Thurs 9:30–8, Sun 12–5:30. (712) 642-2125.

MUSCATINE

River Bend Cove Antique Mall. 418 Grandview Avenue. (319) 263-9929. Antiques, collectibles, lots of glassware. Open 10–5 Mon-Sat, Sun 12–5.

Rivers Edge Antiques. Corner of Second and Walnut Streets. (319) 264-2351. Antiques, collectibles. Plenty of small desirables. Some furniture. Open 10–6 Mon–Sat, Sun 12–5.

NEWTON

Pappy's Antique Mall. Downtown. Take exit 164 from I-80. (515) 729-7774. Large well-stocked 16,000 sq ft mall with good selection of quality antiques and collectibles. Credit cards accepted. Restrooms, ample parking, handicapped accessible. Open Mon–Sat 9–5, Sun 12–4.

Skunk Valley Antique Mall. Go 5 miles west of Newton on I-80 to Exit 159, north 1 block. (515) 729-2361. General line of antiques and collectibles. Nice selection of country collectibles and primitives. Credit cards accepted. Restrooms, ample parking, handicapped accessible. Mall conducts outdoor flea market on the first Saturday of the month from May through October. Open daily.

ONAWA

Onawa Antique Mall. Off I-29 between Sioux City and Omaha. Antique furniture, collectibles, glassware, china, linens, coins, dolls, kitchenware. (712) 423-1487. Open Mon–Sat 10–5, Sun 1–5.

PACIFIC JUNCTION

Antique Junction Mall. Fourteen miles south of Council Bluffs on I-29 at Glenwood exit #35. (712) 622-3532. 24,000 square feet, 138 booths, 80+ dealers. Air-conditioned, tearoom. One of the Midwest's newest and finest malls, worth visiting. This can be a most enjoyable all-day stop. Ample parking, handicapped accessible. Credit cards accepted. Mon–Sat 10–5, Sun 12–5. Market also conducts two large flea markets, spring and fall. Call for new dates.

PELLA

Red Ribbon Antique Mall. 812 Washington Street. 45 dealers. Antiques and collectibles of every description. Open daily. (515) 628-2181.

SPIRIT LAKE

Heritage Square Antique Mall. 1703 Hill. (712) 336-3455. Antiques and collectibles only. No new or reproduction items. Credit cards accepted, restrooms, ample parking, handicapped accessible. Open daily.

THAYER

L & H Antique Mall. Highway 34. 50254. (515) 338-2223. Fourteen miles West of I-35 on Highway 34. Antiques and collectibles. 20 dealers. Mall has extensive selection of Hull pottery. Restrooms, ample parking. Mon–Sat 10–5, Sun 12–5.

WATERLOO

Venice Antiques. Highway 92, halfway between Omaha and Waterloo. Rt. 1, Box 191E, 68069. (319) 359-5782. Sixty-seven dealers. antiques, glass, primitives, toys, books, jewelry, collectibles. Separate furniture building. Mon–Sat 10–5, Sun 1–5.

Antique Galleries. 618 Sycamore Street. Downtown. Kathy Orr (319) 235-9945. Thirty dealers. Antiques, collectibles. Glassware, kitchenware, country primitives, Victorian and Art Deco items, oriental, china. Credit cards accepted. Open 10–5:30 Mon–Sat.

WEST AMANA

West Amana General Store. Main Street, downtown. Antiques, collectibles, gifts, curios. Something here for every budget and interest. 12 dealers. Open daily 10am–5pm. (319) 622-3945.

WEST DES MOINES

Antiqueollectors Mall. 1980 Grand. One mile west of Valley Junction. (515) 224-6494. 60+ dealer mall with general line of antiques and collectibles. Restroom, ample parking, handicapped accessible. Open daily.

KANSAS ✍

ABILENE

Downtown Antique Mall. 313 N. Buckeye Avenue. I-70, Exit 275. (913) 263-2782. General line of antiques, collectibles, and nice selection of Western items. Credit cards accepted. Restrooms, ample parking, handicapped accessible.

ARKANSAS CITY

Summit Antique Mall. 208 S. Summit. (316) 442-1115. Eighty-five-dealer mall with quality line of antiques and collectibles. Credit cards accepted. Restrooms, ample parking, handicapped accessible.

AUGUSTA

Two Fools Antiques Mall. 429 State Augusta, 67010. (316) 775-2588. 60+ dealers. Open daily, except Thursday, 11am–9pm. Mall named tongue-in-cheek for the husband and wife team who operate it.

White Eagle Antique Mall. 2+ miles west of town on Highway 54. Eleven miles east of Wichita. (316) 775-2812. 100+ dealer mall. Good variety of merchandise at this mall. Antiques and collector items in all categories. Credit cards accepted. Restrooms, ample parking, handicapped accessible. Mon–Sat 10–9, Sun 12–7.

BENTON

Benton Antique Mall & Restaurant. Highway 254, halfway between Eldorado and Wichita. (316) 778-1700. One hundred dealers in a 19,000 sq ft facility. Antiques, collectibles, furniture, classic cars for sale. This is one of the area's better malls with lots of interesting items. Restaurant on premises, restrooms, ample parking, handicapped accessible. Credit cards accepted. Open daily.

BONNER SPRINGS

Bunny Patch Craft Mall. 607 Front Street. (K-32 Highway).

Next to Dolly Madison store. (913) 441-6043. Over 60 booths of handmade crafts.

Oak Street Antique Mall. 205 Oak Street. 66012. (913) 441-8999. Twenty-five dealers. Glassware, quilts, china, small desirables, some furniture. Park and enter building from rear.

CANEY

Blackledge Antique Mall. Junction Highways 75 and 166, downtown. (316) 879-2210 or 879-5198. 25,000 square feet building, 2 floors. Quality antiques and collectibles. This mall also has a separate craft area. Open daily. Hours Mon–Sat 10–6, Sun 1–5.

Caney Antique Mall. South edge of town on Highway 75. (316) 879-5478. One hundred dealers. This is a large well-stocked mall with good variety: dolls, toys, glassware, china, jewelry, advertising items, country primitives. Ample parking, restrooms, handicapped accessible. Hours Mon–Sat 9–6, Sun 1–5.

CHETOPA

Mary's Flea Market. 324 Maple Street. Collectibles, tools, and junque. Open Tuesday through Saturday. Closed Sunday and Monday.

DOUGLAS

Treasures Antiques Co. 24 miles SE of Wichita or 12 miles South of Augusta. (316) 746-3131. Antiques, good selection of refinished furniture. Hours 10–5 weekdays and Saturdays, Sun 1–5, closed Tuesdays and holidays.

ELK FALLS

Tiffany Gallery. 601 Montgomery. One block east of Main Street. Open Fri, Sat, Sun, and Mon.

EMPORIA

Wild Rose Antique Mall. 311 Graham Street. 66801. (316) 343-8862 or 342-8662. Fifty dealers. Antiques, collectibles, glass, quilts, jewelry, primitives, and lots of miscellaneous. Mall takes items on consignment. Formerly known as the Junque Yard Antique Mall. Restrooms, ample parking, handicapped accessible. Credit cards accepted. Tues–Sat 11–5, Sun 1–5, Closed Mon.

GALENA
Old Miners Antique and Flea Market Mall. 610 S. Main Street. (316) 733-9814. Crafts, antiques, collectibles, baseball cards, lots of new bookcases, wide variety. Hours Mon–Sat 9:30–5, Sun 12–5.

GARNETT
Emporium on the Square. 415 Oak Street. (913) 448-6459. Nineteen booths with nice antiques, crafts, collectibles. Mon–Sat 10–5, Sun 1–5.

HOLTON
Yesterday's Antique Mall. Downtown, east side of town square. (913) 364-3382. Mall has lots of fine furniture, R.S. Prussia, Roseville, toys, quilts, and jewelry. Mon–Sat 9am–5pm.

HOWARD
Heritage House Mini Mall. 224 N. Wabash Street. (316) 374-2309. Antiques, coins, collectibles, crafts, and furniture. Mon–Fri 9–7, Sat 9–5, Sun 1–5:30.

HUTCHINSON
Yesterday's Treasures Antique Mall & The Tiffany House. #20 S. Main Street. (316) 662-4439. Mall is located in a historic early 1900's building. Quality selection of antiques and collectibles here. The Tiffany House is a very elegant restaurant, with some great desserts. Very fun place to stop. Credit cards accepted. Restrooms, ample parking, handicapped accessible. Open Tues–Sat 10–5, Sundays 1–5.

IOLA
The Treasure Chest. #7 S. Jefferson Street. (316) 365-5419. Forty-five dealers. Antiques, collectibles, crafts, flea market items. Restrooms, ample parking, handicapped accessible. Credit cards accepted. (316) 365-5419.

KANSAS CITY
Antique & Craft City. 1270 Merriam Lane. Take I-35 to the Lamar exit. Harold and Brenda Lynn, (913) 677-0752. Seventy dealers. Coca-Cola collectibles, telephones, lamps, jewelry, good variety of stock. Tues-Sun 9am–6pm. Closed Mondays.

Armoudale Collectibles & Flea Market. 823 Osage. (913) 342-3654. Antiques, collectibles, new and secondhand items, flea market merchandise. Restroom, ample parking, handicapped accessible. Open Mon–Sat 10–5, Sundays 12–5.

LAWRENCE

Antique Mall. 830 Massachusetts. Downtown. (913) 842-1328. 25,000 square feet. 50+ antique and collectible dealers on the first floor. The second floor is devoted to 50+ arts and crafts dealers in a craft mall known as The Artisan's Loft. Lots of nice quality folk art and crafts here. Restrooms, ample parking, building can be difficult to get around in. Open Mon–Sat 10–5:30, Sundays 1–5.

Quantrill's Antique Mall. 811 New Hampshire Street. Antiques and collectibles for every taste and budget. This is a clean, well-stocked mall with over 80 dealers in a 20,000 sq ft facility with a great variety of quality items. Ample parking, restrooms, snack bar. Credit cards accepted. Open daily 10–5.

LEAVENWORTH

11-Worth Antique Mall. Con Denney. 410 S. 5th Street. 66048. (913) 651-2424. Tues–Sat 10–5. If you are superstitious, it is not recommended that you stay overnight in Leavenworth.

Rivermarket Square. 1005 N. 7th Street. (913) 758-0606. 155 booths of arts and crafts, primarily locally produced. Restrooms, ample parking, handicapped accessible. Credit cards accepted. Open daily 9–5.

Collector's Corner Antique Mall. 901 S. 4th Street. (913) 682-5464. Antiques, collectibles, great selection of Victorian and antique oak furniture. Large display of quality collectible glassware, telephones, clocks, primitives. Restrooms, ample parking, handicapped accessible. Credit cards accepted. Open Sun–Fri 12–5, Sat 10–5.

MANHATTAN

On The "Avenue" Antique Mall. 413 Poyntz Avenue, downtown. (913) 539-9116. Antiques, collectibles, furniture, vintage clothing, paper goods, jewelry, books, glassware, quilts. Hours Mon–Sat 10–6, Sun 1–5.

MCPHERSON

Main Street Antique Mall. 119 N. Main Street. (316) 241-7272. 8,500 sq ft in beautifully restored building. China, antiques, collectibles, jewelry, quilts, furniture, dolls, primitives, glassware. Hours Mon–Sat 10–5:30, Sun 1–5.

MISSION

Lincoln Antiques. 5636 Johnson Drive. 66202. Corner of Reeds Road and Johnson Drive. (913) 384-6811. Thirty dealers. General line of antiques and collectibles. Mon–Sat 10–5:30. Sun 12–5:30.

OLATHE

Townsquare Uniques. 138-B South Clairborn. 66032. (913) 829-3661. Antiques, crafts, collectibles. Daily 10–6, Tues 10–8, closed on Sundays.

OSAGE

Section House Antiques. 609 Market Street. Glassware, collectibles, furniture, lamps, clocks, china, pottery, country primitives, kitchenware. (913) 528-8198. Tues–Sat 10–6, Sun 1–5.

OSAWATOMIE

The Old Country Store & Flea Market. 510 Main Street. (913) 755-6595. Antiques, collectibles, furniture, glassware, secondhand and flea market items. Restrooms, ample parking, handicapped accessible. Open Mon–Sat 9:30–5:30. Closed Sundays.

Riff Raff's Ltd. 549 Main Street. (913) 755-3434. Coins, stamps, stained glass, linens, telephones, new items, miscellaneous. Ample parking, handicapped accessible. Open Mon-Thur 10–5. Fri 10-7, Sat 10–5, Sun 12–5.

OSWEGO

Circle C Trading Post. 518 Commercial Street. 67356. (316) 795-3081. Antiques, collectibles, crafts, furniture, clothing, and flea market. Hours, Tues-Sat 11–5. Closed Sunday and Monday.

OTTAWA

Ottawa Antique Mall. Courthouse Square, downtown. (913) 242-1078. New 17,000 sq ft mall featuring a general line of antiques and collectibles. New restaurant, ample parking, handicapped accessible. Credit cards accepted. Open Tues–Sat 10–6, Sundays 12–5.

Big Antique Mall. West 2nd Street. (913) 242-1078.

Antiques, collectibles, gifts. Restroom, ample parking. Open Tues–Sat 10–8, Sundays 11–6.

PAOLA

Magdalena's. Downtown, west side of town square. (913) 294-5048. 10,000 square feet. Antiques, collectibles, and lots of old medicinal remedies. Mall also takes items on consignment. Restrooms, ample parking, handicapped accessible. Credit cards accepted. Open daily.

Park Square Emporium. Downtown on west side of town square. (913) 294-9004. Air-conditioned. 50 dealers. Lots of collectibles, books, comics, records, jewelry, and toys. Mall also has a good selection of model trains, especially HO items. Mon–Sat 9–5:30. Thurs 9–8, Sun 12–5.

PARK CITY

Annie's Antique Mall. 61st Street and N. Hydraulic. $^1/_2$ mile East of I-35. (316) 744-1999. Eighty dealers in a 10,000 sq ft facility. Antiques, collectibles, primitives, furniture, dolls, pottery, quilts, pictures, toys, Coca-Cola items, china, carnival, jewelry. Restrooms, ample parking, handicapped accessible. Credit cards accepted. Open Mon–Tues 10–6, Wed–Sat 10–8, Sun 1–6.

PARSONS

Doogie's Place. 5401 Main Street. Antiques and collectibles of every description including glass, coins, paper and advertising items, linens and quilts. (316) 421-3950. Open daily.

Old Glory Flea Market, Antiques & Crafts Mall. 5021 W. Main Street. Highway 160 W. (316) 421-6326. Seventy-five dealers. Mon–Sat 9–6, Sun 1–6.

PERRY

Perry Antique & Craft Mall. 111 Elm Street. 66073. (Between Lawrence and Topeka on Highway 24). (913) 597-5250. Antiques, jewelry, tools, and Hummels. Handmade local crafts. Mon–Thurs 10–6, Fri–Sat 9–5, Sun 12–5.

PITTSBURG

Jayhawk Antique/Craft Mall & Flea Market. 4030 N. Highway 69. One hundred and seventy-five dealers. Lots of goodies here. Antiques, collectibles, crafts, records/tapes, books, toys, furniture, clothing. Open daily 10am–6pm.

PRATT

Main Street Antiques & Collectibles Mall. 213 S. Main Street. (316) 672-6770. 7,000 sq ft building. Antiques, antique furniture, pictures, dishes, quilts, fishing, railroad and Western items, books, toys, tools. Air-conditioned. Open daily Mon–Sat 10–5:30, Sun 1-5.

PRAIRIE VILLAGE

Mission Road Antique Mall. West 83rd Street and Mission Road. (913) 341-7577. New upscale mall with 250+ dealers featuring general line of antiques and collectibles. Mall also has on premises The Java Garden Coffee and Espresso Bar. Restrooms, ample parking, handicapped accessible. Credit cards accepted. Open Mon–Sat 10–7, Sun 12–6.

SEVERY

Swap Shop Antique Mall. Clarence Pettyjohn. Rt. 1, Box 173. 67137. Two miles west of 99 and Severy Junction on Highway 96. (316) 736-2854. Antiques and collectibles. Good selection of cast iron items, furniture, dolls, toys, Black memorabilia, jewelry, quilts and marbles. Mon–Thurs 9–6, Sun 1–6, closed Tues and Wed.

SHAWNEE

Crafters Creations Craft Mall. 6648 Nieman Road. (913) 962-2646. Craft mall with locally made items. Restrooms, ample parking, handicapped accessible. Open Mon, Wed, Fri 10–6, Tues, Thurs 10–8, Sat 10–5.

STANLEY

J & M Collectibles. 7819 W. 151st Street. 100-dealer mall with antiques, collectibles, crafts, vintage clothing, Indian artifacts, furniture, jewelry, phones, large selection of antique reference books. Lamp, clock/watch and phone repair on premises. Restrooms, ample parking, handicapped accessible. Credit cards accepted. Open Tues–Sat 10–5, Sun 12–5.

TOPEKA

Antique Plaza of Topeka. 2935 SW Topeka Blvd. 29th and Topeka, Holiday Square Shopping Center. (913) 267-7411. Fifty-two booths, 18,000 sq ft building. This mall has an excellent selection of quality antique furniture, flow blue, cameo glass, stoneware, and Staffordshire. Decorator is also available on the premises. Mon–Sat 10–5:30. Sun 12–5.

Topeka Antique Mall. 5427 SW 28th Court. 66614. Just north of I-470 on Fairlawn. (913) 273-2969. Fifty booths. Furniture, stoneware, quilts, jewelry, flow blue, oriental, primitives, pottery. Open daily 10am–5pm.

Wheatland Antique Mall. 2121 SW 37th Street. I-470 off Burlingame Road in the Burlingame South Shopping Center. (913) 266-3266. 4500 square feet, antiques and collectibles. Layaway available. Mall takes items on consignment also. Excellent restaurant, A Lite A'Fare, located next door. Mon–Fri 10–5:30, Sat–Sun 10–5.

Washburn View Antique Mall. 22nd and Washburn Streets. I-40 Exit 5, north 2.2 miles on Burlingame. (913) 234-0949. Over 50 dealers. Dolls, dishes, furniture, antiques, collectibles. Special section of furniture in the rough. Credit cards accepted. Restrooms, ample parking, handicapped accessible. Open daily.

TOWANDA

Towanda Antiques Mall and Blue Moon Saloon & Restaurant. 319 N. Main Street. (316) 536-2544. Forty dealers in an historic setting. Lots of depression glass, jewelry, collectibles, and furniture. This mall has a unique restaurant with an antique soda fountain and old-fashioned entertainment on Friday and Saturday evenings (reservations recommended). Thurs–Sat 11–10, Sun 12–9.

WASHINGTON

George and Martha's Antique Mall. 321 C Street. Downtown. (316) 325-2445. 4,500 sq ft building. Antiques, collectibles, glass, toys, primitives, political items, tools, furniture, pottery, china. Open daily 9–5, Sun 1–5.

WELLINGTON

Antique Merchants Mall. 106 S. Washington Street. (316) 326-8484. Over 35 dealers. Antiques, collectibles, primitives. Open Tues–Sat 10–5, Sun 1–5.

WELLSVILLE

Heartland Antiques. 402 Pendleton. I-35 at Wellsville Exit. Halfway between Olathe and Ottawa. Multidealer shop featuring a general line of antiques and collectibles. Restroom, ample parking, handicapped accessible. Open Mon–Sat 10–5, Sun 1–5.

WICHITA

Castle Antique Mall. 3813 N. 61st Street North. (316) 831-9401. General line of antiques and collectibles. Restrooms, ample parking, credit cards accepted. Open Tues–Sat 10–6, Sun 12–6.

Annie's Antique Mall. 61st Street and North Hydraulic. (Park City area, $^1/_2$ mile east of I-35.) (316) 744-1999. Over 80 dealers, 10,000 sq ft building. Antiques, collectibles, furniture, fishing items, jewelry, lots of Coca-Cola items, and toys. Air-conditioned. Credit cards accepted, restrooms, ample parking, handicapped accessible. Mon–Tues 10–6. Wed–Sat 10–8, Sun 1–6.

Hewitt's Antique Mall. 232 N. Market Street. Downtown. (316) 263-2305. Advertising items, fine art, books, primitives, maps, quilts, jewelry, furniture, glassware, pottery, ephemera. Hours Mon–Sat 9:30–5, Sun 1–5.

Park City Antique Mall. 6227 N. Broadway. I-135, take 61st Street North Exit. West one half mile, mall located in shopping center. (316) 744-2025. Over 200 booths, 20,000 square feet. Large, clean well-stocked antique mall. Credit cards accepted. Restrooms, ample parking, handicapped accessible. Mon–Wed 9:30–6, Thurs–Sat 9:30–7. Sun 9:30–6.

Treasure Mall. 1255 S. Tyler. West Kellogg and Tyler. (316) 729-0560. Antiques, crafts, furniture, dolls, jewelry, primitives, gifts, cookie jars. Dealers welcome. Wed–Sat 10–5, Sun 1–5.

WINFIELD

Antique Mall. 1400 S. Main Street. (316) 221-1065 or 221-0392. Furniture, books, advertising items, toys, jewelry, coins, primitives. Nice selection of reference books for collectors. Hours Mon–Sat 10–6:30, Sun 1–5. Market also has monthly outdoor flea market on Sundays.

KENTUCKY ❧

AUGUSTA

Augusta Antique Mall. Main Street, Downtown, Town Square. (608) 756-2653. Great booths full of fine antiques and collectibles in all categories. Ample parking. Open Thurs–Fri 12–7, Sat and Sun 12–7.

BARDSTOWN

Bardstown Antique Market. 20 N. Third Street. (502) 348-3139. Antiques, collectibles, crafts, Christmas items, nice selection of railroad items. Open Mon–Sat 10–5.

Kimberly Run Antique Center. 200 E. Nohn Rowan Blvd. 40004. (Highway 245). (502) 348-7555. Sixty dealers. Antiques, collectibles, furniture, many unusual lamps, clocks, furniture. Open 10–5 Mon–Sat, Sun 1–5.

Town & Country Antique Mall. N. Third Street. (502) 348-7708. Antiques, collectibles, good selection of locally made crafts. Open daily.

BEAVER DAM

Downtown Antique Mall. 103 N. Main Street. 42320. Glassware, furniture, china, quilts, dolls, advertising, art. (502) 274-4774. Open daily.

BEREA

Chestnut Street Antique Mall. 420 Chestnut Street. (606) 986-2883. Antiques, collectibles, primitives, furniture, majolica, flow blue, R.S. Prussia, Nippon. Open Mon–Sat 10–5, Sun 1–5.

INFORMATION IS SUBJECT TO CHANGE—
ALWAYS CALL AHEAD TO AVOID DISSAPOINTMENT!

Impressions Antique Mall. I-75, Exit 76. A variety of antiques and collectibles can be found at this mall to delight even the most discerning collector. Mon–Sat 10–9, Sun 1–5. (606) 988-8177.

Todd's Antique Mall & Flea Market. Highway 21 West. (606) 986-9087. Antiques and collectibles. Everything has passed through this mall from flow blue plates to Griswold skillets. Credit cards accepted. Open daily 9–5.

BOWLING GREEN

River Bend Antique Mall. 315 Beech Bend Road 42103. (502) 781-6773. Antiques, collectibles, glassware, furniture, primitives. Nice selection of reference books. Credit cards accepted. Hours 10–5 Mon–Sat, Sun 12–5.

BUFFALO

Buffalo Antique Mall. Main Street. (502) 325-3900. General line of antiques and collectibles. Open Mon–Sat 9–5, Sundays 1–5.

CADIZ

Cadiz Antique Mall. Business Route 68, downtown. A typical antique mall, expect to find the unexpected here in quality antiques and collector items. (502) 522-7880. Open daily.

Main Street Antique Mall. Business Route 68, downtown. Collectibles, glassware, vintage jewelry, books, pottery. (502) 522-7665. Open daily.

Simpler Tymes Antique Mall & Frame Shop. Business Route 68, downtown. Expect to find treasures of all kinds: glassware, lamps, decorator items, jewelry, vintage clothing. (502) 522-0214. Open daily.

Starlight Antique Mall. Business Route 68, downtown. Antiques and collectibles in all categories. (502) 522-1410. Open daily.

Blue Moon Antique Mall. Highway 68 East and Bypass. Antique furniture, collectibles, dishes, primitives, china, kitchenware. (502) 522-4245. Open daily.

CORBIN

Past Times Antique Mall. 135 W. Cumberland Gap Parkway. (606) 528-8818. I-75, Exit 29. Behind Super 8 Motel and Burger King. New mall, 30+ dealers. Ample parking, restrooms, handicapped accessible. Open Mon–Sat 9–6, Sun 12:30–6.

DANVILLE

Antique Mall. 158 N. 3rd Street. (606) 236-3026. Mall is located in historic church. Antiques, collectibles. Open Tues–Sat 10–5, Sun 1–5.

DRY RIDGE

White Horse Antiques & Collectibles. #26 Taft Highway. I-75, Exit 159, west $1/4$ mile on U.S. Highway 22. (606) 824-6646. Open Mon–Sat 10–5, Sun 1–5.

ELIZABETHTOWN

Antiques & Things. 618 E. Dixie Highway. I-65, Exit 91.

(502) 769-9691. Thirty booths. Antiques, collectibles. Hours daily 1pm–7pm. Several antique shops located close to mall.

FRANKFORT

Bluegrass Antique Galleries. 1009 Twilight Trail. I-64, Exit 53-A and 127 South. First light, right on Twilight Trail to Building C. (502) 226-4721. Antiques, collectibles, limited edition prints, rugs, glassware, fine furniture. Credit cards accepted. Ample parking, snack bar, handicapped accessible. Open Mon–Sat 10–6. Mall conducts large antique auction on the first Friday of each month.

FRANKLIN

Strictly Country Antique Mall. 5945 Bowling Green Road. (502) 586-3978. Six individual shops located on an 1840's homestead.

Heritage Antique Mall & Collectibles. 111 W. Washington Street. Shop here for a variety of fine antiques and collectibles. (502) 586-3880.

Plain & Fancy Antique Mall. 272 Trotters Lane. Books, quilts, linens, lamps, coins, small desirables, some furniture. (502) 586-4833.

Winnie's Antique Mall. 2736 Nashville Road. Glassware, collectibles, vintage jewelry, books, advertising items, toys, dolls, military items. (502) 586-6104.

GEORGETOWN

Georgetown Antique Mall. 124 W. Main Street. This mall is contained in three large buildings, each with a fine assortment of antiques and collectibles. Open 10–5 Mon–Sat and 1–5 on Sunday. Plenty of parking. (502) 863-1275 or 863-9033.

Central Kentucky Antique Mall. 114 E. Main Street. 7,000 sq ft building. Quality and variety best describe this mall with its booths full to the brim with great antiques and collectibles. (502) 863-4018. Forty dealers. Open Mon–Sat 10–5, Sun 1–5, and Wed 12–5.

Wyatt's Antique Center. 149 E. Main Street. Primitives, kitchenware, glassware, china, silver, pottery, quilts, books. (502) 863-0331. Open Mon–Sat 10–5.

GLASGOW

The Hidden Attic Antique Mall. 609 Columbia Avenue. 42141. (502) 651-8829. Antiques, collectibles, quilts, very nice selection of quality glassware. Lots of antique furniture. Mall has a special warehouse section for dealers and wholesale only. Open Mon–Sat 9am–5pm.

GLENDALE

Glendale Antique Mall. 104 E. Railroad Avenue, 42740. I-65, exit 86. Forty-five dealers. Antiques, collectibles, jewelry, glassware, furniture. Mall has an authentic two-story log cabin on the grounds stocked with crafts and gift items. Open daily.

The Side Track Shops & Antique Mall. Main Street. 42740. (502) 369-8766. Mall features 25 individual shops located in one facility. Antiques, collectibles, wicker, Blue Ridge Pottery, gifts, crafts.

Bennie's Barn Antique Mall. Behind PNC. (502) 369-9677. Glassware and small desirables of all kinds, china, lamps, furniture, crocks, bottles, quilts, Open Tues–Sat 12–9, Sun–Mon 1–6.

GREENSBURG

Glover's Antique Mall. 123 S. Public Square. 42743. (502) 932-5588. 9,000 sq ft facility. Antiques, collectibles, gift items, and locally made crafts. Open daily.

HARRODSBURG

The Antique Mall of Harrodsburg. 540 N. College Street. (606) 734-5191. 130+ dealer mall. Antiques and collectibles in all categories. Open Mon–Sat 10–5, Sun 1–5.

HAZEL

Decades Ago Antique Mall. Main Street. 42049. (502) 492-8140. Seventy-five-dealer mall, antiques, collectibles, primitives, country, depression glass, dolls, telephones, Victorian.

HENDERSON

Henderson Antique Mall. 325 First Street. Corner of First and Green Streets. (502) 826-3007. Over 200 booths and showcases all located on one level. Credit cards accepted. Restrooms, ample parking, handicapped accessible. Open Mon–Sat 10–5, Sun 1–5. Great once-a-month flea market in this town at the race track.

HODGENVILLE

Lincoln Square Mall. Downtown, courthouse square. (502) 358-8513. A mall for all collectors, this one open Mon–Sat 8:30–5:30, Sun 1–5.

HOPKINSVILLE

Main Street Antique Mall. 803 S. Main Street. 42240. (502) 886-9869. Glassware, china, coins, tokens, RR items, military memorabilia, books, dolls, jewelry. Open Mon–Sat 10–5, Sun 1–5.

HORSE CAVE

Country Treasures Antique Mall. East Main Street. General line antiques and collectibles. Open Mon–Sat 8–5.

LEITCHFIELD

Leitchfield Antique Mall. 108 W. Main Street. 42754. (502) 259-5824 or 257-2688. Antiques and collectibles. Everything here from hat pins to perfumes, Fiestaware to Aladdin lamps. Open daily.

LEXINGTON

Antique Mall at Todds Square. 535 W. Short Street. Todd Square. 1 block north of Rupp Arena. Two-story building, 25 dealers. Antiques, clocks, collectibles. Open Mon–Sat 10–5, Sundays 1–5. (606) 252-0296.

Country Antique Mall. Don and Rodna Southworth. 1455 Leestown Road. Meadowthorpe Shopping Center. (606) 233-0075. 14,000 sq ft building, 60 dealers. Open Mon–Sat 10–5, Sun 1–5.

Lexington Antique Gallery. 637 E. Main Street. (606) 231-8197. Forty dealers. Antiques, collectibles, 18th and 19th century furniture, clocks, oriental rugs, prints, silver. Open Mon–Sat 10–5.

LOUISVILLE

Louisville Antique Mall. 900 Goss Ave. 60,000 sq ft. 200+ dealers. Large mall with one of the finest selections of quality antiques in the entire area. Mall has a large showcase section which features the finest items. Credit cards accepted. Open Mon–Sat 10–6, Sun 12–6. (502) 635-2852.

Saint Matthews Antique Market. 3900 Shelbyville Road. (502) 893-7929. Antiques, collectibles, furniture, glassware. Open daily.

Swan Street Antique Mall. 947 E. Breckinridge. (502) 584-6255. One hundred dealer mall in large 30,000 sq ft building. Mall features large showcase room with the cases filled with quality items. Mall also has a rough room for furniture. Open Mon–Fri 10–5, Sat 10–6, Sun 12–6.

MADISONVILLE

Pennyrile Antique Mall. #21 W. Center Street. Downtown. (502) 825-4127. Open Mon, Tues, and Thurs 10–5, Fri and Sat 9–5, Sundays 1–5. Closed Wednesdays.

MCHENRY

Old Brick Mall. Highway 62. (502) 274-4589. Antiques, collectibles. Open Mon–Sat 10–4, Sun 1–5, closed Wednesdays.

MAYFIELD

Remember When Antiques. Route 7 at south edge of town. 15,000 sq ft mall with 75 dealers displaying general line of antiques and collectibles. Credit cards accepted. Restrooms, ample parking, handicapped accessible. Open Mon–Sat 9–5, Sundays 1–5.

NEWPORT

471 Antique Mall. 901 E. 8th Street. (606) 431-4753. 20,000 sq ft mall. Antiques, collectibles, no crafts. Ample parking, buses welcome. Open 10–6 Wed–Sat, Sun 12–6.

NICHOLASVILLE

Antiques On Main Mall. 221 N. Main Street. (606) 887-2767. Antiques, collectibles, glassware, primitives. Open 10–5 Mon–Sat, Sun 1–5.

Coach Light Antique Mall. 213 N. Main Street. (606) 887-4223. Antiques and collectibles. Large well-stocked mall with many quality items. Open Mon–Sat 10–5, Sun 1–5.

The Rocking Horse Antique Mall. 120 N. Main Street. (606) 885-7893. Antiques, collectibles, mall specializes in "country." Open 10–5 daily.

OWENSBORO

Owensboro Antique Mall. 500 W. Third Street. One block in front of Ramada Resort. (502) 684-3003. Fifty-five dealers, antiques and collectibles. Open Mon–Sat 10–6, Sun 12–5.

PADUCAH

Sherry & Friends Antique Mall. 208 Kentucky Avenue. Antiques and collector items of all kinds. Many unique one-of-a-kind finds. (502) 442-4103. Open Mon–Sat 10–5, Sun 1–5.

Chief Paduka Antique Mall. 300 S. Third Street. Collector items for all tastes and all budgets. (502) 442-6799. Open Mon–Sat 10–5, Sun 12–5.

RADCLIFF

Radcliff Antique Mall. 509 S. Dixie Highway. Variety and quality are two words that best describe this mall, with booths displaying antiques and collectibles in all categories. (502) 351–5155. Open Mon–Sat 10–6, Sun 1–6.

RUSSELL SPRINGS

Russell Springs Antique Mall. 224 Dan Street. 42642. A typical mall with a little of this and a little of that in fine antiques and collectibles. (502) 866-7443. Open daily.

RUSSELLVILLE

Russellville Antique Mall. 141 E. 5th Street. 42276. (502) 726-6900. Antiques, collectibles, wicker, china, glassware, furniture. Open Wed–Mon 9:30–4:30.

SHELBYVILLE

Tam Antique Mall. 610 Main Street. (502) 633-3106. Antiques, collectibles, furniture, toys, gifts. Credit cards accepted. Restrooms, ample parking, handicapped accessible. Open Mon–Sat 10–5, Sun 1–5.

Main Street Antique Mall. Main Street. 40065. (502) 633-0721. Two-story building, antiques and collectibles. Open Mon–Sat 10–5, Sun 1–5.

Shelbyville Antique Mall. Main Street. 40065. (502) 633-0720. Antiques, collectibles, glassware, furniture. Open Mon–Sat 10–5, Sun 1–5.

SOMERSET

Cumberland Antique Mall. 6111 S. Highway 27. (606) 561-8622. Antiques and collectibles in all categories: vintage clothing and jewelry, coins, dolls, toys, lamps, banks, glassware.

STAFFORDSVILLE

Antiques & More Antique Mall. 1711 Kentucky Route 40 West. (606) 297-2599. Fifteen-dealer mall with general line of antiques and collectibles. Ample parking. Open Fri 4–9, Sat 9–5, and Sun 12–5.

VERSAILLES

Olde Towne Antique Mall. 161 N. Main Street. (606) 873-6326. Two-story facility full of great antiques and collectibles. Credit cards accepted. Restroom, ample parking. Open 10–5 Mon–Sat. Sun 1–5.

VINE GROVE

Main Street Antique Mall. 116 W. Main Street. Antiques and collectibles of all types. Glassware, china, pottery, silver, linens, primitives. (502) 877-5001. Open Tues–Sat 10–5, Sun 1–5.

WILLIAMSTOWN

Williamstown Antique Mall. 154 N. Main Street. I-75, Exit 154, take U.S. Highway 25 downtown. (606) 824-9897. General line of antiques and collectibles. Open Mon–Sat 8–5, Sun 10–5.

LOUISIANA ✒

BATON ROUGE

Landmark Antiques Plaza. 832 St. Philip Street. (504) 383-4867. Over 70 dealers. Antiques and collectibles of all kinds promise the possibility of found treasure to shoppers who pass this way. Glassware, small desirables, vintage jewelry, decorator finds. This mall also has a fudge factory on premises. Open daily 10am–6pm.

COVINGTON

Claiborne Hill Antique Mall. 72022 Live Oak Street. One block behind Covington Delchamps. (504) 892-5657. Antique furniture, paintings, clocks, collectibles, art glass, pottery. A very nice collection of American fine art can be seen by appointment. Air-conditioned. Thurs–Sat 10–6 pm.

HARAHAN

Harahan Antique Mall. 194 Hickory Avenue. (504) 737-6454. Furniture, primitives, linens, dolls, depression glass, toys, kitchenware, reference books.

Pigott's Antique & Collectibles Mall. 501 Hickory Avenue. Glassware, linens, quilts, kitchen collectibles, books, toys. (504) 737-0641.

LAFAYETTE

Common Market. 3607A Ambassador-Caffreey Street. 70508. (318) 981-4428. Small antique market with 15 dealers. Collectibles, good selection of fine jewelry and watches. Hours 10am–6pm daily.

METAIRIE

Olde Metairie Antique Mall. 1537 Metairie Road. (504) 831-4514. Furniture, primitives, linens, glass, china, antiques, collectibles. Credit cards accepted. Restrooms. Open daily 11–5.

MONROE

Cottonland Crafters Mall. 1127 Forsythe Avenue. (318) 323-2325. Crafts, kitchen collectibles, Victorian prints, gift items. Hours Mon–Sat 10–5:30.

NEW ORLEANS

Aaron's Antique Mall. 2014 Magazine Street. (504) 523-0630. Over 30 dealers, 8,000 sq ft two-story facility with furniture, bric-a-brac, jewelry, dolls, linens. Credit cards accepted. Restrooms. Open daily.

Antiques & Things. 2855 Magazine Street. (504) 897-9466. Thirty-five dealers. Lots of 18th Century furniture and items. Credit cards accepted. Restrooms. Open daily.

Magazine Antique Mall. 2207 Magazine Street. (504) 524-0100. Furniture, vintage clothing, jewelry, pottery, collectibles, porcelain.

Gallagher Antique Mall and Flea Market. 945 Magazine Street. Some true antiques but mostly collectibles. Open daily. (504) 523-8394.

French Market Community Flea Market. 12345 N. Peters Street. (504) 522-2621. Market is located in the middle of the common market area, which is a great tourist attraction. There is a little bit of everything here from great antiques to the most common of imported junk. Lots of great food and drink. Parking and restrooms can be difficult. Hours daily 9am–5pm.

PONCHATOULA

Ponchatoula Antiques. 400 W. Pine Street. Highway 22. Approximately 50 dealers here, inside and outside. Lots of neighboring antique and specialty shops in the area. C/p Jake Walden, (504) 345-2381. Hours Fri–Sun 10–6.

SHREVEPORT

The Antique Mall. 546 Olive Street. (318) 425-8786.

SPRINGFIELD

The Monkey House of Trash & Treasures. 31887 O'Neal Drive. Blood River Landing. (504) 294-3950. Mall specializes in depression glass. Furniture, jewelry, toys, lamps, collectibles, etc.

WEST MONROE

Chandlers's Antique Mall. 318 Trenton Street. Antiques and collectibles in all categories: glassware, vintage clothing and jewelry, art, coins, dolls.

MAINE ✒

BREWER

The Center Mall. #39 Center Street. At the end of the old black bridge. (207) 989-9842. 12,000 sq ft mall with furniture, china, glass, tools, toys, coins, lots of military collectibles. Credit cards accepted. Restrooms, ample parking. Open daily 10–5.

GARDINER

McKay's Antiques. Main Street, downtown. (207) 582-1228. A multidealer mall with a good variety of quality antiques and collector items. Restroom, ample parking. Open daily 10am–5pm.

HALL

Dealers Choice Antique Mall. 108 Water Street. (207) 622-5527. General line of antiques and collectibles. Credit cards accepted. Restrooms, handicapped accessible, ample parking. Open daily.

HAMPDEN

Hampden Flea Market & Antiques. 281 Western Avenue. Route 9. (207) 862-3211. General line of antiques, collectibles, new merchandise, flea market items. Credit cards accepted. Restrooms, handicapped accessible, ample parking. Open daily.

NEWCASTLE

Foster's Antique Mall & Flea Market. Robert Foster, Jr. U.S. Highway #1. (207) 529-5422 or 568-8150. Open May-October. Antiques, collectibles, crafts, secondhand items. The mall conducts a flea market on site on Saturday and Sunday. Credit cards accepted. Restrooms, snack bar, handicapped accessible, ample and overnight parking. Open daily.

WESTBROOK

Annie's Antiques & Flea Mall. Gerry Burns. 1399 Bridgton Road, Route 302. (207) 854-2224. General line antiques, collectibles, glassware, furniture, tools. Credit cards accepted. Restrooms, ample parking. Open daily.

MARYLAND ❧

BOONSBORO

Antique Partners. 23 S. Main Street. (301) 432-2518. Thirty dealers. Antiques, collectibles, furniture, books, war relics, glassware, primitives. Open 10am–5pm daily.

CATONSVILLE

Catonsville Collectors Emporium. 624 Frederick Road. 21228. (410) 744-3634. Twenty-five dealers. Furniture, glassware, linens, old tools, books, bottles, jewelry, Coke items, firearms/knives/war souvenirs. Open Wed–Sun.

CROFTON

Brick House Antiques. 1651 Defense Highway. (Route 450E). ½ mile east of Route 3. Lots of great antiques and collectibles to be found here, from turn-of-the-century treasures to baby boom nostalgia. (410) 721-1400. Open Thurs–Mon.

DENTON

The Denton Attic Antique Mall. Route 404, 15 miles from Route 50E. 1 mile west of Denton. Mall has quality antiques and collector items in all categories. (410) 479-1889. Open daily.

EASTON

Foxwell's Antiques & Collectibles. 7793 Ocean Gateway. (Route 50). (410) 820-9705. Over 80 dealers. A well-maintained multidealer mall with antiques and collectibles for every budget and every taste. Open daily 10–8.

ELLICOTT CITY

Antique Depot. 3720 Maryland Avenue. (410) 750-2674. Across the street from the B&O Railroad Station. Over 100 dealers. Antique furniture, glassware, vintage clothing, pottery, toys, jewelry, and oriental items. Hours Mon–Sat 11–6, Sun 12–6.

Antique Mall. 8307 Main Street. (410) 461-8700. Hours Mon–Sat 10–5, Sun 12–5. Over 60 dealers. Antiques and collector items of all kinds from radios, watches, linens, toys, furniture, glassware, and more.

FREDERICK

Antique Station. 194 Thomas Johnson Drive. Highway 15, exit Motter Avenue. (301) 695-0888. Over 125 dealers. 25,000 sq ft building. Antiques and collectibles. Air-conditioned. Open daily 10–6, closed Wednesdays.

Emporium Antiques. 112 E. Patrick Street. 21701. (301) 662-7099. Over 100 dealers with a good variety of fine antiques. Open daily Mon–Sat 10–6, Sun 12–5.

Fredericktowne Antique Center. 5305 Jefferson Pike. (Route 180W). (301) 473-5070. Over 70 dealers. Formal and country furniture and accessories. Period French, early American, and Deco furniture. Railroad items, tools, glassware, wicker, lamps, quilts, paintings, silver, collectibles, dolls. Open daily, closed Wednesdays.

Old Glory Antique Marketplace. 5862 Urbana Pike. I-70, Exit 54. ¼ mile south. (301) 662-9173. New mall. 100+ spaces. Credit cards accepted. 19,000 sq ft. Antiques and collectibles of every description from turn-of-the-century to baby boom nostalgia items.

HAGERSTOWN

Antique Crossroads. I-70, Exit 32, Route 40 east 1.5 miles. (301) 739-0858. Over 250 antique and collectibles booths along with many showcases. 24,000 sq ft building. Furniture, glassware, jewelry, books, bottles, pottery, paper ephemera, lamps. Handicapped accessible. Hours Thurs–Tues 9–5.

Beaver Creek Antique Market. I-70, Exit 32, Route 40 East 1.5 miles. (301) 739-8075. Over 150 dealers. Modern complex. Furniture, quilts, depression glass, jewelry, collectibles, clocks, comics, lamps, pottery. Credit cards accepted. Open daily 9am–5pm, closed Wednesdays.

HUNTINGTOWN
Southern Maryland Antique Center. 3176 Route 4. (410) 257-1677. Nine individual shops under one roof, with a good selection of antiques and collectibles in every imaginable category. Open Thurs–Sun 10–5.

PRINCESS ANNE
Kings Creek Antique Center. 30723 Perry Road. Route 13 and Perry Road. (410) 651-2776. Fifty-dealer mall with nice selection of antiques, collectibles, furniture, quilts, glassware, and smalls. Open 10am–5pm daily.

SAVAGE
Antique Center. Foundry Street. I-95 to Route 32E, Exit 38A. to Route 1 South. Right on Groman Road. Right on Foundry Street. (410) 792-0173 or (301) 604-2077. 40,000 sq ft complex located at historic Savage Mill. Mill established in 1822. Over 200 dealers. Antiques, furniture, large selection of furniture, Civil War items, dolls, toys, jewelry, china, glassware, linens, silver, victrolas, jukeboxes, Art Nouveau and Art Deco. Credit cards accepted. Buses welcome. Open daily 9:30–5:30.

ST. LEONARD
JAD Center Antiques & Collectibles. 4856 St. Leonard Road. 20685. (410) 586-2740. Advertising items, cut and depression glass, furniture, Hull, McCoy, Roseville, Weller pottery, large selection of quality items. Credit cards accepted. Open daily, 10am–5pm.

ST. MICHAELS
Pennywhistle Antiques. 409 S. Talbot St. 21663. (410) 745-9771. China, quilts, country, period and estate furniture, linens, restored trunks, glassware. Special selection of antique and contemporary working decoys. Open daily 10am–5pm.

WESTMINSTER

The Westminster Antique Mall. 433 Hahn Road. Corner of Route 27 North and Hahn Road. (410) 857-4044. 20,000 sq ft facility with 125+ dealers. Well-stocked mall featuring quality line of antiques and collectibles. Pleasant, clean well-managed mall. Credit cards accepted. Ample parking, restrooms, handicapped accessible. Open daily 10–6.

MASSACHUSETTS ☙

ANDOVER

Andover Antiques. 89 N. Main Street. I-495, Exit 41, One mile south. (508) 582-1228. Multidealer shop well-stocked with fine quality antiques and collectibles. Restroom, ample parking, handicapped accessible. Open daily 10–5, closed Mondays.

BOSTON

Boston Antique Center. 54 Canal Street. (617) 742-1400. Over 100 dealers. Fine quality antiques and collectibles in all categories. Quality is the operative word here. Overall quality of dealers' booths is very high. Credit cards accepted. Restrooms, snack bar, handicapped accessible, ample parking. Open daily.

DENNISPORT

Main Street Antique Center. 691-A Route 28. (508) 760-5700. 50+ dealer mall. Clean, attractive mall with fine quality upscale merchandise. Many fine qualitiy investment items here. Credit cards accepted. Restrooms, ample parking, handicapped accessible. Open daily 10–5.

EAST CAMBRIDGE

Cambridge Antique Market. 201 M'Sgr O'Brien Highway. (617) 868-9655. One hundred and fifty dealers, antiques, collectibles, jewelry, china, toys, ephemera, decorator items, books, vintage clothing. Credit cards accepted. Restrooms, snack bar, handicapped accessible, ample parking. Open Tues–Sun. Closed Mondays.

EASTON

Easton Antique & Design Center. 574 Washington Street. (508) 238-9700. Multi-dealer mall with 9,000 sq ft showroom. Very clean and attractive mall that is well-stocked with quality items. Glassware, pottery, coins, china, silver, dolls, toys. Credit cards accepted. Restrooms, handicapped accessible, ample parking. Open daily.

HADLEY

Hadley Antique Center. 227 Russell Street. (413) 586-4093. Antiques and collectibles of all kinds to be found here. Glassware, china, silver, linens, quilts. Credit cards accepted. Restrooms, handicapped accessible, ample parking. Open daily.

HYANNIS

Hyannis Indoor Flea Market and Antique Mall. Jeff Rose. 500 Main Street. Downtown. (508) 790-3412. Antiques, collectibles, furniture, used and new merchandise. Large variety of mid-range collectibles here along with many quality items. Credit cards accepted. Restrooms, snack bar, handicapped accessible. Open daily.

STURBRIDGE

Sturbridge Antique Shops. 200 Charlton Road. Two miles east of Old Sturbridge Village. (508) 347-2744. Seventy-five dealers here with a general line of antiques and collectibles. Open Mon–Fri 9–5, Sat and Sun 10–5.

WILLIAMSBURG

Flea Market at Colonial Shops. 50 Main Street. Small antique mall with quality antiques, collectibles, coins, glassware. Hours Sat 10am–5pm, Sun 12pm–5pm.

MICHIGAN ☙

ADRIAN

Adrian Antique Mall. 122 N. Main Street. 49221. (517) 265-6266. Antiques, collectibles, oak furniture, nice selection of cookie jars. Open 10–5:30 Mon–Sat, Sun 12–4.

Marsh's Antique Mall. 136 S. Winter Street. 49221. (517) 265-6266. Antiques, collectibles, oak and Victorian furniture. Open Mon–Tues 10–5:30, Thurs–Sat 10–5:30, Sun 1–5. Closed Wednesdays.

ALBION

Harley's Antique Mall. Four miles east of town. I-94, exit 127. (517) 531-5300. Ninety-five-dealer mall. A good variety of antiques and collectibles of all kinds. Ample parking, restrooms, handicapped accessible. Open daily 10am–6pm.

ALLEN

Allen Antique Mall. 9011 W. Chicago Road. Downtown, U.S. Highway 12. (517) 869-2788. Large well-stocked mall with 237 booths. Wide assortment of furniture, collectibles, sports memorabilia, glassware, Indian artifacts. This is one of the area's largest and finest malls. Mall conducts public pig roasts during the summer holidays. Ample parking, restrooms, handicapped accessible. Open Mon–Sat 10–5, Sundays 12–5.

Green Top Mall. Downtown, U.S. Highway 12. (517) 869-2100. Twenty-five-dealer mall with country furniture, crafts, Art Deco, Victoriana collectibles. Ample parking. Open daily 10:30–5.

Antique East Side Mall. 237 E. Chicago Road. (517) 869-2039. Quality line of antiques and collectibles. Open daily 10–5.

ALLENDALE

Grand Valley Antique Mall. 11233 - 68th Street. 49401. North of M-45. (616) 892-6022. Antiques, collectibles. Hours Mon–Sat 9–6, Sun 12–5.

ANN ARBOR

Antiques Mall of Ann Arbor. 2739 Plymouth Road. 48105. Plymouth Road Mall. (313) 663-8200. Quality oriented mall. Very fine selection of high-grade antiques and collectibles. 40 dealers. Credit cards accepted. Open Mon–Sat 11–7, Sun 12–5.

AU SABLE

A Quaint Little Antique Mall. Seasonal market open daily during the summer and fall. Typical array of goods—antiques and collector items for all budgets. (517) 739-4000.

BANGOR

Bangor Antique Mall. Town Square, downtown. (616) 427-8557. Four-story building with over 20,000 sq ft. Carriage barn. Fifties shop under one roof. Open Mon–Sat 10–5, Sun 1–5.

BAY CITY

Bay City Antiques Center. 1010 N. Water. One of the largest malls in Michigan; 41,000+ sq ft. and 150+ booths. Large selection of fine items. New showcase section. Large assortment of stripped pine furniture and quality country accessories. Restaurant in authentic soda fountain setting. Open daily until 5 pm. (517) 893-1116.

BENZONIA

Benzonia Mall. Junction of M-115 and U.S. 31. (616) 882-7063. Antiques, collectibles. Open daily 1–5. Several neighboring antique shops.

BLISSFIELD

Blissfield Antique Mall. 101 U.S. Highway 223. 49228. (517) 486-2236. Two buildings, three floors. Antiques, collectibles, great selection of oak furniture, glassware, toys. Open 10–5:30 Mon–Sat, Sun 12–5.

J & B Antique Mall. Jerry and Beverly Nichols. 109 W. Adrian Street. 49228. (U.S. Highway 223). (517) 486-3544. Sixty dealers with antiques and collectibles. Furniture, pottery, glass, china, tools. Large selection of Jewel Tea items. Open 10–5:30 Mon–Sat, Sun 12–5.

Estes Antiques Mall. 116–118 S. Lane Street. Downtown. (517) 488-4618. Antiques, collectibles, cookie jars, toys, jewelry. Open Tues–Sat 10:30–5, Sun 12–5.

BRIGHTON

Mill Pond Antique Galleries. 217 W. Main Street. 48116. (810) 229-8686. Over 25 dealers. Antiques, collectibles, jewelry, pewter, silver, watches and clocks, oriental rugs, glassware, art. Open daily.

BRITTON

Yesteryears Antique Mall. 208 E. Chicago Street. 49229. (Highway M-50). (517) 451-8600. Quality line of general antiques. Credit cards accepted. Ample parking, restroom, handicapped accessible. Open Sat and Mon 10–5:30.

ALWAYS CALL AHEAD BEFORE TRAVELING LONG DISTANCES TO VERIFY MARKET INFORMATION.

BROOKLYN

Pinetree Centre Antique Mall. 141 N. Main Street. (Highway M-50), downtown. (517) 592-8275. Quality antiques, collectibles, 60+ dealer mall. Credit cards accepted. Ample parking, restrooms, handicapped accessible.

CARSON CITY

Cooks Crossing Antique Mall. 105 W. Main Street. (517) 584-6105. Eight-dealer mall with 8,000 sq ft facility. Collectibles, reproduction furniture, lots of quality junque items. Open Tues–Sat 10–6, Sun 1–5.

CLINTON

First Class Antique Mall. 112 E. Michigan Avenue. (517) 456-6410. General line of antiques, collectibles, garment buttons, and transportation and motorcycle memorabilia. Restrooms, ample parking, handicapped accessible. Open daily 10–6.

COLDWATER

Chicago Street Antique Mall. 34–36 W. Chicago Street. 49036. (517) 279-7555. Twenty-five dealers with antiques and collectibles in all categories: glassware, china, art, furniture. Open Mon–Sat 10–5, Sun 11–5.

DEARBORN

Village Antiques Mall. 22091 Michigan Ave. Thirty-five dealers. Lots of collectibles. Open daily. (313) 563-1230.

FARMINGTON

Hickory Hill Antiques. 32315 Grand River Avenue. 48336. (313) 477-6630. 12,000 sq ft facility with 75+ dealers. antiques, collectibles, furniture. Open daily 10am–6pm.

FLAT RIVER

Flat River Antique Mall. 212 W. Main Street. Downtown. 35,000 sq ft four-story building. Antiques, collectibles, furniture, primitives, jewelry, wicker, toys, good selection of architectural items. Nice restaurant on premises. Restrooms, ample parking. Credit cards accepted. Open Mon–Fri 10–6, Sat 9–6, Sun 9–6.

FLINT

Reminisce Antique Mall. 3514 S. Saginaw Street. (801) 767-4152. Sixty-dealer mall with booths full of great finds in antiques, collectibles, decorator items. Open daily 9am–7pm.

FLUSHING

Antique Center. Rosemary and Jim Allamon. I-75, exit 122. Two and a half miles west. (810) 659-2663. Over 100 dealers. Antiques, collectibles, credit cards accepted. Open daily 10am–5pm.

GALESBURG

Grants Antique Market. 33 W. Battle Creek Street. 49053. Over 30 dealers, 8,000 sq ft building. Quality antiques and collectibles. Tues–Sat 10–5, Sun 12–5.

GRAND HAVEN

West Michigan Antique Mall. Highway 31. 49417. Two miles south of town. (616) 842-0370. 12,000 sq ft building with 75 dealers. Antiques, collectibles, furniture, glassware. Open daily.

GRAND LEDGE

Bridge Street Church Antique Mall. Bridge Street downtown. (517) 627-8637. Antique mall in old church. Restrooms, ample parking. Open Wed–Sat 10–5, Sun 12–5.

GRAND RAPIDS

Antiques By The Bridge. 445 Bridge Street NW. (616) 451-3430. 9,000 sq ft facility. Antiques, collectibles, pottery, china, Beatle and Coke memorabilia. This mall specializes in furniture. Credit cards accepted. Open Tues–Sat 10–5, Sun 12–5.

Plaza Antique Mall. 1410 - 28th Street SE. 49508. (616) 243-2465. Over 65 booths, 9,000 sq ft facility. Antiques, collectibles, glassware, primitives, jewelry, nice selection of antique Christmas items, advertising items, furniture, toys, dolls. Well-stocked section of reference books. Credit cards accepted. Open Mon–Sat 10–7, Sun 1–5.

GRANDVILLE

Memories Antique Mall. 2605 Sanford Street. (616) 538-1010. Forty-dealer mall with general line of antiques and collectibles. Unusual mall, located in large 40,000 sq ft facility with booths, shelves, mini-stores. Restroom, ample parking, handicapped accessible. Open daily.

GRAYLING

Grayling Antique Mall. Downtown at the stoplight. (517) 348-2113. Antique, collectibles, antique furniture, accessories. Open daily.

GREENVILLE
Greenville Antique Center. Corner of Highways M-57 and M-91. 48838. (800) 405-1155 or (616) 754-5540. 24,000 sq ft, 5-story building, Historic Greenville Furniture Building. Over 65 dealers. Furniture, oak, primitives, Victorian, books, linens, quilts, glassware, pottery, jewelry, advertising items. Credit cards accepted. Air-conditioned. Hours Thurs–Sat 11–8, Sun–Wed 11–6.

HOLLAND
Tulip City Antique Mall. 1145 S. Washington Avenue. 49423. (616) 396-8855. Eighty booths. Antiques, collectibles, jewelry, toys, china, pottery, oak and Victorian furniture, restored radios, Indian artifacts, pump organs. Mall is located in one of America's most beautiful cities. Holland holds an annual tulip festival that is one of America's most popular events—a surefire, don't miss happening. Credit cards accepted. Mall open Mon–Sat 10–5:30, Sun 12–5.

HOLLY
Holly Antiques On Main. 118 S. Saginaw. (810) 634-7696. 40+ dealer mall. Large selection of 19th century antiques. No new or reproduction items allowed. Very interesting place to shop for quality items. Restroom, ample parking, handicapped accessible. Open Tues–Sat 10–5, Sunday 11–4, closed Mondays.

Water Tower Antiques Mall. 310 Broad Street. 48442. Antiques and collectibles of all descriptions. Furniture, glass, pottery, china, paper and advertising items, and much more. (313) 634-3500. 10,000 sq ft building. Open Mon–Sat 10–5, Sun 12–5.

HOLT
Antiques Plus. 2495 S. Cedar at Willoughby. Cedar Park Shopping Center. (517) 694-5767. Antiques and collectibles. Ample parking, restrooms, handicapped accessible. Open Mon–Tues 10–5, Wed–Sun 10–9.

HOWELL
Adams Antique Mall. 201 E. Grand River Street. 48843. (517) 546-5360. Antiques, collectibles, primitives, glassware, furniture. Open Mon–Sat 10–6, Sun 10–5.

IONIA

Grand River Country Mall. ¼ mile north of I-96 on corner of M-66 and Grand River Avenue. South of town. A 23-dealer mall with furniture, collectibles, glass, primitives. Credit cards accepted. Ample parking, restrooms, handicapped accepted. Open daily 10–5.

Ionia Antique Mall. 415 W. Main Street. 48846. (616) 527-6720. Plenty of antiques and collectibles to intrigue the most seasoned shopper. Fourteen dealers in a 6,500 sq ft facility. Open daily 10am–5pm, Fri until 8 pm.

JACKSON

Jackson Antique Mall. 201 N. Jackson Street. 49200. (517) 784-3333. Antiques, collectibles. Open Mon–Sat 10–6, Sun 12–5.

KALAMAZOO

Kalamazoo Antiques Market. 130 N. Edwards Street. Downtown. (616) 226-9788. New multidealer market. Wide variety of quality antiques, primitives, Victorian, 50's items. Restrooms, handicapped accessible. Open daily.

KALKASKA

Recycled Time Antiques. 344 S. Cedar Street. (800) 350-9282 or (616) 258-3495. Quality antiques and collectibles, mall specializes in Belleek. Restroom, ample parking. Open Tues–Sat 10–6, Sundays 12–5.

LA SALLE

American Heritage Antique Mall. Mason Bright. 5228 S. Otter Creek Road. 48145. I-75, exit 9. (313) 242-3430. 14,000 sq ft building with 50 dealers. Good selection of antiques and collectibles. Open 10 am daily.

LANSING

Tri-County Craft Mall. 1114 E. Mt. Hope. (800) 482-8090. Nice selection of locally produced quality handmade crafts. Restrooms, ample parking. Credit cards accepted. Open Mon–Fri 10–6, Sat 11–6.

Mid-Michigan Mega Mall. 15487 S. U.S. Highway 27. Two miles South of I-69. Antiques, collectibles, arts, crafts, odds and ends. Restrooms, ample parking. Credit cards accepted. Open daily 11–6.

The Painted Pony Craft Mall. 5812 S. Cedar. (517) 393-0824. Large selection of locally produced crafts. Restrooms, ample parking in rear. Credit cards accepted. Open Mon–Thurs 10–6, Fri 10–8, Sat 10–5.

LAWTON
Lawton Antique Mall. 131 S. Main Street. 49065. I-94, Exit 60, 3 miles south. (616) 624-6157. 8,700 sq ft building, 50 dealers, antiques and collectibles. Hours Mon–Sat 10–5, Sun 12–5.

LIVONIA
Town and Country Antiques Mall. 31630 Plymouth Road. I-96, Exit 175. (313) 425-1344. Approximately 50 dealers, displaying all manner of antiques and collectibles: glassware, books, quilts, primitives, many small desirables. Credit cards accepted. Restrooms, ample parking, handicapped accessible. Open daily 11–6.

LOWELL
Flat River Antique Mall. 212 W. Main Street, downtown. (616) 897-5360. Large 35,000 sq ft, four-story building completely full of great finds in antiques, pictures, primitives, glass, jewelry, wicker, toys, books, collectibles. This is one of the area's largest malls. Restrooms, ample parking, food available. Hours daily 10–6 except Wed and Fri 10–8.

MANCHESTER
Manchester Antique Mall. 116 E. Main Street. (313) 428-9357. Good selection of furniture. Also glass, collectibles, watches, primitives, and jewelry. Credit cards accepted. Restrooms, ample parking, handicapped accessible. Open daily 10am–5pm. (313) 428-9357.

MECOSTA
The Browse Around Antique Mall. 301 W. Main Street. Jerry Albright. (616) 972-2990. Small seven-dealer mall with quality line of antiques and collectibles. Open Mon–Sat 10–5, Sun 12–5.

MT. PLEASANT
Mt. Pleasant Antique Center. 1718 S. Mission Street. 1718 S. Mission Street. (517) 772-2672. A thirty-five dealer mall with general line of antiques and collectibles. Restrooms, ample parking, handicapped accessible. Open Mon–Sat 10–5, Sun 12–6. Closed Wednesdays.

MUSKEGON

Muskegon Antique Mall. 30 E. Clay Street, downtown. Antique furniture, glassware, pottery, china, coins, dolls, toys, lamps, quilts, vintage jewelry. (616) 728-0305. Open Mon–Thurs 10–5, Fri and Sat 10–7, Sun 1–5.

Airport Antique Mall. 1391 Peck Street. All types of antiques and collectibles for every taste and every pocketbook. (616) 726-3689. Open Mon–Sat 11–6, Sun 12–6.

Memory Lane Antique Mall. 2073 Holton Road. (Highway M-120). Fine antiques and collectibles in every category can be found at this mall. (616) 744-8510. Open daily 10am–6pm.

NEW BALTIMORE

Heritage Square Antique Mall. 3682 Green Street. 48047. (Highway M-29). (810) 725-2453. This mall is housed in an historical 1861 house. Eighteen dealers offering a variety of quality antiques and collectibles. Credit cards accepted. Open Tues–Sat 10–5, Sun 11–5.

NILES

Four Flags Antique Mall. 218 N. 2nd Street. (616) 683-6681. Glassware, china, silver, postcards, books, RR items, country primitives, quilts, Victorian era items. Restrooms, ample parking, handicapped accessible. Credit cards accepted. Open Mon–Fri 10–5, Sat 10–6, Sun 12–6.

Michiana Antique Mall. 2423 S. Highway 33. (616) 684-7001. A nice mall with booths full of quality antiques and collectibles. Credit cards accepted. Ample parking, restrooms, handicapped accessible. Open daily 10am–6pm.

Pickers Paradise Antique Mall. 2809 Highway 33 South. (616) 683-6644. A good mall for dealers to shop. Prices reasonable on a wide variety of antiques and collectibles. Credit cards accepted. Restrooms, ample parking, handicapped accessible. Open daily 10am–6pm.

NORTHVILLE

Knightsbridge Antiques. 42305 7 mile Road. Two miles west of I-275, Exit 169. (810) 344-7200. Large, well-stocked, clean 26,000 sq ft mall. Wide variety of antiques and collectibles here. Restrooms, snack bar, ample parking, handicapped accessible. Credit cards accepted. This is a mall that is easy to spend the entire day shopping at. Open daily.

OKEMOS

Farm Village Antique Mall. 3448 Hagadorn Road. 48864. (517) 337-4988. Antiques and collectibles for every want and every budget. Credit cards accepted. Open Mon–Sat 11–6, Sun 12–6.

OTSEGO

Otsego Antiques Mall. 114 W. Allegan Street. Downtown. (616) 694-6440. A thirty-five-dealer mall. General line of antiques, collectibles. Open Tues–Sat 10–6, Sun 1–5.

Heritage Antique Mall. 621 Highway M-89. 2 miles west of town. (616) 694-4226. Sixty-five dealers displaying many hard to find antiques and collectibles. Open Tues–Sat 10–5, Sun 1–5.

OWOSSO

Owosso Midtown Antiques Mall. 1426 N. M-52. (517) 723-8604. Antiques, collectibles. Primitives, quilts, kitchenware, collectibles, decorator finds. Open daily.

PARMA

Cracker Hill Antique Mall. 12000 Norton Road. 49269. I-94, exit 128. Antiques and collectibles in all categories. (517) 531-4200.

RICHMOND

Barb's Country Antiques Mall. Barbara and Paul McConnell. 69394 Main Street. 48067. (810) 727-2826. General line of antiques and collectibles. Mall specializes in quality oak furniture. Credit cards accepted. Restrooms, ample parking, handicapped accessible. Open 12–5 daily, closed Mondays.

ROMEO

Town Hall Antiques. 205 N. Main Street. 48065. (810) 752-5422. Two buildings with 50 dealers selling a wide array of quality antiques and collectibles. Mall has a "General Store" section with three rooms of authentic country store collectibles. Open daily 10am–6pm.

ROYAL OAK

Antiques On Main. 115 S. Main Street. 48068. (313) 545-4663. A 36-dealer co-op with fine antiques and collectibles. Open Mon–Sat 10–6. Many fine neighboring antique shops. This can be a very pleasant all-day stop. Great shopping, great food.

SAGINAW

Antique Warehouse. 1910 N. Michigan Avenue. (517) 755-4343. A 30,000 sq ft building with 70+ dealers. Antiques, collectibles, nice well-stocked mall. Several individual specialty shops within the mall. Very enjoyable stop. Credit cards accepted. Tearoom, restrooms, ample parking, handicapped accessible. Ten neighboring antique shops. Mall open Mon–Sat 10–5, Sun 12–5.

SALINE

Saline House Antiques Mall. 116 W. Michigan. 48176. (313) 429-5112. Excellent selection of antiques, collectibles, furniture, toys, primitives, glassware, art. Open Mon–Sat 10–5, Sun 11–5.

SAUGATUCK

Fannie's Antique Market With Fleas. 3604 - 64th Street. 49453. Antiques to junque, lots of bric-a-brac. Open Tues–Sun 11–5.

SCHOOLCRAFT

Schoolcraft Antique Mall. 209 N. Grand. (Highway 131). (616) 679-5282. Two-story building, antiques, collectibles, toys, primitives. Open Mon–Sat 10–5, Sun 12–5.

SOMERSET

Artesian Wells Antique Mall. Intersection of U.S.12, U.S.127 and U.S. 223, 15 miles south of I-94, Jackson, MI. (517) 547-7422. Located in the historic Irish Hills section. New 15,000 sq ft one-level facility with 135 dealers. General line of antiques and collectibles, nice showcase area. Great selection of furniture. Credit cards accepted. Ample parking, restrooms, handicapped accessible. Open daily 10–6.

SPRING LAKE

Spring Lake Antique Mall. 801 W. Savidge. (616) 846-1774. Antiques, collectibles, glassware, furniture. Open Mon–Thurs 10–6, Fri 10–8, Sun 12–6.

TECUMSEH

Hitching Post Antiques Mall. 1322 E. Monroe Road. 49286. Two miles west of town on M-50. John Nerlson. (517) 423-8277. Antiques, collectibles, hardware, good selection of reference books. Credit cards accepted. Mall open daily 10am–5:30pm. Mall conducts large outdoor flea markets on Memorial Day, 4th of July, and Labor Day.

L & M Antique Mall. 7811 Monroe Road. 49286. (Highway M-50). (517) 423-8441. Antiques and collectibles. Ample parking, restroom, handicapped accessible. Open Tues–Sun, closed Mondays.

Tecumseh Antique Mall I. 112 E. Chicago Blvd. 49286. (Highway M-50). (517) 423-6441. Thirty dealers, antiques and collectibles. Open Mon–Sat 10–5, Sun 12–5.

Tecumseh Antique Mall II. 111 W. Chicago Blvd. 49286. (Highway M-50). (517) 429-6082. One hundred dealers selling antiques and collectibles in all collector lines. Open Mon–Sat 10–5, Sun 12–5.

TRAVERSE CITY

Chum's Corner Antique Mall. 4200 U.S. Highway 31 South. (616) 943-4200. General line of antiques, primitives, glass, china, collectibles, vintage accessories. Very nice antique furniture showcase. Credit cards accepted. Ample parking, restrooms, handicapped accessible. (616) 943-4200.

Wilson's Antiques. 123 S. Union Street. Downtown. (616) 946-4177. Four-floor building with antiques, collectibles, 50+ dealers. Ample parking in rear, restrooms, handicapped accessible. Open Mon–Sat 10–6, Sun 11–5.

TROY

Troy Corners Antiques. 90 E. Square Lake Road. 48098. (810) 879-9848. Eighteen dealers with antiques and collectibles. Lots of furniture—American and English country. Also, primitives, chests, desks, etc. Open Mon–Sat 10am–5pm.

WATERFORD

The Great Midwestern Antique Emporium. 5233 Dixie Highway. 48329. (U.S. Highway 24). (810) 623-7460. 5,500 sq ft building. 50 dealers, quality antiques and collectibles. Open Tues-Sun 10am–5pm.

WATERVLIET

Annette's Antique Mall. 340 N. Main Street. (616) 463-3554. Antiques and collectibles. Open 10–5 daily, closed Tuesdays.

Historic House Antique Mall. Karen and Dan Stice. 349 N. Main Street. (616) 463-2888. Antiques, collectibles, Indian artifacts, nice selection of Civil War items, furniture, graniteware, glassware. Open Mon–Sat 10–5:30, Sun 12–5.

WEST OLIVE

Lake Shore Antique Shop. 10300 W. Olive Road. 49460. (Highway 31). (616) 847-2429. Over 60 dealers. Antiques, collectibles. Hours Mon–Sat 10–6, Sun 12–5.

WILLIAMSTON

Antique Mall of Williamston. 1039 W. Grand River Road. 48895. (517) 655-1350. Seventy-five dealers in a 15,000 sq ft building. Antiques and collectibles. Open Mon–Sat 10:30–5:30, Sun 12–5:30.

Putnam Street Antiques Mall. 122 S. Putnam. Glassware, paper and advertising items, vintage clothing and jewelry, coins, dolls. (517) 655-4521. Open Mon–Sat 10:30–5, Sun 12–4.

Consignments of Williamston. 115 W. Grand River Avenue. (517) 655-6064. Consignment shop with collectibles. This is a market where occasional treasures can be discovered. Open Tues–Sat 10–6, Sun 1–6.

YALE

Yale Antiques Mall. 110 S. Main Street. 48097. (810) 387-2261. New mall. 6,500 sq ft, quality antiques and collectibles. China, pottery, dolls, linens, quilts, glassware. Open daily.

MINNESOTA ❧

ANOKA

Antiques on Main. 212 E. Main Street. (612) 323-3990. Two-story facility with 50+ dealers. General line of antiques and collectibles. Restroom, handicapped accessible. Credit cards accepted. Open daily 9–6.

BLOOMINGTON

A-Frame Antiques. 801 E. 78th Street. (612) 851-9391. Forty-dealer mall. Restroom. Ample parking. Open Mon–Sat 11–6, Sun 12–5.

CANNON FALLS

Country Side Antique Mall. 51 Old Highway 52. 55009. Next to John Deere dealership. (507) 263-0352. 12,000 sq ft facility with 45 dealers. Antiques and collectibles. Restrooms, ample parking, handicapped accessible. Hours 9:30am–5pm, Sun 12pm–5pm.

CAMBRIDGE

Memories on Main. 103 S. Main Street. Quality antiques and collectibles, glassware, china, silver, linens, country primitives, Victorian and Art Deco items, oriental collectibles. Open 10am–5pm daily. (612) 689-1950.

CANNON FALLS

Country Side Antique Mall. 31752 - 65th Avenue. (Old Highway 52) South. 15,000 sq ft facility. Thirty-five dealers. Collectibles, plenty of small desirables. Open daily. (507) 263-0352.

HOPKINS

Blake Antiques. Excelsior Blvd. Fifty dealers. Good selection of antiques, bric-a-brac, collectibles. Open Mon–Sat 11–6, Sun 12–5. (612) 930-0477. Fax (612) 933-9777.

Main Street Antique Mall. 901 Main Street. Twenty minutes west of Minneapolis. 65 exhibitors. Open daily at 11. Closed on holidays. (612) 931-9748.

HUTCHINSON

Main Street Antiques. 122 N. Main Street. 40 dealers with booths of interesting antiques and hard to find collectibles of all kinds. Open daily. (612) 587-6305.

ISANTI

Isanti Antique Mall. 16 W. Main Street. New mall. Glassware, collectibles, lots of small desirables, china, art, furniture, oriental items. Open daily. (612) 444-5522.

LITCHFIELD

Sibley Antiques. Downtown. 25 dealers. Antiques and collectibles for everyone from casual to serious collectors.

Restrooms, ample parking, handicapped accessible. Open daily. (612) 693-7335.

LOWRY

Memory Mercantile Antiques & Collectibles. Highway 55. Thirteen miles South of I-94. (612) 283-5120. Large, well-stocked 20,000 sq ft mall. Restrooms, credit cards accepted. Ample parking, restrooms. Open Mon–Sat 10–6, Sun 1–6.

MANKATO

Earthly Remains. 731 S. Front Street. 25 dealers. Glassware and small desirables, collectibles, kitchen nostalgia, primitives, Victorian era items, paper, advertising, vintage jewelry. Open Mon–Sat 10–5. (507) 388-5063.

MAPLE PLAIN

Steeple Antique Mall. 5310 Main Street. (612) 479-4375. Town is located 20 miles west of Minneapolis.

Country School House Shops. 5300 U.S. Highway 12. (612) 479-6353. A 100-dealer mall located in old three-story school building. Antiques, collectibles, jewelry, primitives, wildlife, and sporting collectibles. Mall offers furniture refinishing and repair. Credit cards accepted. Restrooms, ample parking. Open Mon–Fri 10–7, Sat and Sun 10–6.

MINNEAPOLIS

Antiques Minnesota. 1516 E. Lake Street. (612) 722-6000. Large, clean, friendly, well-stocked mall with wide variety of antiques and collectibles. Credit cards accepted. Restrooms, ample parking. Open Mon–Sat 10–5, Sundays 12–5, closed Tuesdays.

Cobblestone Antiques. 1010 W. Lake Street. Corner of Dupont and Lake Streets. 90+ dealers. Large well-stocked mall, 22,000 sq ft, with great selection of quality antiques and collectibles. Credit cards accepted. Restrooms, ample parking. Open daily 11–6. (612) 823-7373.

Antiques Riverwalk. 210 Third Avenue N. (612) 339-9352. Mall features many well-stocked booths of high-quality antiques and collectibles. Credit cards accepted. Restrooms, ample parking. Open Tues–Sat 10–5:30, Sun 11–5:30.

Great River Antiques. 210 - 3rd Avenue North. Historic warehouse district downtown. 40+ dealers. Open Tues–Sat 10–5:30, Sun 11–5:30. (612) 338-1109.

OWATONNA

Uncle Tom's Antique Mall. Highway 14 W. ¾ of a mile west of I-35. 7,000 sq ft facility. Antiques and collectibles. Glassware, china, quilts, flow blue to RR timetables. (507) 451-2254. Open 10–5 Mon–Fri, Sat 10–4, Sun 12–4.

ROGERS

Antique Mall of Rogers. 12905 Main Street. (612) 422-4873.

Gateway Antique Mall. I-94 and Highway 101. (612) 428-8286.

SHAKOPEE

The Country Collection Antiques. 213 E. First Avenue. 55379. (612) 446-1500. Fifteen dealers, 3,200 sq ft building. Antiques, collectibles, decoys, stoneware, folk art, great selection of country furniture and country collectibles. Open daily.

ST. CLOUD

Depot Antique Mall. I-94 and Highway 23W, exit 164. (612) 253-6573. Three-story facility with general line of antiques and collectibles. Credit cards accepted. Restrooms, ample parking, coffee shop on premises. Open daily 10–8.

ST. PAUL

Antiques Minnesota. 1197 University Avenue. (612) 646-0037. Large well-stocked mall, great selection of quality items here. Credit cards accepted. Restrooms, ample parking. Open Mon–Sat 10–5, Sundays 12–5. Closed Tuesdays.

TNT Antique Mall. 1815 Shelby Avenue. (612) 644-1557. A 35-dealer mall featuring antiques and collectibles. Restroom. Ample parking. Open daily.

STILLWATER

American Gothic Antiques. 236 S. Main Street. (612) 439-7709. Very quality oriented mall, nice selection of high-grade antiques and collectibles. Credit cards accepted. Restrooms, ample parking. Open daily.

The Mill Antiques. 410 N. Main Street. 55082. (612) 430-1816. Over 80 dealers. Mall is located in an historic sawmill. Large selection of collectibles, antiques, and lots of memorabilia. Restrooms, ample parking. Getting around the building here can be a little difficult. Open daily 10am–6pm.

Mulberry Point Antiques. 270 N. Main Street. 55082. (612) 430-3630. Sixty-five dealers in four-level building. Furniture, china, silver, pottery, art, glassware, collectibles in all categories. Open daily.

More Antiques. 312 N. Main Street. 55082. (612) 439-1110. Sixty-five dealers selling antiques and collectibles of all kinds. From furniture to miniatures, china to table linen. Open Mon–Sat 10–5, Sun 11–5.

MISSISSIPPI ☙

GULFPORT

Back In Time Antique Mall. Steve Baudier. 205 Pass Road. (601) 868-8246. A 30-dealer mall with antiques, collectibles, glassware, Civil War items. Mall offers repair and restoration service for many antiques. Credit cards accepted. Restroom. Ample parking. Open Mon–Sat 10–6.

HATISBURG

Calico Mall Antique Flea Market & Crafts Show. Town Square, downtown. (601) 582-4351 or 583-2971. Antiques, collectibles, furniture, jewelry. Great selection of locally made crafts including quilts. Credit cards accepted. Restrooms, handicapped accessible, ample parking. Open Friday through Sunday.

JACKSON

Jackson Antique Mall. 950 N. State Street. (601) 352-7310. Antiques, collectibles, mall has large selection of antique clocks. Credit cards accepted. Restrooms, ample parking. Open Tues–Sat 10–4:30.

MADISON

Antique Alley. Route 463. I-55, Madison Exit, 1 mile east. (601) 853-1349. A multidealer mall with a great variety of fine antiques and collector items. Glassware, china, silver, clocks, lamps, collectibles, vintage jewelry, furniture. Credit cards accepted. Restrooms, handicapped accessible, ample parking. Open daily.

OSCEOLA

Wisner's Antique Mall. Highway 13. Antiques and collectibles of all descriptions can be found in the rows of booths at this well-maintained mall. Primitives, china, silver, coins, toys, dolls. Everything from turn-of-the-century treasures to baby boom nostalgia can be found here. Open daily. (417) 646-8555.

PASS CHRISTIAN

Old Community Antique Mall. 301 E. 2nd Street. 39571. (601) 452-3102. Thirty-two dealers with antiques and collectibles. Country and Victorian era items, pocket watches, primitives, quilts, knives. Open 10am–5pm daily. Closed Tuesdays.

RIDGELAND

Antique Mall of the South. 367 Highway 51. (601) 853-4000. Fifty dealers, 14,000 sq ft facility. Antiques, collectibles, jewelry, silver, linen. Credit cards accepted. Restrooms. Ample parking. Open daily 10–6.

MISSOURI ☙

ANDERSON

Anderson Main Street Flea Market. Highway 71 and Highway 59. (417) 845-6941. Fifty booths, two floors, crafts, antiques, collectibles, new and used merchandise. Restrooms, ample parking. Open daily.

AURORA

Madison Place Flea Market and Antiques. Downtown, Courthouse Square. Antiques, collectibles, bric-a-brac, furniture, cookie jars, watch fobs, dolls, lots of flea market items. Restrooms, handicapped accessible, parking can be tough. Credit cards accepted. Open Mon–Sat 10–5:30.

AVA

Back Country Antiques. Downtown courthouse square. (417) 683-2715. Antiques, collectibles. Restrooms. Open Mon–Sat 9–5.

BELTON

Unique Craft & Antique Alley. 420 D Street. Virginia Spence, (816) 322-7030. Restrooms, ample parking, handicapped accessible.

Evans Antiques & Auction Service. 1016 N. Scott Street. (816) 322-4040. Antiques, collectibles, miscellaneous.

Restrooms, ample parking, snack bar, handicapped accessible. Mall operates a large auction center next door.

BETHANY

Bethany Antique Mall. 410 S. 38th Street. Junction Highway 136 and I-35. (816) 425-6020. Antiques, collectibles, and primitives. Restrooms, handicapped accessible, ample parking. Open Mon–Sat 9–5:30. Sun 12–5.

BEVERLY

Beverly Hills Antique Center. Junction of Highways 45 and 92. (816) 546-3432. Antiques and collectibles in every imaginable category. Glassware, china, silver, dolls, vintage jewelry, advertising items. Restrooms, snack bar, ample parking, handicapped accessible. Credit cards accepted. Tues–Sun 10–5.

BLUE SPRINGS

Decorator's Touch Craft Mall & Decorating Center. 1035 S. Highway 7 (Next to Hobby Lobby). (816) 224-9252. Mon, Wed, Fri, and Sat 10–5, Tues and Thurs 10–8, Sun 12–5.

Once Upon A Time Collectible Mall. 411 S. Highway 7. 64014. (816) 224-2555. Collectibles, Jewel Tea, books, Shawnee, McCoy, Wagon Wheel, Frankoma. Music rolls, records, and even a player piano. Memorabilia and fine antiques. Mon–Sat 10–7, Sun 12–5.

Yesterday's Treasures Antiques & Flea Market. 1305 W. Highway 40 (816) 224-9997. Antiques, collectibles, new items, used merchandise. Restrooms, ample parking, handicapped accessible. Credit cards accepted. Open Tue–Fri 10–6, Sat 10–5, Sun 11–5.

Victorian Rose Antique Mall. 3500 W. Highway 40. (816) 229-3045. Glassware, linens, quilts, lamps, furniture. Restrooms, ample parking, handicapped accessible. Credit cards accepted. Mon–Sat 10–6, Sun 1–5.

BOLIVAR

Hidden Treasures Flea Market. Old Morrisville Road and Highway 13. (417) 326-4499. Seventy-five dealers, antiques, primitives, collectibles, furniture, glass pottery, books. Restrooms, ample parking, handicapped accessible. Open daily.

BOONEVILLE

Boone Village Antique Mall. I-70, Exit 103. Approximately 50 dealers. Open daily, 10am–5pm.

BRANSON

Hillbilly Peddler. Highway 76, two miles West of Silver Dollar City. Jane and David Dunn (816) 338-5413. Antiques, collectibles, flea market. Restrooms, ample parking. Open Mon–Sat 10–5, Sun 12–5.

Fugitt's Famous Flea Farm. Highway 165, 4 miles from Highway 76. Between Lawrence Welk Theatre and Branson Belle Show Boat. Nell Terral (417) 337-8337. Aprox 50 booths. Antiques, collectibles, crafts. Restrooms, ample parking, handicapped accessible. Food nearby. Open daily.

BRUNSWICK

Brunswick Antique Mall. Downtown. (816) 548-3739. Antiques, collectibles, crafts, primitives, large selection of antique furniture. Restrooms, ample parking, handicapped accessible. Open Tues–Sat 10–5, Sun 12–6, closed Mondays.

BUCKNER

Antique & Auction Center. Highway 24. (816) 373-1247 or 249-9488. Twenty dealers. Mall conducts monthly consignment/retail auctions. Mon–Sat 10–5, Sun 1-5.

Granny's Attic. 323 S. Hudson, Downtown. (816) 249-3717. Seventeen dealers. Antiques, crafts, collectibles, miniatures, Fenton glass. Mon–Sat 10–5:30, Sun 12–5.

CAPE GIRARDEAU

Antique Centre Mall. 2121 William. Behind Hardees. Furniture, lots of small desirables, glassware, silver, pottery, primitives. Open daily. (314) 339-5788.

Croxton Antique Mall & Flea Market. 111 N. Sprigg. (314) 651-4338. Open Mon–Sat 10–4:30, Sun 12–4:30.

Heartland Antiques. 701 William Street. (314) 334-0102. Antiques, collectibles. Restrooms, ample parking. Credit cards accepted. Open Mon–Sat 9–5, Sundays 12–5, Closed Tuesdays.

Antique Furniture & Craft Mall. 18 N. Sprigg Street. (314) 339-0840.

CARROLLTON

Country Cellar Antique Mall. Downtown, north side of town square. (816) 542-2588. Twenty-seven dealers. Antiques, collectibles, tins, stoneware, quilts, antique jewelry, furniture. Mon–Sat 10–5.

CARTHAGE

Deans Antique Mall & Flea Market. 1200 Oak Street. (417) 358-6104. Over 100 dealers with a little bit of everything antique and collectible. Glassware, furniture, books, vintage clothing and jewelry, and more.

Goad's Unique Antique Mall. Downtown, north side of town square. (417) 358-1201. Antiques, collectibles, books, primitives, furniture, glassware. Mon–Sat 10–5, Sun 1–5.

Oldies & Oddities Mall. Downtown, west side of town square. Books, decorator finds, glassware, china, art, pottery, watches, coins. Collectibles and antiques of all kinds on two floors. (417) 358-1752.

CLAYCOMO

Claycomo Antique Mall & Flea Market. Claycomo Plaza Shopping Center. I-35 and I-435 at Highway 69. (816) 455-5422. Over 130 dealers in a 10,000 sq ft facility. Clean, well-stocked mall with nice selection of quality antiques and collectibles. Restrooms, ample parking, snack bar, handicapped accessible. Tues–Sun 10–6.

Remember When Antiques & Collectibles. 349 Highway 69. (816) 455-1815. Antiques, collectibles, and lots of oak furniture. Mon–Sat 10–6, Sun 1–5, Closed Tues and Wed.

CLINTON

Junction Antique Mall. Highways 7 and 13 North. (816) 885-8575. Quality antique furniture, Coca-Cola memorabilia, lots of nice glassware, Heisey, Fenton, Fostoria, Stangl, Roseville, Frankoma, advertising items. Very nice craft area. Approximately 70 dealers. Open daily.

COLUMBIA

Midway Antique Center. Exit 121, I-70 and Highway 40. Three miles west of Columbia. (314) 445-6717. Forty-five dealers. Open daily 10–5.

CRANE

Country Treasures Antiques & Flea Market. 209 Main Street. 16 booths featuring depression glass, primitives, old records, antique furniture. Restrooms, ample parking. Open Mon–Sat 10–4, Sun 1–4.

CREVE COEUR

Creve Coeur Antique Mall. 1275 Castillon Arcade. 1-¾ miles west of I-270. New high-quality mall in suburban St. Louis. Many museum quality items and collections here. Restrooms, snack bar, ample parking. Handicapped accessible. Credit cards accepted. Open daily.

DEARBORN

Lick Skillet Antique & Craft Mall. 210 Main Street. (816) 992-8776. Lots of country crafts. Good selection of toys and wind-ups, primitives, lots of country furniture. Great selection of quality items here. Mall also sells country food, jams, preserves, sorghum, and such. Ample parking, restrooms, snack bar, handicapped accessible. Credit cards accepted. Mon–Sat 10–5, Sun 1–5.

EDGERTON

White Rabbit Antique Mall. Z Highway. (816) 227-3637. Collectibles, primitives, glassware, furniture, jewelry, pocket watches. Restrooms, ample parking, handicapped accessible. Open Wed–Sat 10–5, Sundays 11–5.

EOLIA

Feed Store Antiques & Mall. Highway 61, Eolia exit (D) ¼ mile to downtown. (314) 485-7000. 6,000 square feet. Antiques, collectibles, furniture, primitives, glassware, gift items, quilts, and handcrafted items. Open Mon–Sat 9–6, Sun 11–6.

EUREKA

Ice House Mall. Downtown. 14 dealers. Good selection of collectibles. Several neighboring shops. Open daily. (314) 938-6355.

Aunt Sadie's Antique Mall. 515 N. Virginia. I-44, Exit 264. (314) 938-9212. Large house with 17 rooms of antiques, Indian artifacts, sports collectibles, toys, glassware, jewelry, pottery. Restrooms, ample parking. Open Mon–Thurs 9–8, Fri–Sat 9–6, Sundays 10–5.

EXCELSIOR SPRINGS

Excelsior Trade Fair. 1220 Jesse James. (816) 630-8000. Open Mon–Sat 10–5, Sundays 1–5.

FARMINGTON

Shopper's Paradise. Highway 67 North. 63640. (314) 756-5437. Nice indoor mall with new merchandise, imports, gifts, sportswear, furniture, and some collectibles. Open daily.

Farmington Antique Mall. 4618 Highway 67. (314) 760-0033. Antiques, collectibles, crafts, new items, gifts, and imports. Restrooms, ample parking, handicapped accessible. Open daily 10–5, closed Wednesdays.

The Old Village Store Antique Mall. 102 S. Jackson. (314) 756-8060. Antiques, collectibles, lots of quality smalls. Separate building for crafts. Large quilt store and woodworker next door. Hours Mon–Sat 10–5, Sun 1–5.

FESTUS

Vintage Peddler Antique, Collectible, Craft Mall. 16 Main Street. Exit 175 from I-55, left to Main Street. (314) 937-1050. Antiques, collectibles, furniture, lots of locally made crafts. Restrooms, handicapped accessible, difficult parking. Open daily.

GOODMAN

Kelly Springs Antique Mall & Flea Market. Highway 71 south of town. (417) 364-8508. Collectibles, Coca-Cola memorabilia, cast iron items, quilts, dolls, glassware. Thurs–Sun 10am–5pm.

GRAIN VALLEY

Main Street Mall Antiques. 518 Main Street. (Three blocks south of I-70 exit). Glassware, collectibles, antique furniture, decorator finds. (816) 224-6400. Mon–Sat 10–5, Sun 12–5.

GRANDVIEW

Truman Corners Antique & Furniture Mall. 12346 S. 71 Highway. 64030. Truman Corners, between Sams Wholesale and Wards Outlet Store. Highway 71 and Blue Ridge Exit. (Kansas City). (816) 761-2221. Lots of furniture, some very high-quality pieces, police memorabilia, trunks, cookie jars, crafts, good selection of Disney items. Lots of "stuff" at this mall for treasure hunters to prowl through. Mon–Fri 10–8, Sat 10–7, Sun 12–6.

GREENWOOD

Greenwood Antiques and Country Tea Room. 5th and Main Streets. (816) 537-7172. Seventy individual shops in 15,000 sq ft building featuring country and fine antiques. Delightful country tearoom on premises. Restrooms, ample parking, handicapped accessible. Credit cards accepted. Mon–Sat 10–5, Sun 12–5.

HAMILTON

Antique Market Antique Mall. C/p Mike Ford/owner. Downtown. Furniture, antiques, and collectibles of all descriptions, in all price ranges. From hat pins to graniteware. (816) 583-2300. The boyhood home of J. C. Penney is located in this town.

Over the Hill Mini Mall. I-35 and Highway 36. Box 187, Cameron, MO 64429. (816) 632-7807. Sixty dealers. Antiques, collectibles, and crafts. (816) 632-7807.

Penney Mall. Downtown. Antiques, collectibles, gifts.

HALLTOWN

Richards SW Antiques. I-44, Halltown Exit. (417) 491-4411. Small mall with mostly collectibles and used items. Restroom, ample parking. Open daily.

HANNIBAL

Market Street Mall. 1408 Market Street. 63401. (314) 221-3008. Antiques, collectibles, quilts, furniture. 30 dealers. Mon–Sat 10–5. Historic river town, home to Mark Twain. Lots of antique shops, old homes, and museums to tour. An excellent place to spend a few days. The city also hosts several popular special events during the year. Contact the Hannibal Chamber of Commerce for more information.

HARRISONVILLE

Fountain Square Antique Mall. 311 S. Independence Street. Downtown on the town square. (816) 884-2119. Eighty dealers. Crafts, collectibles, primitives, good all-around selection and atmosphere. Cafe on premises. Restrooms, ample parking, handicapped accessible. Credit cards accepted. Mon–Fri 9–6, Sat 10–6, Sun 1–5.

Harrisonville Trade Fair. 2301 S. Commercial Street. (816) 884-5413. Over 100 dealers in large 38,000 sq ft facility. Antiques, collectibles, lots of handmade items, especially glass and jewelry, new reproduction and used furniture. Large showcase area. Restrooms, snack bar, ample parking, handicapped accessible. Credit cards accepted. Mon–Sat 10–5, Sun 12–5.

Harrisonville Trade Fair Annex. 1405 S. Commercial. (816) 380-3716. New antique mall featuring general line of antiques and collectibles. Restrooms, ample parking, handicapped accessible. Credit cards accepted. Open Mon–Sat 10–5, Sundays 12–5.

HIGHLANDVILLE

Eagle's Nest Flea Market. Highway 160 at 0 Highway. 18 miles South of Springfield. (417) 443-7710. Collectibles, antiques, salt and peppers, dolls, clocks, antique and vintage furniture, pottery, fishing collectibles, knives, depression glass, primitives. Restrooms, ample parking, handicapped accessible. Open daily.

INDEPENDENCE

Adventure Antiques. 11432 E. Truman Road. (816) 833-0303. 10,000 square feet, collectibles and furniture. Tues–Sat 10–5, Sun 12–5.

Back Alley Antiques & Auction. 1400 W. Turner Street. (816) 254-5855. New shop. Antiques and collectibles only. Mon–Sat 10–5, Sun 12–5.

Country Meadows Antique Mall. 17200 E. Highway 40. (816) 373-0410. 35,000 square feet, 200+ dealers. Large mall with excellent assortment of quality items. Serious collectors will like this mall. It also puts on many weekend special events that are free to the public. They have a quaint tearoom on premises. Reservations are welcome. Mon–Sat 9–9, Sun 9–6.

Keepsake Kupboard. 212 W. Maple Street. 64050. (816) 252-6653. Eighty craft booths. Ceramics, rugs, florals, dolls, lamps, stained glass, wood crafts. Mon-Sat 10am–5pm.

Covered Wagon Mart. 125 E. Lexington. (816) 461-9367. Antiques, collectibles, and flea market items. Open Sat and Sun only, 10–5.

JEFFERSON CITY

Missouri Boulevard Antique Mall. (314) 636-5636. New large well-stocked mall with lots of quality antiques and collectibles. Strong on name glassware. Restrooms, ample parking, handicapped accessible. Credit cards accepted. Open Mon–Fri 9–5, Sat 9–4, Sundays 11–4.

JOPLIN

Connie's Antiques. 3421 N. Rangeline. 64801. Five miles north of I-44 on Highway 71. (417) 781-2602. Large well-stocked mall with over 500 booths of antiques, crafts, new items, lots of high quality collector items here. This is a good place to put on your regular shopping list if you can overcome the crabby employees. Restrooms, ample parking, handicapped accessible. Credit cards accepted. Sun–Fri 9–6, Sat 9–7.

The Meeker Antique Mall. 1101 E. 7th Street. (417) 781-5533. Mall is located in a very large old (Meeker) factory building. Large, well-lighted, well-stocked and very interesting place to shop. Two floors. Mon–Thurs 9–6, Fri–Sat 9–8, Sun 1–6.

North Main Street Antique/Craft Mall & Flea Market. Five miles north of I-44 on Highway 43 (Main Street). (417) 781-9700. Over 100 booths. Air-conditioned. Mon–Sat 9–5, Sun 12–5.

Gingerbread House Antique Mall. I-44 and Highway 43 South, Exit 4. On North Outer Road. (417) 623-6690. 16,000 sq ft new facility with 120 booths. General line of antiques and collectibles. Mall features an old-fashioned soda fountain and sandwich shop. Ample parking, restrooms, handicapped accessible. Credit cards accepted. Open Sun–Thurs 7–8, Fri 7–3:30. Closed Saturdays. Yes that is 7 am.

Southside Antique Mall. 2914 E. 32nd. ½ mile north of I-44 on Rangeline at 32nd Street. (417) 623-1000. 18,000 square feet, antiques, collectibles, Precious Moments, large selection quality glassware, Roseville and Hull. Restrooms, parking can be difficult, handicapped accessible. Credit cards accepted. Open Mon–Sat 9–6, Sun 9–5.

KANSAS CITY

Volker Village Antique Mall. 200 Main Street. Kansas City, MO. (816) 421-0911. Located in Kansas City's historic downtown river market area, next to the water tower. Hours

Mon through Fri 10:30 am to 6 pm. Sat 9 am to 7 pm. Sun 10 am to 5 pm. Large mall with over 18,00 square feet of dealer-occupied space. Market has unusually large amount of firefighter memorabilia.

Mid America Antique Mall. 3501 Red Bridge Road. Terrace Lake Shopping Center. 64137. (816) 763-0979. 5,000 square feet. Quality furniture, collectibles, primitives, good selection of Hummels. Large selection of Barbie and G.I. Joe items. Restrooms, ample parking. Mon–Sat 10–5:30, Sun 12–5.

State Line Antique Mall. 4510 State Line. (913) 362-2002. 7,000 square feet. 40 dealers. Collectibles, antiques, silver, toys, orientalia, and original artwork. Restrooms, ample parking. Mon–Sat 10–5, Sun 12–5.

Antique Mall of America. 400 E. 135th Street. Open daily. Antiques and collectibles in all descriptions and price ranges. (816) 941-2119.

Claycomo Antique Mall. 433 N.E. Highway 69. (816) 455-5422. Over 125 dealers. 10,000 sq ft building. Antiques, collectibles, flea market. Hours 10–6 Tues–Sun, closed Mondays.

Waldo Antiques & Flea Market. 226 W. 75th Street. (816) 333-8233. Twenty-five shops open Wednesday through Sunday and flea market on the weekends.

River Market Antique Mall. 115 W. 5th Street. (816) 221-0220. New mall with antiques and collectibles. Mall features a complete antique furniture floor. Restrooms, ample parking, handicapped accessible. Open Mon–Fri 10:30–5, Sat 9–6, Sundays 10–5.

Rachael's Junque & Antique Mini Mall. 5715 St. John. (816) 241-2174. Antiques, collectibles, furniture, jewelry, primitives, lamp repair on premises, lots of secondhand and flea market items. Restrooms, ample parking. Open Mon–Sat 10–6, Sun 12–5. Closed Tuesdays.

LAKE OZARK

What-Ever Antiques Flea Market. Highway 54 to east 42 Highway. (314) 348-6112. Lots of furniture, dishes, records, quilts, and junk. Mall is located in a beautiful tourist area. Lake country. Open daily 9am–5pm.

KIRKWOOD

Pierce House Antiques. 132 W. Monroe. (314) 821-2931. Nine dealers in remodeled historic house. Quality antiques, furniture, quilts, glassware, collectibles. Restroom. Parking can be difficult, handicapped accessible.

KNOB NOSTER

B&B Swap & Shop Flea Market & Large Variety Mall. ½ mile east of town on Highway 50. Antiques, collectibles, crafts, glassware, primitives, canopies, sports cards, antique furniture, new merchandise, and lots of secondhand items. Restrooms, ample parking, handicapped accessible. Credit cards accepted. Open Mon–Wed 10–5, Fri 10–5, Sat and Sun 9–5. Closed Thursdays.

LEADINGTON

Parkland Pavilion Antiques & Auction Gallery. Corner of Main Street and Woodlawn. (800) 827-2887 or (314) 431-6094. Fax (314) 431-7031. Highway 67 to 32 West. Leadington exit. Mall is located in an old Pepsi-Cola plant. New antique mall. This is one of my favorite malls. There are some real treasures here at very good prices. Very pleasant, helpful people operate this mall.

LEBANON

General Store Antique Mall. 112 E. St. Louis Street. (618) 537-8494. Five-room house of antiques, collectibles, furniture, glassware, pottery, primitives, breweriana. Restroom, ample parking, handicapped accessible. Open Tues–Sat 10–5, Sun 11–4. Closed Mondays.

LEES SUMMIT

American Heritage Antique Mall. 220 S. Douglas Street. 64063. (816) 524-8427. Over 40 dealers. Primitives, folk art, furniture, jewelry, vintage clothing, lots of Fenton glassware. Tues–Sat 10–5:30, Sun 1–5:30.

Gingham Goose Antiques. 302 SW Main Street. (816) 524-4015. Antique furniture, primitives, glassware, collectibles, gnomes. Mon–Sat 10–5:30, Sun 1-5.

Sandy's Mall. 101 SW Market Street. (816) 525-9844. Antiques, crafts, art collectibles, and gifts. Restrooms, handicapped accessible. Open Mon–Sat 10–5, Sundays 1–5.

LEXINGTON

Cannon Ball Antique Mall. 900 Main Street. (816) 259-6580. Open every day.

Rivertown Antique Mall. 914 Main Street. (816) 259-4102. Antiques and collectibles. Mon–Sat 10–5, Sun 11–5.

LIBERTY

Liberty Antique Mall. 1 E. Kansas Street. Downtown on the town square. 40 dealers, two floors, large selection of primitives, tools, vintage clothing, collectibles. Mon–Wed 10–5, Thurs–Sat 10–8, Sun 1–5.

Liberty Antique Mall #2. 1005 N. 291 Highway. (816) 781-3190. Seventy-five dealers in newly remodeled building. Quality antiques and collectibles displayed in attractive nostalgic setting. Snack bar, restrooms, ample parking, handicapped accessible. Open daily 10–6.

LINCOLN

Lincoln Antique Mall. S. Highway 65. (816) 547-2448. Antiques, collectibles, large selection of outdoor concrete ornaments. Ample parking, restrooms, handicapped accessible. Open daily.

LOUISIANA

Old English House of Antiques Mall. Janis Bartolin. 300 N. Main Street. 63353. Seven blocks west of Highway 79. Twenty dealers. (314) 754-5992. Furniture, glassware, jewelry, old dolls. Very interesting old river town; worth a day's stop here.

MARIONVILLE

Kountry Korner. Junction Highways 60 and 265. Don and Ruth Rickman, (417) 463-2923. Furniture, Indian artifacts, primitives, toys, glass, picture gallery collection.

MARSHFIELD

His Heritage Antique Mall. I-44 at Marshfield exit. Ben Franker, Rt. 2, Box 174E. Marshfield, 65706. (417) 468-3303. Fifty booths, air-conditioned, soda fountain. Primitives, furniture, antiques, radios, jewelry, collectible, lots of Coca-Cola stuff and Aladdin lamps. Custom framing and old prints. Open Mon–Sat 9–5:30.

Bobbie's Wishing Well. Bobbie Reed, 222 S. Crittenden. (417) 468-6380. Antiques, collectibles, good junque, approximately 20 dealers. Hours Mon–Sat 9:30–5, Sun 12:30–5.

KD'S Antiques & Woodcrafts Mall. Town square, old Sears building. (417) 468-4469. Lots of locally made woodcrafts. Hours Mon–Sat 9–5, Sun 1–5.

MT. VERNON

Nana's Antique Mall. Exit 46 from I-44 and Highway 39. A convenient highway stop. Antiques, collectibles, crafts, flea market items. 100+ dealers. Well-stocked mall operated in the true Ozark manner. A very enjoyable place to stop and shop. Restrooms, snacks, ample parking. Handicapped accessible. Open daily. (417) 466-2646.

NAPOLEON

Ma & Pa's Riverview Antique and Collectible Mall. Downtown, on Highway 24. (816) 934-2698. Twenty-four dealers, antiques, collectibles, furniture. Ample parking, restrooms, handicapped accessible. Open Mon–Sat 9:30–5, Sundays 12–5.

NEOSHO

Neosho Gallery & Flea Market Antique Mall. 900 N. College Street. (Business Route 60). (417) 451-4675. Over 100 booths. Antiques, furniture, collectibles, glassware, and toys. Restrooms, ample parking, handicapped accessible. Credit cards accepted. Tues-Sun 9–5.

Special Treasures. 902 N. College Street. (417) 451-3080. Forty booths, glassware, furniture, consignments, toys, antiques, and collectibles. Hours Tues–Thurs 10–6, Fri–Sun 9–6, closed Mondays.

NEVADA

Crossroads Antique & Collectibles Mall. 1617 E. Ashland. (417) 667-7775. General line of antiques and collectibles. Restrooms, ample parking, handicapped accessible. Credit cards accepted. Open daily.

Nevada Flea Market. Highway 71 and Highland. Antiques and collectibles. Restrooms, ample parking. Open Thursday through Monday.

NEW HAVEN

New Haven Antique Mall. 117 Front Street, downtown historic district. (314) 237-2420. Antiques, collectibles, and a year-round Christmas store with many Christmas collectibles and Christmas decorator items. Open daily.

NIANGUA

Niangua Antique Mall. Downtown. (417) 473-6335 or 473-6291. 10,000 sq ft building with antiques, collectibles, and secondhand items. Open daily.

NIXA

Old Theater Mall. Junction Highways 160 and 14. (417) 725-3939. 11,500 sq ft building. Antiques, furniture, collectibles. Excellent bakery with fresh bread and delicious pies. Open daily 9am–6pm.

OAK GROVE

Olde Stone Church Antiques. 200 E. 12th Street. (816) 625-7797. Collectibles, primitives, flea market. Tues–Sat 10am–5pm.

Inge's Oak Grove Flea Market. 1120 Broadway. (816) 690-8885. Antiques, collectibles, furniture, tools. Restrooms, ample parking, handicapped accessible. Credit cards accepted. Open Mon–Sat 10–6, Sundays 1–6

ODESSA

Country Corner Treasures Antique & Craft Mall. 102 S. 2nd Street. (816) 633-4393. Daily 10am–5pm, Sun 1pm–5pm. Closed Wednesdays.

O'FALLON

I-70 Antique Mall. 1174 W. Terra Lane. 63366. Exit 216, I-70.(314) 272-0289. Furniture, toys, elegant glass, jewelry, collectibles, primitives. Very pleasant place to shop. Ample parking, restrooms, handicapped accessible. Credit cards accepted. Open daily 10am–5pm.

OWENSVILLE

Antique Mall. Junction Highways 19 and 28. (417) 581-3253. Ten-dealer mall with quality antiques, collectibles, oil paintings, new wooden items. Restroom, ample parking. Open Mon–Sat 9–4.

OZARK

Best Friends Antiques and Collectibles Mall. Riverview Plaza Shopping Center. Business Rt. 14. (417) 485-0307. Antiques, collectibles, lots of glassware and jewelry. Open daily.

Maine Street Mall. 1994 Evangel. (800) 553-2575 or (417) 485-2575. Two-story building, 25,000 sq ft. Antiques, collectibles, furniture, jewelry, toys, Jewel Tea items, depression glassware, dolls, quilts, primitives. Restrooms. Plenty of parking. Credit cards accepted. Open daily 9–6.

Ozark Antique Mall. 200 S. 20th Street. New mall, One level. Handicapped accessible. Primitives, toys, sporting goods, old-time ice cream shop. Plenty of parking. (417) 485-5233.

Riverview Antique Center. 909 W. Jackson. Riverview Plaza. Over 100 dealers. 18,000 sq ft one-story facility. Very interesting mall with a great selection and variety of quality items. Particularly quality toys. Restrooms, ample parking, snack bar, handicapped accessible. Credit cards accepted. Mon–Sat 10–5, Sun 12–5.

Country Junction Flea Market. 205 E. South Street (Highway 14 East). (417) 581-8116. Antiques, collectibles, jewelry, housewares, linens, sports cards, carnival glass, hardware and tools. Large selection of antique reproduction furniture. Restrooms, snack bar, ample parking. Handicapped accessible. Open daily. Mall has outside swap meet during summer.

Ozark Flea Market. East Highway 14, Southtown Center. (417) 581-8544. Antiques, collectibles, glassware, Coke items, gifts, Ertl toys, primitives, furniture. Restrooms, ample parking, handicapped accessible. Open daily.

Applejacks Country Store. Highways 65 and 14. New crafts mall featuring Ozark country crafts, quilts, needlework, and wood items. Also gifts, imports. Restrooms, ample parking, food nearby, handicapped accessible. Credit cards accepted. Open daily.

Finley River Heirlooms. Corner of Highways 65 and 14. (417) 581-3253. Nice, clean, well-stocked mall with good variety of antiques, collectibles, and country items. Credit cards accepted. Restroom, ample parking, handicapped accessible. Full service cafe and bakery. Open daily 9–6.

PARK HILLS

Pat's Antique Mall. 233 W. Main Street. (314) 431-6950. Collectibles, jewelry, smalls, dolls, china, costume jewelry, lots of Avon products.

Southern Hills Antique Mall. 201 E. Main Street. (314) 431-3499. Antiques, collectibles, secondhand items, some crafts. Hours Mon–Fri 9–6, Sat 9–5, Sun 12–4.

PECULIAR

(Yes Virginia, there is a Peculiar, MO). *Dorothy's Den Antiques.* Highway 71 and Peculiar Exit. 15 dealers. (816) 758-6910. Mon–Sat 10–5, Sun 11–5.

Peculiar Antique Mall. Highway 71 and Peculiar Exit. (816) 758-9511. Forty dealers. Depression glass, pottery, antiques and collectibles. Outdoor flea market held on second Sunday of each month during warm weather. Mall is undergoing extensive remodeling and a large increase in size. Mon–Sat 10–5, Sun 12–5.

Vintages. 208 C Highway. (816) 758-5456. Antiques, collectibles, gifts. Mon–Sat 10–5, Sun 12–5.

PEVELY

Pevely Antique Mall. (314) 479-7755 or 479-3215. Market is located at the Pevely Flea Market on Highway 61-67 at the I-55 Pevely Exit. Mall has many fine quality antiques and a good selection of quality collectibles. Flea market is held on Sat and Sun both outside and indoors and is far and away Missouri's finest flea market. Mall open Wed–Sun 9–4.

PLATT CITY

I-29 Antique Mall. Junction of I-29 and HH Highway. Six miles north of KCI Airport. (816) 431-2921. 12,000 square feet, 65 dealers. Lots of advertising items, Art Deco, coin-op, country furniture, primitives, telephones, toys, quilts, and Fiesta ware. No crafts or flea market items. Clean, pleasant well-stocked mall. Restrooms, ample parking, snack bar, handicapped accessible. Credit cards accepted. Open 10am–6pm, 7 days a week.

W. D. Pickers Antique Mall. Exit 20, off I-29 at the Weston/Leavenworth exit. (816) 243-8645 or 431-3100. Over 100 dealers, lots of Indian artifacts, always a good Jewel Tea selection, advertising, furniture, primitives, granite,

Coca-Cola, toys. Restrooms, ample parking, snack bar, handicapped accessible. Credit cards accepted. Mall has a flea market the second weekend of each month. Open daily 10am–6pm.

PLATTSBURG

Spease Antique Mall. 202 N. East Street. (816) 539-3170. Antiques, collectibles, an exceptional assortment of fine Victorian furniture. Tues–Sat 10–5, Sun 1–5, Thurs 10–8.

116 Highway Swap 'N Shop. 3-½ miles west of Plattsburg on Highway 169. Virginia Smith (816) 539-3522. Antiques, glassware, furniture, toys, miscellaneous. Restrooms, ample parking, handicapped accessible. Open Wed–Sat 8–5, Sundays 11–4.

PLEASANT HILL

Traders Market. 100 First Street. Downtown. (816) 986-5592. Two floors, toys, dolls, records, primitives, collectibles. Mon–Fri 11–5, Sat–Sun 12–5.

Simmons General Mercantile Antique Mall. 124 First Street. (816) 987-5999. Wed–Fri 11–5, Sat 10–5, Sun 1–5.

POPLAR BLUFF

Strawberry Hill Antiques. Highway 67 North. (314) 686-3184. Antique and collectible mall with 60 booths and 24 showcases. Restrooms, ample parking, handicapped accessible. Food next door. Open Mon–Sat 9–5, Sun 12–5.

RAYTOWN

A Step Above Craft Mall & Gift Store. 6614 Blue Ridge Extension. (816) 356-2890. Open Mon–Sat 10–6.

REEDS SPRING

The Old Spring Flea Market. Highway 13. (417) 272-3173. Antiques, primitives, collectibles, tools. Restrooms, handicapped accessible. Food and lodging nearby. Open daily, 9–6.

ROCHEPORT

Missouri River Antique Mall. I-70, Rocheport exit 115. Glassware, china, furniture, silver, dolls, toys. Don Brumm, (314) 698-2066.

ROCK PORT

Country Creek Mall. 323 S. Main Street. 64482. (816) 744-

2345. Antiques, Precious Moments. Mall has an old-fashioned candy counter and a crafter's loft. Mon–Sat 9am–5pm.

ROCKAWAY BEACH

Captain Ed's Antiques and Collectibles Mall. 2637 Highway 176. (417) 561-4389. Lots of great modern collectibles such as Disney, Precious Moments, Cherished Teddies, Ertl banks, and more. Restrooms, ample parking. Credit cards accepted. Open 9–5 daily from March 1 through November 1.

SALISBURY

General Store & Antique Mall. 2nd and Broadway, downtown. (816) 388-5030. Antiques, collectibles, gifts, lots of Missouri food items. Religious bookstore. Mon–Sat 9–5:30.

SAVANNAH

Savannah Square Mini Mall. 427 W. Main Street. Downtown. (816) 324-3984. Antiques, primitives, collectibles, tools, dolls, cookie jars, depression glass. Restrooms, ample parking, handicapped accessible. Open Mon–Sat 10–5, Sundays 12–5.

SEDALIA

Marriott Antiques. Three miles south of 50-65 Junction. (816) 826-5894. Furniture, glassware, primitives. Restrooms, ample parking, handicapped accessible. Open Mon–Sat 9:30–5, Sun 12:30–5.

Maple Leaf Antique Mall. 106 W. Main Street. Downtown. Large well-stocked mall. Year-round Christmas and Holiday Shoppe. Large selection of antique furniture. Victorian country gift and craft shop. Restrooms, ample parking. Very quaint Maple Leaf Tea Room on premises. Handicapped accessible. Credit cards accepted. Open Mon–Sat 10–5, Sun 11–5.

SMITHVILLE

Down on Main Street. 113 E. Main Street. Antiques, crafts, gifts. Mon-Fri 1–5, Sat 10–5.

Pack Rats Antiques. 103 E. Main Street. (816) 532-3363. Antiques, furniture, jewelry, and toys. Mon 9–5, Tues–Sat 10–5.

ST. CHARLES

St. Charles Antiques Mall. #1 Charlestown Plaza. Three miles south of I-70 on Highway 94. (314) 939-4178. Large well-stocked mall, 25,000 sq ft, with a wide variety from fine antiques, collectibles to crafts and new merchandise. Mon–Sat 10–8, Sun 11–5.

ST. GENEVIEVE

Kaegel's Country Collectibles. 252 Merchant Street. Al and Marty Kaegel, (314) 883-7996. Thirty-five dealers. Collectibles, antiques, crafts. Thurs–Tues 10–5, closed Wed. Mall is located in very old and quaint historic river town. There are many fine antique and craft shops here. Worthy of spending a couple of days in one of the many fine bed and breakfast inns in the area.

ST. LOUIS

South County Antiques Mall. 13208 Tesson Ferry Road. I-270, south two miles on Tesson Ferry Road. (314) 842-5566. Large one-level mall with over 400 booths. Very pricey. Open daily, Mon–Sat 9–8, Sun 10–6.

Noble House Antique Mall. 7345 Watson Road. (314) 963-9397. Large well-stocked mall with antiques and collectibles, very uninteresting mall. Restrooms, ample parking, handicapped accessible but very difficult entrance. Open daily 9–9.

ST. JOSEPH

Alabama Street Mall. 715 Alabama (Highway 752). Thirty dealers, primarily collectibles. Mon–Sat 10–5.

Belt Highway Antique Mall. 407 S. Belt Street, one block south of Venture. (816) 232-0568. New mall. Chandeliers and lamps, lots of WW II Memorabilia, carousel horses, dolls, toys, Victorian items, crafts. Well-stocked mall. Mon–Sat 10–5, Sun 1–5.

Central Station Mall. 710 S. 9th Street. (816) 232-6171. Located in the old police/jail building. 15,000 square feet. Lots of dolls and quilts, collectibles of all descriptions, also furniture, glassware, and pottery. Mon–Sat 10–5, Sun 1–5.

Felix Street Mini Mall. 518 Felix Street. (816) 233-7676. Over 50 dealers. Antiques, collectibles, crafts, primitives, glassware, and new merchandise. Mon–Sat 10–6, Sun 12–6.

Horns Antique Emporium. 502 Felix Street. Downtown, One block east of Civic Arena. (816) 364-3717. Sixty-five dealers, fine antiques and collectibles. Two large furniture rooms. Mon–Sat 10–5, Sun 12–5.

Kaleidoscope Antique Mall. 2717 Pear Street. (816) 232-8775. Antiques, furniture, collectibles, art glass, pottery, jewelry, layaways available. Mon–Sat 9–5, Sun 1–4.

One of a Kind Gallery & Gifts. Connie Tabony. 2239 N. Belt, Woodlawn Center. 64506. (816) 232-0441. Eighty-five artists booths. Original artwork, stained and etched glass, jewelry, pottery, lots of high-quality art and crafts. Mall has free special events for the public every weekend. Mon–Fri 10–6, Sat 10–5.

Penn Street Square Antique & Craft Mall. 12th and Penn Streets. (816) 232-4626. Two-story mall, located between the Jesse James House and the Pony Express Stable. Across the street from the Patee House Museum. Open daily. Antiques and collectibles of all kinds. Some unique and hard to find items amid the booth displays and bric-a-brac.

United Antique Mall. 6th and Felix Street. Downtown. (816) 364-2881. Over 100 booths. Furniture, glassware, collectibles. Mon–Fri 11–6, Sat 10–6, Sun 12–6.

Olde Towne Antique Mall. 4529 S. 169 Highway. I-29 at exit 44 then 500 ft east. (816) 364-0408. Collectibles, glassware, furniture. Open daily.

ST. MARY'S

St. Mary's Antique Mall. 777 Seventh Street. Exit 141 east from I-55. Follow signs closely, difficult to locate. Large one-level building with antiques, collectibles, crafts, new, and flea market items. Restrooms, snack bar, ample parking, handicapped accessible. Open Sun–Thurs 10–6, Fri–Sat 10–7.

SEDALIA

Country Cottage Craft Mall. 105 S. Osage. Downtown. (816) 826-2164. Lots of local country crafts of all types. Mon–Fri 9–5:30, Sat 9–5.

Crafters Mall. 809 Thompson Blvd. 65301. (816) 826-6606. Lots of locally made crafts. Mon–Sat 10–5.

Evie's Country Village. 4005 S. Highway 65. (816) 827-2877. Antiques, collectibles. 25+ dealers.

Maple Leaf Antique Mall. 106 W. Main Street. (816) 826-8383. Large antique mall in downtown area. Well-stocked mall with wide variety of good items. Also a large selection of country gifts and crafts, new merchandise, new oak and pine furniture. For the added enjoyment of shoppers, there is an excellent tearoom. The mall also has a year-round Christmas and Holiday Shoppe. Mon–Sat 10–5, Sun 11–5.

Marriott Antiques. The Pink Mall. Rt. 2, Box 340. Three miles south of Highways 50-65 junction. Furniture, glassware, nice primitives. Mon–Sat 9:30–5, Sun 12:30–5.

SIKESTON

River Birch Antique Gallery. 901 S. Kingshighway. River Birch Mall. (573) 472-4700. Large new 65,000 sq ft antique mall. Fine antiques and collectibles. Restrooms, ample parking, handicapped accessible. Open Mon–Sat 10–8, Sun 1–5.

SPRINGFIELD

Bass Country Antique Mall. 1832 S. Campbell. Mall is located directly across the street from the Bass Pro Store, an adventure in itself. Lots of fine antiques and collectibles here. The serious shopper will like this 100+ dealer mall. Crabby owners and no restroom facilities. Mon–Sat 10–6, Sun 12–5.

Traders Market Antiques & Gifts Mall. 1845 E. Sunshine. 65804. (417) 889-1145. Fax 882-0261. New indoor mall.

Antique Emporium. Highways 65 and CC. Behind Lambert's Cafe. (417) 581-2029. 12,000 sq ft one-level facility. Nice clean newer mall stocked with lots of quality collectibles. Antique repair service on grounds. Restrooms, ample parking, handicapped accessible. Be sure to visit Lambert's Cafe next door for a truly unique dining experience. Open Mon–Sat 9–9, Sun 9–5.

Coachouse Antique Mall, Craft Mall & Flea Market. 2051 E. Kearney. (417) 869-8008. Antiques, collectibles, toys, sports items, coins, advertising items. Restrooms, ample parking, handicapped accessible. Open Mon–Fri 10–6, Sat 10–9, Sun 11–5.

S.T.D. and Flea Market East. 1820 E. Trafficway. (417) 831-6367. General line of antiques and collectibles, lots of sports items, flea market items. Restrooms, ample parking, handicapped accessible. Credit cards accepted. Open daily 10–6.

S.T.D. and Flea Market West. 651 S. Kansas. (417) 831-6331. General line of antiques and collectibles, lots of sports items, flea market items. Restrooms, ample parking, handicapped accessible. Credit cards accepted. Open daily 10–6.

SULLIVAN

Showcase Antique Mall. 201 N. Service Road. Open daily 10am-6pm. (314) 481-1068.

VERONA

Charlotte's Web. Highway 60 West. (417) 678-6580. Forty-five dealers, dolls, collectibles, books, jewelry, primitives, furniture, good selection of locally made Ozark crafts. Open Tues–Sat 10–5, Sun 12–5.

WARRENSBURG

Those Were The Days Mall. ½ mile south of town on Highway BB at Highway 13. (816) 747-8799. Collectibles and lots of secondhand items. Mon–Sat 10–5, Sun 1–5.

Trash & Treasures Shopping Mall. 138 W. Pine Street. (816) 747-3123. 7,500 square feet. Antiques, crafts, collectibles, lots of low dollar items and junk here. Mon–Fri 9–5, Sat 10–4:30.

WARSAW

Warsaw Antique Mall. 245 W. Main Street. Next to Drake Harbor. (816) 438-9759. Mall is located in 1917 building with antiques and collectibles tastefully displayed. No flea market items. Restrooms, ample parking, food and lodging nearby. Handicapped accessible. Credit cards accepted. Open daily.

Valley Flea Market and Antique Mall. Old Highway 65 North. (816) 438-6633. Over 100 dealers. Quality antiques, collectibles, furniture, primitives, glassware, jewelry, and brass. Very interesting and picturesque town with lots of antique shops and other fun things to do. This is a nice vacation area.

WAVERLY

Gospel Truth Antique Mall. 100 W. Kelling. Downtown. (816) 493-2354. Mall is in an historic 1800's church. Antiques, collectibles, lots of Roseville and carnival glass. Mon–Sat 10–5, Sun 1–5.

WEBB CITY

Broadway Antiques & Collectibles. 210 E. Broadway. (417) 673-2327. Open Mon–Sat 10–5, Sun 12–5. Closed.

Steve's Fleas and More. 1506 S. Madison. (417) 673-4224. Collectibles, toys, flea market items, crafts, new, and used merchandise. Restrooms, ample parking. Open Mon–Sat 10–7, Sun 1–5.

WEST PLAINS

Downtown Antique Mall. City Square, downtown. 60 dealers. Quality line of antiques and collectibles. Restroom, ample parking, handicapped accessible. Open Mon–Sat 9–5:30, Sun 1–5. (417) 256-6487.

WESTON

Main Street Galleria Antiques & Gifts. 501 Main Street. (816) 386-2796. Antiques, collectibles, gifts, new items. Restrooms, ample parking, an old-fashion soda fountain. Handicapped accessible. Open daily.

Old Brewery Antique Mall. 500 Welt Street. 6,000 sq ft old brewery building. Furniture, glassware, jewelry, stoneware, pottery, advertising, railroad items, and large selection of primitives. Mall features a large quilt shop. Restrooms, ample parking. Open Fri–Sat 10–6, Sun–Thurs 10–5.

MONTANA ☞

BILLINGS

Lind Antique Mall. 1600 Main Street. 9,000 sq ft building. Furniture, primitives, china, lots of Western collectibles. (406) 252-2870. Closed Mondays.

Collectors Emporium Antique Mall. 114–118 N. 29th Street. Downtown. 35 dealers. Antiques, collectibles, lots of Western items. (406) 259-3314. Hours weekdays 9–9, Sat 9–5:30, Sun 12–5.

BOZEMAN

"Montana's Largest Antique Mall." 612 E. Main Street. 14,000 sq ft building. 40+ dealers. Antiques and collectibles of all kinds. Glassware, country, and Victorian items, kitchen collectibles, linens, quilts, vintage jewelry, art. (406) 587-5281.

HELENA

Quigley's Last Chance Antique Mall. 5944 Highway 12 West. Mile marker 36. (406) 449-8878. Over 25 dealers with good selection of small antiques and collectibles. Restroom, ample parking, handicapped accessible. Open daily 10am–6pm. No, Tom Selleck does not work here.

KALISPELL

Glacier Antique Mall. Highway 93, Four miles north of town. Some furniture, lots of small antiques and collectibles. Glassware, china, silver, toys, dolls, decorator finds. (406) 756-1690.

LAUREL

Lind Antique Mall. 101 W. 1st Street. (406) 628-1337. 9,000 sq ft facility with nice selection of antique furniture, china, primitives, and large selection of Western items. Restrooms, ample parking, handicapped accessible.

NEBRASKA ❧

BELLEVUE

Enamel & Lace Antiques. 908 Ft. Crook Road South. (Highway 75). 68005. (402) 291-4781. Thiry-five dealers with fine antiques and collectibles of all kinds. Credit cards accepted. Restrooms, ample parking. Mon–Fri 10–6, Sat 10–5, Sun 12–6.

COLUMBUS

Billy Bob's Antique Mall. 2707 - 13th Street. (402) 562-8408. 5,000 sq ft facility with general line of antiques and collectibles. Open Mon–Fri 10–5, Sat 10–4.

EAGLE

Eagle Antiques. 517 S. 4th Street. Over 30 dealers with a general line of antiques and collectibles including: glassware, primitives, vintage jewelry and clothing, advertising items. Open daily.

FAIRBURY

Fredericks Antique Mall. W. Highway 136. (402) 729-5105 or 729-5126. Five buildings full of furniture, primitives, glassware, collectibles. Property has a beautiful, restored Victorian house. Open Mon–Sat 10–5, Sun 1–5.

FREMONT

Park Avenue Antiques. 515 N. Park Avenue. Downtown. (402) 721-1157. Over 25 dealers with a variety of antique desirables. Also, a large assortment of oak and pine furniture, both finished and unfinished, and a good selection of stoneware. Open daily.

KEARNEY

Kaufmann's Antiques. 2200 Central Avenue. (308) 237-4972. 8,000 sq ft facility with 60+ dealers of antiques and collectibles. Restrooms, ample parking, handicapped accessible. Credit cards accepted. Open Mon–Sat 10–5, Sun 1–5.

Granny's Antique Co-Op. 229 S. Central. Multidealer shop with a bit of everything antique and collectible to be found, from turn-of-the-century family pictures to vintage wind-up toys. Open Mon–Sat 10–5, Sun 1–5.

Plum Tree Antique Mall. 2006 E. Highway 30. Glassware, china, pottery, art glass, collectibles. Open Tues–Sat 10–5, Sun 12–5. (308) 236-5777.

LEXINGTON

Antique Mall. I-80, Exit 237, ¼ mile north. Antique mall and 11 individual shops located here. Open daily. (308) 324-2816.

LINCOLN

The Antique Market. 48th and Old Cheney Road. 68516. (402) 423-4805. Antiques and collectibles. 55 dealers. Lincoln is the home of the University of Nebraska. They have attempted to learn to play football there, but so far, unsuccessfully.

Platte Valley Antique Mall. I-80, Exit 420. Midway between Lincoln and Omaha. (402) 944-2949. 150 dealers with quality antiques and collectibles. No reproductions or flea market merchandise. Restrooms, ample parking, handicapped accessible. Credit cards accepted. Open daily 10–8.

Burlington Arcade Antique Mall. Corner 7th and P Streets. Antique and collector items in all categories. Open daily. (402) 476-6067.

St. George Antique Mall. 1023 O Street. 7,000 sq ft building. Everything for the casual collector or serious investor. Some treasures hidden here amid the run-of-the mill collectibles. Open daily. (402) 477-4400.

Lincoln O Street Mall. 1835 O Street. (402) 435-3303 or 434-3747. Sixty dealers, furniture, primitives, jewelry. Credit cards accepted. Open daily Mon–Sat 10–6, Sun 12–5.

Antique Corner Cooperative. 1601 S. 17th Street. (402) 476-8050. Collectibles and good selection of oak furniture. Open daily.

Cornhusker Mall. 2130 Cornhusker Highway. 120 booths, antiques, collectibles, gift items. Restrooms, ample parking, handicapped accessible. Open Mon–Sat 9–5:30, Sun 12–5:30.

MCCOOK

Magic City Mall. 112 E. 2nd Street. (308) 345-7473. Great selection of quality collectibles.

NORFOLK

Antique Arcade Mall. Four miles north of town on Highway 81. (402) 379-0533. Antiques and collectibles. Open Mon–Sat 9:30–5, Sun 12–5.

OMAHA

Meadowlark Antique Mall. 10700 Sapp Brothers Drive. (800) 730-2135. Large 25,000 sq ft mall on I-80. Well-stocked with booths and showcases of quality antiques and collectibles. Ample parking, restrooms, handicapped accessible. Credit cards accepted. Open daily 9–9.

Brass Armadillo Antique Mall. Exit 440 from I-80. (402) 896-9600. Large 30,000 sq ft mall with over 350 dealers displaying quality lines of antiques and collectibles. This is a great mall to shop at. Restrooms, snack bar, ample parking, handicapped accessible. Open daily 9–9.

Treasure Trove Flea Mall. E. 8806 Groer Street. I-80, exit 72nd Street. 16,000 sq ft building, antiques, collectibles, new merchandise, flea market items. Credit cards accepted. Restrooms, handicapped accessible, ample parking. Open 9–6 daily. (402) 397-6811.

PAPILLION

Papillion Collectors Market. Papillion exit, I-80. Antiques, collectibles, furniture, primitives, farm items, quilts, silver, jewelry, toys, bric-a-brac. Credit cards accepted. Restrooms, ample parking. Open daily 10–5.

VENICE

Venice Antiques. Highway 92, 10 miles west of town. (402) 359-5782. Over 60 dealers. Antiques, furniture, primitives, glass, pottery, collectibles. Open daily.

NEVADA ✎

LAS VEGAS

Red Rooster Antique Mall. I-15 and Charleston. (702) 382-5253. 25,000 sq ft mall. Mall is clean and well-stocked with collectibles, furniture, jewelry, glass, primitives, antiques. Credit cards accepted. Restrooms, handicapped accessible, ample parking. Open daily.

The Sampler Shoppes. 6115 W. Tropicana. (702) 368-1170. 40,000 sq ft facility. Antiques, decorator items, furniture, jewelry, dolls, toys, glassware. Tearoom. Credit cards accepted. Restrooms, handicapped accessible. Open daily.

Westside Antique Mall. 3020 W. Charleston. (702) 877-5944. Antiques, collectibles, glassware, and small desirables of all varieties. Credit cards accepted. Restrooms, handicapped accessible, ample parking. Open daily.

Gypsy Caravan Antique Mall. 624 S. Maryland Parkway. Corner of Charleston and Maryland Parkway. (702) 384-1870. 24,000 sq ft facility. Antiques, collectibles, and large selection of decorator items from ridiculous to spectacular. Restrooms, ample parking, handicapped accessible. Open Mon–Sat 10–6, Sun 12–5.

AH Antique Mall. 2016 E. Charleston Blvd. (702) 388-1202. General line of antiques and collectibles. Credit cards accepted. Restrooms, handicapped accessible, ample parking. Open daily.

RENO

Antique Mall. 1215 S. Virginia Street. (702) 324-1003. 12,000 sq ft building. 60 dealers. General line of antiques and collectibles. New mall. Open daily. Credit cards accepted. Restrooms, handicapped accessible, ample parking. Open daily.

Image of the Past Antique Mall. 1000 S. Virginia Street. (702) 827-2355. 25,000 sq ft building with quality antiques and collectibles. Credit cards accepted. Restrooms, handicapped accessible, ample parking. Open daily.

The Antique Collective. 400 Mill Street. (702) 322-3989. Collectibles and antiques of all kinds. Credit cards accepted. Restrooms, handicapped accessible, ample parking. Open daily.

Nevada Collectibles. 290 California Avenue. (702) 324-0909. New mall, featuring casino items, postcards, and general lines of antiques and collectibles. Credit cards accepted. Restrooms, handicapped accessible, ample parking. Open daily.

NEW HAMPSHIRE 🐚

GROVERTON
Potato Barn Antiques. Route 3. Four miles north of Lancaster Fairgrounds. Ernie and Janice Yelle. (603) 636-2611. Multi-dealer shop with a wide selection of antiques and collectibles, featuring, old tools, costume jewelry, vintage clothing, and accessories. Ample parking, restroom, handicapped accessible. Open daily 9–5, closed Wednesdays.

MEREDITH
Burlwood Antique Center. Rt 3. Approximately 170 exhibitors. Market has a good variety of antiques and collectibles. No crafts or secondhand merchandise, very quality oriented establishment. Open May–October, daily 10am–5pm. (603) 279-6387.

NEW JERSEY 🐚

ASBURY PARK
Asbury Casino Antiques & Flea Market. Boardwalk and Ocean Avenue. (908) 988-8585. Antiques, collectibles, furniture, bric-a-brac, toys, secondhand items, linens, tools. Credit cards accepted. Restrooms, snack bar, handicapped accessible, ample parking. Open daily.

BRIELLE
Brielle Antique Center. 609 Higgins Ave. 08730. Garden State Parkway, Exit 98, 5 miles. (908) 528-8570. Twenty dealers. Country, furniture, vintage clothing, linens, Victorian, art

pottery, glassware. Credit cards accepted. Restrooms, handicapped accessible, ample parking. Open 10–5 Mon–Sat, 12–5 Sun.

DEERFIELD

Deerfield Village. Highway 77. (609) 451-2143. Fine antiques, collectibles, and specialty shops. Credit cards accepted. Food available. Restrooms, handicapped accessible, ample parking. Open Thurs–Mon 10–6.

EGG HARBOR TOWNSHIP

The Delilah Outlet Market. 6550 Delilah Road. (609) 652-4044. ¾ mile east of Atlantic City Airport circle. 20,000 sq ft facility with antiques and collectibles, which was formerly the Smithville Antique Center. Credit cards accepted. Restrooms, handicapped accessible, ample parking. Open Wed–Sat 10–9, Sun–Mon 10–6.

FREEHOLD

Freehold Antique Gallery. Victoria Collins, 21 W. Main Street. 07728. (908) 462-7900. 10,000 sq ft building. Antiques, collectibles, lots of smalls, and nice decorator items. Credit cards accepted. Restrooms, handicapped accessible, ample parking. Open Mon–Wed 11–6, Thurs and Fri 11–8, Sat and Sun 10–5.

HADDONFIELD

Haddonfield Antique Center. #9 Kings Highway E. (609) 429-1929. General line of antiques and collectibles. Credit cards accepted. Open 10–5 Mon–Sat.

HOPEWELL

Tomato Factory Antiques. Hamilton Street. (609) 466-9833. Forty individual shops featuring a wide range of antiques, collectibles, furniture, silver, linens, jewelry. Credit cards accepted. Restrooms, food available, handicapped accessible, ample parking. Open daily.

LAMBERTVILLE

Fox's Den Antiques & Collectibles. 7 N. Main Street. 08530. (609) 397-0877. Two large buildings, consignment gallery, fine furniture, collectibles, accessories, silver, art, jewelry, glassware, textiles. Credit cards accepted. Restrooms, handicapped accessible, ample parking. Open Mon–Fri 10–5, Sat and Sun 10–6.

Lambertville Antique Market. 1864 River Road. 1-½ miles south of town on Route 29. (609) 397-0456. Three large buildings of quality antiques and collectibles, mall has four showrooms and over 50 display cases. Mall also has outdoor market on Wed, Sat, and Sun from 6–4. Credit cards accepted. Restrooms, snack bar, handicapped accessible, ample parking. Mall is open Wed–Fri 10–4, Sat and Sun 8–4.

MIDLAND PARK

Brownstone Mill Antique Center. #11 Paterson Avenue. (201) 444-5046. Twenty individual shops located here featuring a wide range of quality antiques, collectibles, and decorator lines. Credit cards accepted. Restrooms, handicapped accessible, ample parking. Open Wed–Sat 10:30–5.

MT. HOLLY

Country Antique Center. Route 38. 08060. (800) 264-4694, (609) 261-1924. Over 60 dealers. Primitives, jewelry, glassware, Roseville, Heisey, furniture. Credit cards accepted. Restrooms, handicapped accessible, ample parking. Hours daily 10–5.

MULICA HILL

The Old Mill Antique Mall. #1 S. Main Street. 08062. (609) 478-9810. Thirty dealers located in picturesque old mill setting. Furniture, glassware, china, ephemera, tools, vintage clothing, linens, toys, jewelry. Air-conditioned. Credit cards accepted. Restrooms, snack bar, handicapped accessible, ample parking. Open daily 11–5.

POINT PLEASANT

Point Pleasant Antique Emporium. Clara Johnson. Bay and Trenton Avenues. 08742. (908) 892-2222 or (800) 322-8002. Over 100 dealers. Full range of quality items. This is a very well-stocked mall. Credit cards accepted. Restrooms, handicapped accessible, ample parking. Open daily 11–5.

Shore Antique Center. 300 Richmond Avenue. 08742. Route 35 South. (908) 295-5771. Twenty-five dealers, antiques, furniture, glass, collectibles, silver, paintings, scrimshaw, art glass, bronzes, jewelry. Credit cards accepted. Restrooms, handicapped accessible, ample parking. Hours 11–5 daily.

RED BANK

The Antiques Center of Red Bank. Front Street. 07701. Garden State Parkway, Exit 109. (908) 741-5331. Three large buildings, 150 dealers with a wide range of antiques and collectibles. Many neighboring antique shops. Credit cards accepted. Restrooms, handicapped accessible, ample parking. Open Mon–Sat 11–5, Sun 12–5.

SMITHVILLE

Smithville Antique Center. Route 9. 08201. Ten minutes north of Atlantic City. (609) 652-4044. Over 100 dealers. Two-story building with general line of antiques and collectibles. Credit cards accepted. Restrooms, ample parking. Open daily 11–6.

NEW MEXICO ☙

ALBUQUERQUE

Antique Specialty Mall. 4516 Central SE. 87108. (505) 268-8080. 18,000 square feet. Approx 57 dealers. American and English furniture, glassware, jewelry, Victorian, Deco, fishing items, specialty shops with Western, Indian items, and lots of books. Nice selection of old vending machines. Credit cards accepted. Restrooms, handicapped accessible, ample parking. Mon–Sat 10–6, Sun 12–5. Mall highly recommended for dealers.

Antique Connection. 12020 Central Avenue SE. 87123. (505) 296-2300. Over 50 dealers, furniture, dolls, glassware, pottery, lamps, china, quilts, books, toys, several nice old vending machines. Credit cards accepted. Restrooms, handicapped accessible, ample parking. Hours Mon–Sat 10–6, Sun 12–5.

Classic Century Square. 4616 Central SE. (505) 265-3161. 125 shops, paper, books, glassware, furniture, Indian art, toys, collectibles, primitives, gifts, dolls. Credit cards accepted. Restrooms, handicapped accessible, ample parking. Open daily Mon–Sat 10–6, Sun 12–9.

Classic Century Square. 3100 Juan Tabo NE. (505) 294-9904. 125 shops, paper, books, glassware, furniture, Indian art, toys, collectibles, primitives, gifts, dolls. Credit cards accepted. Restrooms, snack bar, handicapped accessible, ample parking. Open daily, Mon–Sat 10–6, Sun 12–9.

I-40 Antique Mall. I-40 and 12th Street. (505) 243-8011. New mall, 10,000 sq ft facility. Well-stocked with nice variety of antiques and collectibles, Western items, toys, linens. Credit cards accepted. Restrooms, snack bar, handicapped accessible, ample parking. Open daily 10–6.

HOBBS

The Downtown Antique Mall & Shoppers Emporium. 200 W. Broadway. (505) 397-1614. General line of antiques and collectibles, with nice selection of furniture. Credit cards accepted. Restrooms, snack bar, handicapped accessible, ample parking. Open Mon–Sat 10–6.

LAS CRUCES

Main Street Antique Mall. 2301 S. Main. I-10, Exit 142. (505) 523-0047. General line of antiques and collectibles with a good selection of Western items. Credit cards accepted. Restrooms, handicapped accessible, ample parking. Open daily.

SANTA FE

Antique Merchants. 2461 Cerrillos Road. Open daily. (505) 471-6303. Good selection of quality antiques, collectibles, furniture, silver, jewelry, and linens. Credit cards accepted. Restrooms, handicapped accessible, ample parking. Open daily.

SILVER CITY

Silver City Trading Post. 205 W. Broadway. (505) 388-8989. Antique mall with general line of antiques, collectibles, cowboy and Indian items. Mall has a very nice free doll museum. Restrooms, ample parking, handicapped accessible. Credit cards accepted. Open daily.

NEW YORK ✒

AVON

Avon Antique House. Barb and Bill Hulbert. 65 E. Main Street. 14414. Junction Routes 5 and 20. (716) 226-8360. Twenty-five dealers in two-story building with general line of antiques, collectibles, and smalls. Open Wed–Sun 11–5.

BLOOMFIELD

Jan's Early Attic. 6900 Routes 5 and 20. 14443. (716) 657-

7446. Fifty dealers. Furniture, glass, china, art pottery, Indian artifacts, dolls, toys, primitives, collectibles. Open Mon–Sat 10–5, Sun 12–5.

ENDWELL

Charlie Brown's Antiques & Used Furniture. Charles Bystricky. 100 Endwell Plaza. Corner of North and Main Street. (Route 17C). (800) 758-0761 or (607) 785-0761. 3,500 sq ft facility. Antiques, used furniture, large selection of tools, custom wood carvings, military items, glassware, primitives, marbles, silver, vintage clothing. Open daily.

FAYETTEVILLE

Seymour June House. 203 S. Manlius Street. (315) 637-1749. Mall is in a restored 1838 two-level building. Antiques, collectibles, glassware, furniture, art. Credit cards accepted. Restrooms, handicapped accessible, ample parking. Open daily.

FULTONVILLE

Hillcrest Antique Mall. Junction Routes 5A and 30A. Mall has 20+ dealers with general line of antiques and collectibles. Open daily. (518) 853-4550.

HOOSICK

Hoosick Antique Center. Troy-Bennington Road. (Route 7). 12089. (518) 686-4700. Sixty dealers. Antiques, collectibles, general lines. Very picturesque location. Open 10–5 daily.

HUNTINGTON STATION

Browsery Antique Center. 449 E. Jericho Turnpike. 11746. One mile east of Loop 110. Antiques, collectibles, secondhand items.

Yankee Peddler Antiques. 1038 New York Avenue. Three-story building with 30 dealers. Antiques, collectibles, furniture, clocks, china. (516) 271-5817.

MARATHON

Riverbend Antiques Center. Route 11 North. I-81, exit 9. (607) 849-6305. Two-story building with 40 dealers. Primitives, period furniture, majolica, Staffordshire, clocks, quilts. Open Tues–Sun 10–6.

Peck Street Antiques. Corner of Peck and Brink Streets. (607) 849-6367. Open Wed–Sun 10–5:30.

MILFORD

Brockmann's Antique Center. Route 28. 13807. Five miles south of Cooperstown. (607) 547-9192. Two large buildings, well-stocked with antiques, collectibles, new baskets, crafts, pine furniture, and decorative accessories. Open 10–5 Mon–Sat, Sun 12–5.

> **SHOPPING SMART—**
> FOR HELP IDENTIFYING ANTIQUES AND COMPARATIVE SHOPPING, THERE IS NOTHING WRONG WITH TAKING YOUR FAVORITE PRICE GUIDEBOOK ALONG ON YOUR SHOPPING TRIP TO THE ANTIQUE MALL.

NEW YORK CITY

Chelsea Antiques Building. 110 W. 25th Street. Large 12-floor building with shops, antiques, co-ops, galleries, and stores. Lots of high-quality estate items here. Open 10–6. (212) 929-0909.

PINE VALLEY

Serendipity II. Route 14. 14872. Route 17, exit 52N. (607) 739-9413. Antiques, collectibles, paper, sewing items, books. Open Mon–Fri 10–5, Sat and Sun 11–4.

PINE WOODS

The Cobblestones. Junction Routes 20 and 46. 13310. One mile west of Bouckville. (315) 893-7670. Country, primitive and oak furniture, glassware, kitchen collectibles, ironstone, bottles, fishing tackle, tools. Open 10–5 daily.

PRESTON HOLLOW

Antique Center of Preston Hollow. 961 Main Street. 12469. Route 145. (518) 239-4251. Twenty-five dealers. Antiques, collectibles. Open 10–5 daily.

ROCHESTER

Lee Way Antique Co-Op. 1221 Lee Road. 35 dealers. Credit cards accepted. Open daily until 5. (716) 458-3990.

Route 104 Antiques Center. Corner of Route 104 and Dean Parkway. Ten miles east of Rochester. (716) 265-3280. Fax (716) 265-1390. Large well-stocked mall with showcases of beautiful quality items. Credit cards accepted. Open daily Mon–Fri 9–8, Sat and Sun 9–5.

SYRACUSE

Antiques Underground. 247 W. Fayette Street. (315) 472-5510. Antiques, collectibles, paintings, jewelry, orientals, silver. Credit cards accepted. Restrooms, handicapped accessible. Open daily.

NORTH CAROLINA 🐾

ABERDEEN

Town & Country Antique Mall. Town & Country Shopping Center. (919) 944-3359. Twenty dealers. General line of antiques and collectibles. Credit cards accepted. Restrooms, handicapped accessible, ample parking. Open Mon–Sat 10–5, Sun 1–5.

ASHEBORO

Collector's Antique Mall. David and Janet Rich. 211 Sunset Avenue. Downtown. 25,000 sq ft two-story building. (919) 629-8105 or 672-1867. Antiques and collectibles. Open daily, Mon–Sat 10–6, Sun 1–5.

Cedar Creek Mall. Downtown. Open Fri, Sat, and Sun. (919) 625-1521.

64 East Antique Mall. 4660 Highway 64. 27248. (918) 824-1542. Hours 10–6 daily.

ASHEVILLE

Asheville Americana. 43 Rankin Avenue. 28801. (704) 253-3634. Antiques, collectibles. Credit cards accepted. Restrooms, handicapped accessible, ample parking. Open Mon–Sat 10–5.

Corner Cupboard Antique Mall. 49 N. Lexington Avenue. 28801. (704) 258-9815. Thirty dealers, antiques, collectibles. Credit cards accepted. Restrooms, handicapped accessible, ample parking. Open 10–6 Mon–Sat.

BREVARD

Brevard Antique Mall. 53 E. Main Street. 28712. (704) 885-2744. Two-story building with 30 dealers with a general line of antiques and collectibles. Restrooms, ample parking. Open 9:30–5:30 Mon–Sat.

CARY

The Cary Antique Emporium. 305-B Asheville Avenue.

27511. (919) 233-8668. Thirty dealers, antiques and collectibles. Open daily.

CASHIERS
Cashiers East Antique Mall. Downtown. (704) 743-3580.

CHARLOTTE
Antique Malls of the Carolinas. 8829 E. WT Harris Blvd. Outlet Marketplace. I-77, Exit 90. (704) 536-5220. General line of antiques and collectibles. Credit cards accepted. Restrooms, handicapped accessible, ample parking. Open Mon–Sat 10–9, Sun 1–6.

Pineville Antiques Center. I-77, Exit 90. General line of antiques and collectibles. Credit cards accepted. Restrooms, handicapped accessible, ample parking. Open Mon–Sat 10–5, Sun 1–5.

Queen City Antiques. 3892 E. Independence Blvd. (704) 531-6002. Antiques, collectibles, furniture, Persian rugs, fine jewelry, linens, silver, glassware. Credit cards accepted. Restrooms, handicapped accessible, ample parking. Open Mon–Sat 10–6, Sundays 1–6.

CONOVER
Conover Antique Mall. Villa Park Shopping Center. 28613. I-40, exit 128. Forty dealers. Collectible glassware, toys, trains, antique clocks, estate jewelry, furniture. Open Tues–Sat 10–6, Sun 1–6. (704) 465-0300.

DURHAM
Downtown Flea Mall. 317 N. Main Street. (919) 688-5872.

FUQUAY/VARINA
Bostic & Wilson Antiques. 105 S. Main Street. 12,000 sq ft. Thirty-eight dealers. Wide selection of antiques, collectibles, country, primitives, Victorian, glassware, pottery, and oak roll-top desks. Mall has very nice tearoom. (919) 552-3248. Mon–Sat 10–5.

GREENSBORO
Cotton Mill Square. 801 Merritt Drive. Large century-old cotton mill converted into a shopping mall. Antiques, crafts, museum, restaurant, and a monthly auction. High-quality antiques, art, and collectibles here and an outdoor weekend flea market. (919) 299-2427. Open Mon–Sat 10–9, Sun 1–6.

O'Henry Antique Mall Antiques & Collectibles. 3224 N. O'Henry Blvd. (Highway 29 North). (919) 375-0191. Antiques, collectibles, furniture, primitives, silver, linens, glassware. Credit cards accepted. Restrooms, handicapped accessible, ample parking. Open 10–5:30 Mon–Sun.

HAMPSTEAD

Thee Mall Antiques. Highway 17, 28443. Four miles north of town. (919) 270-2168. Ten dealers, general line of antiques and collectibles. Credit cards accepted. Open 10–5 Mon–Sat.

HAMPTONVILLE

Yadkin Valley Antique Mall. Highways 421 and I-77. Exit 73A. (919) 468-4333. Eighty-five dealers, Two buildings, antiques and collectibles. Credit cards accepted. Restrooms, ample parking. Open daily 10–6.

HICKORY

Hickory Antiques Mall. 348 Highway 70. I-40, Exit 123. (704) 322-4004. Over 80 dealers. 15,000 sq ft building. Furniture, glassware, good variety of merchandise here. Credit cards accepted. Restrooms, handicapped accessible, ample parking. Open daily.

HILLSBOROUGH

Antique Mall. Daniel Boone Village. I-40 Exit 261, I-85 Exit 164. (919) 732-8882. Twenty-five dealers, 6,000 sq ft building. Collectibles, fishing lures, furniture, glassware. Credit cards accepted. Restrooms, handicapped accessible, ample parking. Open Mon–Sat 10–5, Sun 1–5.

JACKSONVILLE

Thrift Lords Thieves Market. 733 Bell Fork Road. 28540. (919) 577-7188. Antiques, collectibles, new and used furniture. Credit cards accepted. Restrooms, ample parking. Open daily.

Memory Lane Antique Mall. 657 N. Marine. (Highway 17). 28540. (919) 347-6006. Antiques, collectibles, and mall has an auction every other Saturday night. Credit cards accepted. Restrooms, snack bar, handicapped accessible, ample parking. Open daily.

KANNAPOLIS

Cannon Village Antique Mall. I-85 at the Factory Outlet

Shopping Center. (704) 932-2529. New Mall with 50+ dealers. Antiques, collectibles, furniture, linens, kitchen collectibles, primitives. Restrooms, handicapped accessible, ample parking. Open Mon–Sat 10–6, Sun 1–6

LENOIR

321 Antique Mall. 606 NE Blowing Rock Blvd. 28645. (704) 754-0910. General line of antiques and collectibles. Credit cards accepted. Restrooms, handicapped accessible, ample parking. Open Mon–Sat 10–6.

MATTHEWS

Antique Alley. 1325 Matthews-Mint Hill Road. (704) 847-3003. Thirty-five dealers. Antiques, collectibles, large selection of antique and country furniture, primitives, linens. Credit cards accepted. Restrooms, handicapped accessible, ample parking. Open daily.

MOORESVILLE

Twice Treasured Antique Mall. 132 S. Main Street. I-77, exit 36. Timothy Cook, (704) 664-6255. 10,000 sq ft facility featuring quality line of antiques and collectibles. Credit cards accepted. Ample parking, restrooms, handicapped accessible. Open Mon–Sat 10–6, Sun 1–6.

NEW BERN

Poor Charlie's Flea Market & Antiques. 206–8 Hancock Street. Across the street from the Farmers Market. (919) 638-2798. Seventeen booths, furniture, antiques, collectibles, heirloom jewelry, unique gifts, and furniture. Carnival-like atmosphere of old-time flea markets in an old historic ivy-clad warehouse. Credit cards accepted. Restrooms, food available, handicapped accessible, ample parking. Open daily.

NORTH WILKESBORO

Forester's Antique Mall. Corner of Tenth and Main Streets. 919 838-2271. Lots of toys, antiques, glassware, furniture, pottery, primitives, vintage clothing. Credit cards accepted. Restrooms, handicapped accessible, ample parking. Open daily.

PITTSBORO

Antiques & Collectibles. 52 Hillsboro Street. 9 dealers. (919) 542-5649. Numerous shops located here.

RALEIGH

Carolina Antique Mall. 2050 Clark Avenue. 27604. (919) 833-8227. Large selection of furniture, jewelry, crystal, silver and art. Credit cards accepted. Restrooms, handicapped accessible, ample parking. Open Mon–Sat 10–5:30.

Oakwood Antique Mall. 1526 Wake Forest Road. (919) 834-5255. 10,000 sq ft. 40+ dealers. Wide variety of furniture, glass, jewelry and 50's memorabilia. Ample parking, restrooms, handicapped accessible. Credit cards accepted. Open Tues–Sat 10–6, Sun 1–5.

Gresham Lake Antique Mall. 6917 Capital Blvd. 27604. (919) 878-9381. Antiques, jewelry, collectibles, primitives, glassware. Credit cards accepted. Restrooms, handicapped accessible, ample parking. Open Mon–Sat 10–7, Sun 1–6.

SALISBURY

The Salisbury Emporium. 230 E. Kerr Street. 28144. (704) 642-0039. Antiques, fine art, handcrafts. This stop is a collection of shops and galleries located in a renovated historic landmark adjacent to the architecturally acclaimed Salisbury Train Station. Credit cards accepted. Restrooms, handicapped accessible, ample parking. Open daily.

Antiques on Main Street. 106 S. Main Street. I-85, exit 76B. (704) 642-0660. General line of antiques and collectibles. Credit cards accepted. Hours Mon–Sat 10–5.

SOUTHPORT

The following malls all are located within walking distance and have a wide selection of antiques, collectibles, furniture, glass, silver, imports, books, toys, jewelry, prints, lamps, gift shops, and fine restaurants.

The Antique Mall. 108 E. Moore Street. (919) 457-4982.

Etcetera. 112 E. Moore Street. (919) 457-6119.

Northrop Mall. 111 E. Moore Street. (919) 457-9569.

Palm Tree Passage. 111 S. Howe Street. (919) 457-9200.

STATESVILLE

Duck Creek Antiques & Collectibles Mall. I-77, Exit 45, south ½ mile. (704) 873-3825. 12,000 sq ft building with 50 dealers. Large selection of antiques and collectibles. Credit cards accepted. Restrooms, handicapped accessible, ample parking. Open Mon–Sat 10–6, Sun 1–6.

Riverfront Antique Mall. 1441 Wilkesboro Road. (704) 873-9770. Large well-stocked new mall, 60,000 sq ft facility with over 350 dealers carrying a complete line of antiques and collectibles. Ample parking, restrooms, snack bar, handicapped accessible. Credit cards accepted. Open Mon–Sat 10–8, Sun 10–6.

WAXHAW
Waxhaw Antique Village. Highways 16 and 75. (704) 843-2181. Hours Wed–Sat 10–5, Sun 1–5. 4,000 sq ft mall and 23 separate specialty shops and restaurants. This is a quaint turn-of-the-century town.

NORTH DAKOTA ❧

JAMESTOWN
Antique Attic. 219 First Ave S. Downtown. (701) 252-6733. Open Mon–Fri 12:30–5:30, Sat 10–4.

MANDAN
Antique Gallery. 300 W. Main Street. Open Mon–Sat 9–6, Sun 12–5. (701) 667-2829.

OHIO ❧

AKRON
West Hill Antiques. 461 W. Market Street. 44303. (Highway 18). (216) 762-6633. Five dealers with quality line of antiques and collectibles. Mall is located in Akron's antique row with many neighboring shops. Hours daily 10–6.

ARCANUM
Olde Tyme Treasures Antiques & Collectibles Mall. Judy Holster. Corner of West George and High Streets. 45304. Open Tues–Sat 10–5, Sun 12–5.

Victorian Babes Antiques Mall. Vickie Bruss Harter. 20 W. George St. 45304. (513) 548-3349. Open Tues–Sat 11–5, Sun 1–5. Closed Mondays.

Smith's Big Antique Store. 109 W. George Street. 45304.

(513) 692-8540. Sixty dealers. Open Tues–Sat 10–5, Sun 12–5.

ASHLAND

Antiques on Main. 143 West Main Street. 44805. Downtown. (419) 289-8599. Multidealer shop with general line of antiques and collectibles.

Pumphouse Antiques. 400 Orange Street. 44805. 22,000 sq ft Three-story building with over 100 dealers of antiques and collectibles. First floor is quality antiques from all periods. Second floor is the collectors mart. Antiques and creative art. Third floor is the lost treasures and elegant junque. Air-conditioned. Good food at the Pumphouse Cafe on premises. Open daily.

AVON

Country Heirs. 35800 Detroit Road. 44011. (Route 254). (216) 937-5544. Fifteen dealers, antiques, collectibles, crafts, wreaths, woodcrafts, primitives, Christmas items. Hours daily 11–5.

BARNESVILLE

Barnesville Antique Mall. 202 N. Chestnut Street. 43713. (614) 425-2435. Three-story building with antiques, collectibles, secondhand and used merchandise. Open daily 9–5.

BERLIN

Berlin Antique Mall. 4898 W. Main Street. (216) 893-3051. Antiques, handmade furniture, crafts, quilts. Ample parking, snack bar, restrooms, handicapped accessible. Open Mon–Sat 9–5.

BLANCHESTER

Broadway Antique Mall. 102 S. Broadway. 45107. (513) 783-2271. Eighty-five booths, antiques, collectibles. Hours Mon–Sat 10–5, Sun 12:30–5.

Broadway Antique Mall #2. Junction Routes 28-123-133. 45107. (513) 783-2271. 10,000 sq ft building, 85 booths. Antiques, collectibles, primitives, glassware, furniture, dolls, and toys. Hours Mon–Sat 10–5, Sun 12:30-5. Mall conducts retail consignment auctions the first Thursday of each month.

BROOKFIELD

Valley View Expo Center and Antique Mall. 7281 Warren Sharon Road. (800) 587-2535. This is one of the new mega-malls that have sprung up around the country. Too large, too much of everything, including all the amenities. Too big for me. Open Mon–Sat 10–8, Sun 10–6.

CAMBRIDGE

Penny Court Antiques. 637 Wheeling Avenue. 43725. (614) 432-4369. Over 100 dealers, antiques and collectibles. Mon–Sat 10–6, Sun 12–5.

CARROLL

Soper's Antique Palace Mall. Junction Route 33 and Coon-path Road. 43112. (614) 756-4411. Four miles north of Lancaster. Four buildings full of antiques and collectibles. Mall specializes in old furniture and jewelry. Open Wed–Sun 11–5:30.

CASTALIA

Cloud's Antique Mall. Mark and Trina Cloud. Route 269. 44824. (419) 684-7566. Fifty dealers, antiques, collectibles. Mall features 35 showcases. Very quality oriented establishment. Open 10–5 daily.

CHADRON

Antiques On The Square. 101 Main Street. 44024. (216) 286-1912. Twenty-dealer mall on the town square, several antique shops neighboring. Hours Mon–Sat 10–5, Sun 12–5.

CHESTERLAND

Antiques of Chester. 7976 Mayfield Road. 44026. (Route 322). (216) 729-3395. Eleven dealers in a restored 1830 farmhouse. Fine antiques, collectibles, country oak, Victorian, nautical, tools, quilts, glassware. Hours Tues–Sat 11–5, Sun 12–5.

CHESTERVILLE

Chesterville Antiques. Junction Routes 95 and 314. Two miles east of I-71, exit 151. (419) 768-3979.

CINCINNATI

Duck Creek Antique Mall. 3715 Madison Road. 45209. (513) 321-0900. New mall. 130 dealers, 20,000 sq ft.

Antiques, furniture, glassware, jewelry, pottery, china, toys. Credit cards accepted. Hours Mon–Sat 10–5, Sun 12–5.

Special Things Antique Mall. 5701 Cheviot Road. 45247. I-74, exit 14, 1 mile north. (513) 741-9127. Dealer co-op, 10-room farmhouse with fine antiques and collectibles. Hours 10–5 Mon–Sat, Sun 12–5.

Antique Mall & Collectibles Market. 3742 Kellogg Avenue. 45226. (Highway 52). (513) 871-5560 or 321-0919. 30,000 sq ft building, antiques, collectibles, fine furniture, Art Deco, vintage clothing, dolls, toys, estate jewelry. 909 dealers. Credit cards accepted. Restaurant on premises. Hours Wed–Fri 10–5, Sat and Sun 9–6.

CIRCLEVILLE
Brewer's Antique Mall. 105 W. Main Street. Open Mon–Sat 10–6, Sun 12–5.

CLIFTON
Clifton Antique Mall. 301 N. Main Street. 45316. (513) 767-2277. Antiques and collectibles. Hours Wed–Sun 11–5.

Weber's Antiques. Clay Street. (513) 767-8581.

CLYDE
Maplewood Gallery. 1012 E. U.S. Route 20. (419) 547-9175. Antique mall with quality line of antiques and collector lines. Open Mon–Fri 8–8, Sat 8–5, Sun 12–5.

COLUMBUS
Greater Columbus Antique Mall. 1045 S. High Street. (614) 443-7858. Large 5-story facility, 11,000 sq ft with quality antiques and collectibles. 70+ dealers. Credit cards accepted. Mall open 11–8 daily.

COSHOCTON
Coshocton Antique Center. Clark Stuart. 309 S. 4th Street. 43812. (614) 622-3223. Hours 10–5 Mon–Sat, Sun 1–5.

CRIDERSVILLE
The Antique Arcade. 608 E. Main Street. 45806. I-75, exit 118. (419) 645-4563. Antiques, collectibles, furniture. Hours Mon–Sat 8–5, Sun 12–5.

DEFIANCE
Another Man's Treasures Antique Mall. 235 Hopkins 43512.

(419) 784-4589. 4,000 sq ft building, antiques, collectibles, furniture. Hours Tues–Fri 10–5, Sat–Sun 12–4.

DELPHOS

Miami-Erie Antique Mall. 132 S. Delphos Street. 45833. (419) 695-6926. Mall is located in 1880's train station hotel. Antiques, collectibles, lots of antique furniture displayed in the hotel's 30 rooms. Open Mon–Fri 10–6, Sat and Sun 11–4.

DELTA

Delta Antiques Market. 301 Main Street. 43515. (Highway 2). (419) 335-0156. Hours Tues–Sat 10:30–5. Sun 12:30–4.

DENNISON

250 Antique Mall. 9043 State Route 250 SE. 44621. (800) 247-3704 or (614) 922-3811. Over 50 dealers, 13,000 sq ft building. Quality line of antiques and collectibles. Mall has a year-round Christmas shop. Hours daily 10–5.

DEXTER CITY

Dexter City Antique Mall. Highway 821. I-77, exit 16, 2 miles north. (614) 783-5921. Two-story building with 45 dealers. Large selection of furniture at this mall, general line of antiques and collectibles. Lots of quality glassware here. Hours Mon–Sat 10–6, Sun 12–6.

DOVER

Dover Antique Mall. 416 W. 8th Street. Rear of building. (216) 343-3336. Antiques and collectibles. Open Mon–Sat 10–5.

ETNA

H & R Antique Mall. 1063 Pike Street. I-70, exit 118. ½ mile north to Pike. (614) 927-4053. Antiques and collectibles. Open Wed–Sat 10–5, Sun 1–5.

FINDLAY

Clover Farms Antiques Emporium. 130 E. Sandusky Street. 45840. (419) 424-8833. Mall is located in historic old building. Antiques, collectibles, nice selection of oak, walnut, cherry furniture. Lots of architectural antiques. Open Tues–Sat 11–5, Sun 1–5.

Jeffrey's Antique Gallery. Bryan Jrick. 11326 Township Road 99. 45840. (419) 429-7500. I-75, exit 161. Large well-stocked mall, over 300 dealers, many high-quality and investment-grade pieces here. Credit cards accepted. Open daily 10–6.

FOSTORIA

Fostoria Town Center Antique Mall. 116 N. Main Street. 44830. (419) 435-1989. Open Tues–Sat 10–6, Sun 12–5.

GREENTOWN

Union Station Antiques. 9815 Cleveland Ave. NW. 44630. Located at Coach House Square. (216) 966-0658. Fifteen dealers, 4,000 sq ft, 2-story building. Credit cards accepted. Hours Mon–Sat 10–5, Sun 12–5.

GREENVILLE

Biddlestone Antique Mall. 126 W. 4th Street. 45331. (513) 548-3180. Antiques, collectibles. Open Mon–Sat 10–5, Sun 1–5.

HARPSTER

Old General Store Antique Mall. 7223 State Route 294. 43323. (614) 496-2532. Antiques, collectibles. Open Mon–Fri 11–6, Sun 1–5.

HILLSBORO

Old Parts Factory Mall. 135 N. West Street. (513) 393-8934. Nice selection of quality antiques and collectibles. Hours 10–6 Mon–Sat, Sun 1–5.

HOMERVILLE

Homerville Antique Mall. Junction of Highways 224 and 301. 44235. (216) 625-2500. Antiques, collectibles, country, kitchen items, primitives, furniture, depression glass, decorator items. Open Thurs 11–5, Fri–Sat 11–7, Sun 11–5.

JOHNSTOWN

Village Antique Mall. 42 S. Main Street. 43031. (614) 967-0048. 6,000 sq ft facility. Antiques, collectibles, pottery, books, depression glass, primitives, cookie jars. Hours Mon–Sat 9–6.

INFORMATION IS SUBJECT TO CHANGE—ALWAYS CALL AHEAD TO AVOID DISSAPOINTMENT!

KIDRON

Village Antique Mall. 4750 Kidron Road. 44636. (216) 857-1040. Antiques and collectibles, 20 dealers. Hours Mon–Sat 10–5.

KUNKLE

Kunkle Schoolhouse Antique Mall. Don Ackley. 119 Elm Street. 43531. (419) 737-2571. New mall.

LANCASTER

Lancaster Antique Emporium. 201 W. Main Street. (614) 653-1973. Open daily.

LEBANON

Broadway Antique Mall. 17 S. Broadway. 45036. (513) 932-1410. 10,000 sq ft building, 80 dealers, antiques and collectibles. Open 10–5 Mon–Sat, Sun 12–5.

Lebanon Antique Exchange. 15 E. Main Street. (513) 933-9935. Open 10–5 Mon–Sat, 12–5 Sun.

LITHOPOLIS

Lithopolis Antique Mart. #9 E. Columbus Street. (614) 837-9683. 5,000 sq ft, 4 levels, 50 dealers. Antiques, collectibles, furniture. Hours 10–8 Tues, 10–5 Wed–Sat, Sun 1–5.

LOGAN

Logan Antique Mall. 145 W. Main Street. 43138. (614) 385-2061. Sixty dealers, 3-story building. Hours Mon–Sat 10–5:30, Sun 12–5.

MANSFIELD

Mid-Ohio Antique Mall. 155 Cline Avenue, corner of Cline and Lexington Avenue. (Route 42S). (419) 756-5852. 2-story building. Open daily 10–5.

MARYSVILLE

Marysville Antique Mall. 117 S. Main Street. (513) 642-9393. New mall with general line of antiques and collectibles. Open Mon–Sat 10–6, Sun 12–5. Closed Tuesdays.

MEDINA

Brothers Antique Mall. 6132 Wooster Pike. 44256. (Route 3). Five miles north of I-76, Exit 2. Antiques, great selection of cookie jars, Watt pottery, 40's and 50's collectibles. Mall does furniture stripping, repair, and refinishing. (216) 723-7580. Open daily 10–5, Sun 12–5.

MENTOR
Mentor Village Antiques. 8619 Mentor Avenue. 44060. (Route 20). (216) 255-1438. Furniture, linens, glass, primitives, pottery, paper, porcelains. Hours Mon–Sat 11–5.

MIDDLETOWN
The Bronze Horse Antiques Mall. 1200 Central Avenue. Rob or Dana Roberts, (513) 727-9133. New 25,000 sq ft antique mall. Open daily.

MILLERSBURG
Antique Emporium. 113 W. Jackson. 44654. (216) 674-0510. Antiques, collectibles, country furniture, china, Victorian, glassware, primitives. Great selection of antique furniture in the rough. Country crafts and decorator items. Open Mon–Sat 10–5, Sun 10–4.

MONTPELIER
Village Trading Post. 123 Empire Street. 43543. (419) 485-4996. Credit cards accepted. Hours Mon–Sat 10–5, Sun 1–5.

NEW BALTIMORE
Mack's Barn Old-Tiques & Ant. Cheryl Himebaugh. State Route 44, between Routes 619 and 224. (216) 935-2746. Antiques and collectibles. Hours Mon–Sat 11–5, Sun 12–5, closed Tuesdays.

NEW PHILADELPHIA
Riverfront Antique Mall. 1203 Front Street. 44663. I-77, Exit 81. (800) 926-9806 or (216) 339-4448. 80,000 sq ft building, all on one floor. 250+ dealers. One of the largest and best-stocked malls in the country. Many showcases and room settings very attractively displayed. Very large antique furniture showroom and separate area for furniture in the rough. Dealer quality throughout the mall is very high. This mall is almost a vacation in itself. It is located in the heart of Amish country, a great area to spend a couple of days. Restrooms, snack bar, handicapped accessible, ample parking. Hours Mon–Sat 10–8, Sun 10–6.

NEW VIENNA
Village Antique Mall. 191 Main Street. 45159. (513) 987-

2932. 4,000 sq ft facility. Antiques and collectibles. Hours 10–5 Mon–Sat, Sun 1–5.

NORTH RIDGEVILLE

Hatchery Antique Mall. 7474 Avon Belden Road. 44039. (216) 327-9808. 5,000 sq ft building with 30 dealers. Mall features a 16-showcase room filled with very desirable smalls. Hours 10–6 daily.

OLMSTED FALLS

Trackside Antique Mall. 9545 Columbia Road. 44138. (Route 252). (216) 235-1166. Antiques, collectibles, early toys, glass, advertising items, china. Hours 11–4:30 daily.

PERRYSBURG

Perrysburg Antiques Market. Marty Kruser. 118 Louisiana Avenue. 43551. (419) 872-0231. Fifteen dealers, antiques, collectibles, furniture, jewelry, watches, always a nice selection of fireplace mantels. Open Tues–Sat 10:30–5:30, Sun 11–4.

PIONEER

Pioneer Antique Mall. 103 Baubice Street. 43554. (419) 737-2341. Credit cards accepted. Hours Mon–Sat 10–6, Sun 1–5.

Tri-State Antique Mall. State Route 15. Ohio Turnpike, exit 2, 1 mile north. (419) 485-5610. Credit cards accepted. Hours Tues–Sat 10–5:30, Sun 1–5.

POWELL

Depot Street Antique Mall. Merrill and Bunny Wells, 41 and 47 Depot Street. (614) 885-6034. Two buildings with 6,000 sq ft of antiques and collectibles. Credit cards accepted. Hours Tues–Sat 10–5, Sun 12–5.

RIPLEY

Olde Piano Factory Antique Mall. 307 N. 2nd Street. 45167. (513) 392-9243. Antiques, collectibles, furniture. Open 10–4 Mon–Sat. Sun 12–5.

ROSS

Venice Antique Mall. Junction of State Routes 128 and 126. (513) 738-8180. 12,000 sq ft facility, 3 floors, 70+ dealers. Antiques and collectibles. Open 11–7 daily.

Early Days Antiques. 71 W. Olentangy Street. (614) 848-4747. Antiques, collectibles, gifts. Open Tues–Sat 11–5, Sun 1–5.

Liberty Antique Mall. 22 N. Liberty Street. (614) 885-5588. Thirty dealers, antiques, collectibles, furniture, toys, paper, jewelry, glassware. Open Tues–Sat 12–5, Sun 1–5.

SMITHVILLE

Smithville Antique Mall. 637 E. Main Street. 44677. (Highway 585). (216) 669-3332. Antiques and collectibles. Hours Mon–Sat 10–5, Sun 12–5.

SOUTH BLOOMFIELD

South Bloomfield Antique Mall. Route 23 North. (614) 983-4300. Twenty-five dealers. General line of antiques and collectibles. Open Mon–Sat 10–5, Sun 12–5.

SPENCERVILLE

Spencerville Antique Mall. 127 N. Broadway. (419) 647-4050. Antiques and collectibles. Hours Mon–Sat 11–5, Sun 1–5, closed Thurs.

Ohio Antique Market. 113 S. Broadway. (419) 647-6237. Forty dealers, antiques and collectibles. Mon–Sat 10–6, Sun 12–5, closed Wed.

SPRINGFIELD

AAA I-70 Antique Mall. 4700 S. Charleston Pike. (513) 324-8448. New mall. Deli in mall. Credit cards accepted. Hours 10–6 daily.

STRASBURG

Strasburg 77 Antiques & Collectibles. 780 S. Wooster. 44680. (216) 878-7726. I-77, exit 87. ¼ mile west. Antique mall, 3 antique shops and 2 weekend indoor flea markets are all located at this stop. Mall is open Tues–Sun 11–5.

SUGARCREEK

Dutch Valley Antique Mall. Old Route 39. (216) 852-4026. 4,000 sq ft mall with antiques and collectibles. Great restaurant next door. Hours Mon–Sat 9–8.

SUNBURY

Sun-Berry Antique Mall. 20 S. Vernon Street. (614) 965-2279. Twenty dealers. Country, collectibles, jewelry. Hours Mon–Sat 10–5, Sun 1–5.

Weidner's Village Square Antique Mall. 31 E. Granville Street. (614) 965-4377. Forty dealers. Quality antiques, coins, furniture, artifacts. Mall has a large selection of display cases and accessories. Hours Mon–Sat 10–6, Sun 1–5.

TOLEDO

Downtown Antiques & Collectibles Mall. Jim Wagner. 333 N. Superior Street. (419) 255-5252. Antiques, collectibles, books, coins, glassware, estate jewelry, pottery, dolls. Hours Mon–Sat 10–6, Sun 10–4.

Cobblestone Antique Mall. 2635 W. Central Avenue. (419) 475-4761. Over 40 dealers, antiques, collectibles. Mon–Sat 10–5, Sun 12–5.

Old West End Collector's Corner. 2502 Collingwood Blvd. 12,000 sq ft consignment center. Antiques, collectibles, credit cards accepted. Open Mon–Fri 12–6, Sat 10–6.

VAN WERT

Years Ago Antique Mall. 108 W. Main Street. 45891. (419) 238-3362. Antiques, collectibles. Open Mon-Fri 9–5.

WADSWORTH

Wadsworth Antique Mall. 332 College Street. 44281. (216) 336-8620. Good selection of quality antiques and collectibles. Hours Wed–Fri 10–5, Sat 10–3, Sun 1–5.

WAPAKONETA

Auglaize Antique Mall. 116 W. Auglaize Street. (419) 738-8004. 17,000 sq ft, two levels. Credit cards accepted. Hours Mon–Sat 10–5, Sun 12–5.

WATERVILLE

Mill Race Antiques Mall. 217 Mechanic Street. 43566. (419) 878-6822. Antiques, collectibles.

WAYNESVILLE

Bittersweet Antiques Mall. 57 S. Main Street. 20 dealers. Antiques, collectibles.

Waynesville Antique Mall. 69 S. Main Street. (513) 897-6937. Over 20 dealers. Antiques and collectibles. (513) 897-6937. Open daily 11–5.

WESTERVILLE

Westerville Antique Mall. 34 E. College Avenue. (614) 891-6966. Antique clocks, Victorian linens, quilts, furniture, primitives, glass, china, collectibles. Hours Mon–Sat 10–5.

Heart's Content Antique Mall. #7 N. State Street. (614) 891-6050. Country furniture, restored trunks, classic fountain pens, bottles, linens, kitchen collectibles. Open Mon–Sat 10–5.

ZANESVILLE
Old Towne Antique Mall. 529 Main Street. 43701. (Route 40). (614) 452-1527. 20,000 sq ft building with 80 dealers. Quality line of antiques and collectibles here. Good selection of antique furniture and quality pottery. Mall atmosphere is set in 1890's Western town with a "General Store" and an auction house. Open daily. Many neighboring antique shops.

OKLAHOMA ✒

ADDINGTON
Cow Creek Mini Mall. Highway 81. (405) 439-6489. Located on old Chisholm Trail in an authentic, historical ghost town, 20 miles South of Duncan. Antiques, lamps, farm items, lots of Southwestern and Indian items. Nice tearoom. Credit cards accepted. Restrooms, handicapped accessible, ample parking. Open Tues–Sat 10–5:30, Sun 1–5.

ANADARKO
Anadarko Antique Mall. 307 SW Sixth Street. (405) 247-5744. More than 25 dealers. Antiques, collectibles, Western items, and lots of Indian-related merchandise. Credit cards accepted. Restrooms, handicapped accessible, ample parking. Anadarko is rich in Indian heritage. Several very interesting Indian cultural facilities to visit here. Mall open daily.

ARDMORE
Peddler's Square Antique Mall. 117 W. Main Street. (405) 223-4255 or 223-MALL. Mall is located in the old Ritz Theater Building, 3 floors, 100 dealers. Antiques, collectibles, and a special Christmas attic. Nice restaurant on premises. Hours Mon–Sat 10–6.

BARTLESVILLE
Apple Tree Mall. 3900 SE Frank Phillips Blvd. 74006. (918) 335-2485. Open Mon–Sat 10–6.

BIXBY
Rebecca's Memories. 13161 S. Memorial. 74004. (918) 369-

6255. Antiques and collectibles mall, 3 miles South of Tulsa. Located in the North Forty Shopping Center. 8,000 square feet. Vintage Victorian. Hours Mon–Sat 10–5, Sun 1–5.

BLANCHARD

Glenda's Antiques & Craftworks. 115 N. Main Street. (405) 485-9211. Collectibles, antiques, primitives, crafts, glass. Hours Tue–Fri 10–6, Sat 10–5.

Yesterday's Best Antique Mall. 109 N. Main Street. (405) 485-2550. Twenty-five dealers, antiques, collectibles. Open Tue–Fri 10–6, Sat 10–5.

The Mercantile Mall. 113 N. Main Street. (405) 485-3131 or 321-2456. Fifteen dealers, antiques, collectibles. Hours Tue–Fri 10–6, Sat 10–5.

BROKEN ARROW

The Picket Fence. corner 71st and 161st Streets. (918) 258-2969. Antiques, arts, crafts, collectibles, 150 booths.

CLAREMORE

Chamwood Mall. 2409 E. Highway 20. (918) 341-7817. Antiques, knives, tools, collectibles, depression glass. Open Thurs–Sun 9–6.

Frontier General Store & Antique Mall. 710 S. Lynn Riggs. (918) 341-3442. Fifty booths. Antiques, collectibles, Rowe pottery, Glenda Turley prints, Handcrafted oak furniture. Hours Mon–Sat 10–6.

Hoover's Have All Mall. 714 W. Will Rogers Blvd. (918) 341-7878. Forty-five individual shops located here featuring a quality line of antiques and collectibles including furniture. Restrooms, ample parking, handicapped accessible. Credit cards accepted. Open daily.

San Bear Antique Mall. 510 W. Will Rogers Blvd. (918) 341-6227. Antiques and collectibles. Large selection of marbles. Restrooms, ample parking.

Route 66 Mall & Flea Market. 1660 North Lynn Riggs Blvd, 74017. (918) 341-4100. Over 80 individual shops under one roof. Antiques, Route 66 souvenirs, lots of old toys, crafts.

CHICKASHA

Yellow Rose Antique Mall & Flea Market. 516 W. Chickasha Avenue. 73018. (405) 222-2112, or 224-7257. Antiques, collectibles, secondhand and new merchandise, tack shack. Tues–Sat 9:30–5:30, open on Thurs until 7 pm.

CHOUTEAU

Frailey's Antiques & Country Mall. Highway 69 South. (918) 475-6581. Antiques, collectibles, crafts, primitives, country decor items. Restrooms, ample parking. Open daily.

Antique Mall of Chouteau. Highway 69. (918) 476-6188. Open daily 10–6.

CLINTON

Antique Mall of Clinton. 815 Frisco. Downtown. (405) 323-2486. 10,000 sq ft building. Furniture, glassware, jewelry, collectibles, toys, quilts, primitives, nice selection of Ertl banks. Hours Mon–Sat 10–6, Sun 1–5.

COLLINSVILLE

Rainbow's End Mall. 10th and Main Streets. On Highway 20, between Highways 169 and 75. (918) 371–5226. Antiques and collectibles. Open daily.

DAVIS

Dusty Steamer Mall. Don and Verdie Franklin. 222 E. Main Street. (405) 369-3723. Large mall with unusually nice quality items, furniture, glassware, pottery, primitives, quilts, collectibles. Very quality oriented establishment. Open daily except Sundays.

Honey Creek Emporium. 214 E. Main Street. (405) 369-3524. Ninety dealers. Crafts, antiques, collectibles, furniture, glassware, lots of nice collectibles. Open Mon–Sat 10–6, Sun 1–6.

DEWEY

Auntie Que's Junktion Antique Shoppe & Mall. Betty Brown. 815 N. Osage. (Highway 75). 74029. (918) 534-2525. Twenty-eight dealers. Antique furniture, glassware, primitives, collectibles, lots of unusual items here. Mall also conducts many estate and garage sales. Hours Mon–Sat 10–5. Sun 1–5.

DUNCAN

The Antique Market Place. 726 W. Main Street. (405) 255-

2499. 10,000 sq ft building, 50 dealers. Furniture, tools, jewelry, toys, glassware, antiques, collectibles, quilts. This mall has a very nice Victorian tearoom. Open Mon–Sat 10–6.

The Penny Farthing Antique Mall. 920 Main Street. (405) 255-2552. 16,000 sq ft building. Antiques, collectibles, consignments. Open Mon–Sat 10–5:30.

EDMOND

Aunt Bea's Attic. 320 E. Hurd Street. (405) 340-6517. Antiques, collectibles, and unusual gifts. Shop is located in three-story historic house that is rumored to be haunted.

Broadway Antique Mall & Diane's Tea Room. 114 S. Broadway. (405) 340-8215. Mon–Sat 10–5:30.

Carriage House Antique Galleries. 6 N. Broadway. (405) 359-1240. Forty individual booths in gallery like setting. High-quality items here. Very attractive and interesting place. Open Mon–Sat 10–6.

Courtyard Antique Market & McKibbins Tea Room. 3005 S. Broadway. (405) 359-2719. Twenty-five dealers, lots of American and European furniture. Tearoom serves full lunch and afternoon tea.

Edmond Antique Mall. 907 S. Broadway. (405) 359-1234. 12,000 sq ft. Quality antiques and collectibles only. Hours Mon–Sat 10–6.

Among Friends. 24 W. Main Street. (405) 359-6800. Small mall, antiques, collectibles, gifts, crafts. Mall features custom sewing and vintage clothing. Hours Mon–Fri 10–7, Sat 10–4.

EL RENO

Route 66 Antique Mall. Highway 66. (405) 262-9366. 24,000 sq ft building. 100+ dealers. Antiques, collectibles, toys, jewelry, glass furniture, advertising items, nice selection of Western and Indian collectibles. Mall has a 50's soda shop. Tues–Sat 10–6, Sun 1–5.

Old Opera House Antique Mall. 110 N. Bickford. (405) 422-3232. Antiques, crafts, collectibles, one of the largest malls in the area. It features an excellent tearoom. Hours Mon–Sat 10–5, Sun 1–5.

ELK CITY

Old Route 66 Antique Mall. 401 E. Third Street. (405) 225-9695. Over 20 dealers. Jewelry, collectibles, furniture, primitives, dolls, quilts, glassware. Hours Mon–Sat 10–6, Sun 1–5.

EUFAULA

317 N. Main Street. 74432. (918) 689-7177. Dolls, collectibles, glassware, furniture. Hours Mon–Sat 10–5, Sun 1–4.

FAIRVIEW

Antique Mall of Fairview. 117 N. Main Street. (Highway 60). (405) 227-2900 or 227-2235. 4,000 sq ft, 15 dealers. Air-conditioned. Clocks, jewelry, silver, glassware, pottery, furniture, china cabinets, books, primitives. Open Tues–Sat 10:30–5.

GUTHRIE

Dee's Antiques & Collectibles. 115 W. Harrison. (405) 282-8788. 5,000 sq ft building. Great selection of glassware and china. Furniture, primitives, collectibles, pottery, quilts, dolls, jewelry. Nice selection of collector guidebooks. Credit cards accepted. Open daily.

King's Antique Mall. 107 W. Oklahoma St. 73044. (405) 282-0534. Downtown. Mall has 60 dealers and also features 30 showcases of nice items. Closed Tuesdays. Several antique shops are also located in this downtown area.

89er Antique Mall. 119 W. Oklahoma. 73044. (405) 282-2661. Forty-two dealers. Furniture, primitives, vintage cloth-

---

SHOPPING SMART—TRY TO AVOID TAKING VERY YOUNG CHILDREN ON YOUR SHOPPING TRIP TO THE ANTIQUE MALL. LITTLE ONES DEARLY LOVE TO RUN AND PICK UP EVERYTHING THEY SEE. YOU WILL BE DRIVEN NUTS TRYING TO KEEP THEM IN TOW. ANTIQUE MALLS CAN CERTAINLY BE WONDERFUL LEARNING EXPERIENCES FOR OLDER CHILDREN. BUT FOR THE YOUNGER SET, THERE ARE MANY MORE APPROPRIATE PLACES TO SHARE WITH THEM. DON'T FORGET THE "PRETTY TO LOOK AT. NICE TO HOLD. BUT, IF YOU BREAK ME...CONSIDER ME SOLD!" RULE OF SHOPPING APPLIES AT MOST MALLS.

ing, paper, pottery, collectibles and lots of toys. Mon–Thurs 10–5, Fri–Sat 10–7, Sun 1–5.

HENRIETTA

Attic Treasures Mall. Galen and Arlene Benton. 115 N. Second Street. (918) 652-2484 or 652-9779. 7,000 sq ft building with 52 booths. Mall specializes in American primitives. Glassware, jewelry, furniture, collectibles, quilts, Indian artifacts. Open Mon–Sat 9–5, Sun 12–5.

JENKS

Antique Affair. 217 E. Main Street. (918) 299-7700. New mall, 10-15 dealers. Glassware, primitives, antiques, collectibles. Hours Mon–Sat 10:30–9.

Main Street Antique Mall. 105 E. Main Street. (918) 299-2806. Twenty dealers. Furniture, collectibles, antiques, glassware, primitives, and crafts. Hours Mon–Sat 10–5, Sun 12–5.

KINGFISHER

Kingfisher Antique Mall. 1109 S. Main Street. (405) 375-3288. Antiques, collectibles, furniture, linen, glass, primitives, quilts, pictures, pottery, china. Open Mon–Sat 10–5:30, Sun 1–5.

LINDSAY

Rocking Chair Mall. 104 S. Main Street. (405) 756-3941 or 756-4046. Antiques, collectibles, jewelry, furniture, pottery, very nice selection of Southwestern and Indian items. Hours daily 10–6.

MCALESTER

Maggie's Antique & Craft Mall. Highway 69. Open daily 9–6. (918) 423-9203.

Main Street Junction. 1301 N. Main Street. 74501. (918) 426-3513 or 423-9031. New mall. Antiques, collectibles, crafts, decorator items. Mon–Sat 10–6, Sun 1–4. If you are superstitious, it is not recommended that you stay overnight in McAlester.

MIDWEST CITY

Remember Me Crafters Gift Emporium & Antiques and Collectibles. 129 W. Atkinson Plaza. 73110. (405) 741-3114. I-40, Exit 157. Mall is located directly across the street from Tinker AFB. 17,000 sq ft, 200 booths. Credit cards accepted.

Nice, clean, well-managed mall with primarily crafts. Limited antiques and collectibles. Open Mon–Thurs 10–6, Fri–Sat 10–7:30, Sun 1–5.

MINCO

Our House Antique Mall. 215 W. Main Street. (405) 352-5007. Twenty-five dealers. Glassware, jewelry, collectibles, nice selection of antique furniture. Hours Tues–Sat 10:30–5.

MOORE

Southern Antiques Mall & Treasure House. 2635 N. Shields Blvd. (405) 794-9898 or 799-2509. Exit 19A off of I-35 South. 12,000 square feet. 40+ dealers. Antiques, furniture, glassware, primitives, crystal, quilts, china, Fenton glass, clocks. Credit cards accepted. Open Mon–Sat 10–6, Sun 12–6.

MUSKOGEE

Old America Antique Mall. Highway 69 South. (918) 687-8600. 12,000 sq ft building. 100+ dealers. Restrooms, ample parking, handicapped accessible. Open 10–6 daily.

Old America Too Antique Mall. 24th Street and W. Shawnee (Highway 62). (918) 686-8600. A 100+ dealer mall with nice selection of antiques and collectibles. Restrooms, ample parking, handicapped accessible. Open daily 10–6.

NOBLE

Remember When Mall. 119 S. Main. (Highway 77). (405) 872-8484. 7,000 sq ft building. Antiques and collectibles only. No crafts, or secondhand items.

NORMAN

The Company Store Antique Mall. 300 E. Main Street. (405) 360-5959. 7,000 sq ft building. 55 dealers, antiques, collectibles. Hours Mon–Fri 10–6, Sat 10–5, Sun 1–5. Enjoyable city to visit. This is the home of the Oklahoma Sooners, where football was developed to a fine art.

Kensington Antique Mall. 208 E. Gray. I-35, Exit Robinson eastbound. (405) 364-8840. Over 50 dealers, collectibles, lots of furniture. Hours Mon 12–8, Tue–Fri 10:30–5:30, Sat 10–5, Sun 1–5.

NOWATA

Bear Necessities Antique Mall. 104 E. Cherokee. (918) 273-

3463 or 273-3427. Antiques, collectibles, marbles, Red Wing, nice selection of Keen Cutter items. Open Mon–Sat 10–4:30.

OKLAHOMA CITY

The Bare Necessities. 2842 NW 10th Street. (405) 943-2238. Ten dealers with nice selection of quality antiques. Credit cards accepted. Hours Mon–Sat 10–5, Sun 1–4.

Crow's Nest Antique Mall. 2800 NW 10th Street. (405) 947-4343. Fax (506) 946-1844. Jewelry, glassware, furniture, primitives, pottery, Disney items. Very large section of military items; just about everything military related, except the tank. Hours daily 10–5.

Antique Market. 311 S. Klein. (405) 239-2273. Thirty shops located in historic public market.

Antiquities Antique Market. 1433 NW Expressway. (405) 843-5063. Open daily, Mon–Sat 10–6, Sun 1–6.

The Colonies. 1116 NW 51st Street. (405) 842-3477. Antiques, 50 dealers set up in individual rooms. Very quality-oriented mall with some very fine pieces here. Tearoom, on premises, is excellent. Hours Tues–Fri 11–5, Sat 10–5.

Diane Lee's. 7210 N. Western. (405) 843-1651 or 842-7200. Antiques, artwork, silver, furniture, decorative accessories.

Antique Co-Op. 1227 N. May Avenue. (405) 942-1214. 25,000 sq ft building. 65 dealers. Oak and Victorian furniture, primitives, collectibles, glassware. Mall offers refinishing and upholstery services. Credit Cards accepted. Open Mon–Fri 1–6, Sat 10–5, Sun 1–5.

May Antique Mall. 1515 N. May. I-40 and May exit. (405) 947-3800. Fifty dealers. Mall is located in old movie theater building. 70+ dealers with a wide range of furniture, quilts, jewelry, primitives, collectibles, glassware, pottery. No crafts and no secondhand items. Open Mon–Sat 10–5:30.

Villa Antique Mall. NW 23rd Street and Villa. Mall is located in north end of Shepherd Mall, a very large retail mall. (405) 949-1185. 13,000 sq. ft. facility. Antiques and collectibles. Mon–Sat 10–9, Sun 1–6 pm.

Apple Tree Antique Mall. 1111 N. Meridian. I-40, exit Meridian, north 1 mile. (405) 947-8999. Forty dealers.

Glassware, collectibles, toys, primitives, furniture, dolls, jewelry. Open Mon–Sat 10–6, Sun 1–5.

Southern Mall Antiques and Treasure House. 2635 N. Shields. I-35, 4 blocks west on 27th Street exit. (405) 794-9898. 12,000 sq ft building. Antiques, antique furniture, china, glassware, advertising items, collectibles, primitives. Hours Mon–Sat 10–6, Sun 11–6.

OKMULGEE
On the Square Antique Mall. 114 W. 7th Street. (918) 756-2400. 9,000 square feet. Lots of crafts, antiques, collectibles, clocks, Indian items and artifacts. Credit cards accepted. Mon–Sat 10–5:30, Sun 1–5.

PAWNEE
Antique Mall of Pawnee. Corner of 7th and Harrison Streets. Downtown. (918) 762-3134. Collectibles, Jewel Tea items, advertising items, depression glass, furniture, toys, pottery, Southwestern and Indian items. Hours Tues–Sat 10–5:30, Sun 1–5.

PERRY
Antique Mall. 1224 First St. 73077. (405) 336-2811. Furniture, glassware, primitives, nice selection of collectibles. Hours Mon–Sat 10–5, Sun 1–5.

PONCA CITY
The Granary Antique Co-Op. 121 W. Central. (405) 762-5118 or (800) 690-5118. Antique furniture, primitives, and collectibles. 6,000 sq. ft. Ample parking. Credit cards accepted. Hours Mon–Sat 10–5, Sun 1–5.

POTEAU
Bright's Antique Mall. 223 Dewey Ave. (918) 647-7134. Antiques, collectibles, crafts, consignments. Hours Mon–Sat 9–5, Sun 1–5.

Homesteader Antique Mall. 212 Dewey Ave. (918) 647-3675. 7,000 sq ft facility. Antiques, crafts, collectibles. Mall specializes in early primitives from Ohio and Pennsylvania and early Amish goods. Restroom, ample parking, handicapped accessible. Open Mon–Sat 10–5.

PRAGUE
Broadway Antique Mall. Diane and Gary Srader. 815 S.

Broadway. (405) 567-4417. Ten dealers with glassware, dolls, quilts, kitchen collectibles, pottery, furniture, advertising items. Hours Mon–Sat 8–5.

PRYOR

Almost Anything Mall. Frank McFarland. Highway 69. Across street from Kentucky Fried Chicken. (918) 825-6658. Forty-five dealers with antiques and collectibles of all descriptions. Hours Tues–Sat 9–5:30, Sun 1–5.

Melton's Mall. Virginia Cunningham, Highway 69 South, across street from the Pizza Hut. (918) 825-5181. Thirty-five shops, good selection of antiques and collectibles. Open Tues–Sat 10–7, Sun 1–5.

Heritage Antique Mall. 122 S. Adair Street. 74361. (One block east of Highway 69). (918) 825-5714. Mall is located in an historic, turn-of-the-century home, next door to several antique shops. Antiques, collectibles. Hours Tues–Sat 10–5:30, Sun 1–5.

The Country Connection. Diane Bryant. 14 S. Mill, Highway 69 South. (918) 825-0093. Thirty dealers. Lots on new and general merchandise items. Hours Wed–Sat 10–5:30, Sun 12–5.

PURCELL

Auntie Mae's Antiques & Collectibles. Sam Vaughn. 127 W. Main Street. (405) 527-5214. 9,000 sq ft building. Antiques, collectibles, memorabilia, furniture, pottery, quilts, glassware, fine art. Hours Mon–Sat 10–6.

RUSH SPRINGS

Janies Art and Antiques. 312 W. Blakely St. Lots of Indian and local artwork, primitives, furniture, collectibles, prints, lighting. Hours Mon–Fri 10–6.

SALLISAW

Sallisaw Antique Mall. Highway 64. Downtown. Across from the depot. Antiques and collectibles. (918) 776-0221. Hours Mon–Sat 9:30 to 5:30.

SAND SPRINGS

Humdinger's Antique & Crafts Mall. 8500 Keystone Expressway. (918) 245-4777 or (800) 206-4777. Next to K-Mart. New mall, 26,000 sq ft, 175 booths. Open Mon–Sat 10–8, Sun 12–6.

SAVANNA

Maggie's Antique & Craft Mall. One mile north of town on Highway 69. (918) 423-3101 or 548-3354. 8,000 sq ft. Antiques, collectibles, primitives, crafts. Credit cards accepted. Open daily.

SAYRE

Old Town Mall. 103 W. Main Street. (405) 928-5845. Collectibles, glassware, furniture, quilts, dolls, crafts. Open Mon–Sat 10–5, Sun 1–5.

SKIATOOK

Skiatook Antique Mall. 101 W. Rogers. West of Highway 75 on Highway 20. Forty dealers. Furniture, glassware, primitives. Open Mon–Sat 10–6, Sun 1–5.

STILLWATER

Antique Mall of Stillwater. Arlene Brooks. 116 E. 9th Street. 74074. (405) 372-2322. Eighty booths. 20,000 sq ft building. Antiques, collectibles, memorabilia, jewelry, books, Coke items, vintage clothing, Indian items, quilts, tools, signs. New tearoom. Large clean, well-stocked and managed mall. Hours Mon–Wed, Fri 10–6, Thurs 10–8, Sat 10–5, Sun 1–5.

Remember When Antiques. 715 S. Main Street. (405) 372-4013. Twenty-five dealers. Antiques, collectibles, furniture, glassware, pottery, good selection of cookie jars, consignments. Hours Mon–Sat 10–5:30.

STROUD

Horn's Gallery of Art, Antiques and Collectibles. 412 W. Main Street (Route 66). (918) 968-2761. Antiques, collectibles, jewelry, glassware, primitives, kitchenware. Great selection of Indian art. Mall holds summer flea market outdoors on Saturdays. Hours Mon–Sat 10–5.

TAHLEQUAH

Tahlequah Antique Mall. 204 S. Muskogee Street. (918) 456-2400. Antiques, collectibles, glass, jewelry, furniture, primitives, quilts. Credit cards accepted. Hours Mon–Sat 10–5:30, Sun 1–5:30.

TONKAWA

Antique Annie Mall. Ricky and Liz Greene. 110 E. Grand. I-35, exit 211 or 214, 2 miles to town. (405) 628-5046 or 628-3608. Over 50 dealers. Antiques, collectibles, memorabilia, furniture, glassware. Clean, pleasant mall. Credit cards accepted. Restrooms, handicapped accessible, ample parking. Open Mon–Sat 10–5, Sun 1–5.

Tonkawa Mall. 117 E. Grand Street. (405) 628-2622. New mall. Antiques, collectibles, primitives. Credit cards accepted. Restrooms, snack bar, handicapped accessible, ample parking. Open Mon–Sat 10–5, Sun 1–5.

TULSA

Great American Flea Market and Antique Mall. 9212 E. Admiral Place. (918) 834-6363. Antiques, furniture, extensive book section, collectibles, jewelry. One of the more interesting places in the area to shop at. Restrooms, snack bar, ample parking, handicapped accessible. Credit cards accepted. Open Tues–Sun 10–6.

Crafters Market Mall. 9120 E. 31st Street, #C. Briar Village Center, next to Drug Warehouse. (918) 622-0512. 150 booths. A vast amount of fine handmade and locally produced crafts. No antiques. Credit cards accepted. Mon–Sat 10–6. Thurs 10–7, Sun 1–5.

The Centrum Antiques. 8144 S. Lewis. Plaza Center. (918) 299-3400. Large 17,000 sq ft facility with 100 dealers, clean, well-stocked with quality items. Restrooms, ample parking, handicapped accessible. Credit cards accepted. Open Mon–Sat 10–6, Sun 1–5.

Persimmon Hollow Antique Village. One block east of 71st Street and Garnett, then 1 block north. (918) 252-7113 or 749-4707. Forty-five shops located on three acres. Art deco, oak furniture, lots of old advertising items, Coca-Cola merchandise. Fun place to shop. Restrooms, handicapped accessible, ample parking. Credit cards accepted. Open on Sat and Sun 9–5.

Tulsa Antique Mall. 2235 E. 51st Street. 74105. (918) 742-4466. 9,000 sq ft. General line of antiques and collectibles. Ample parking, restrooms, handicapped accessible. Credit cards accepted. Hours 10–5:30 weekdays and Saturdays. Sunday 1–5.

VINITA

Maxine's Collectors Palace. 113 E. Canadian. (918) 256-8010. Antiques, collectibles, dolls. Restrooms, ample parking, handicapped accessible. Credit cards accepted. Open Mon–Sat 10–6.

Ripley's Antique Mall. 133 S. Wilson, 74301. Downtown. (918) 256-5754. 10,000 sq ft, 50 dealers. Restrooms, ample parking, handicapped accessible. Open daily.

WAGONER

D.J.'S & Dovecot Antique Mall. 3700 S. Highway 69. 2-½ miles south of town. (918) 485-8191 or 485-4195. Antiques, collectibles, primitives. Outside space available on weekends. Mon–Sat 10–6, Sun 1–5, closed Wednesdays.

Robins Nest Antique Mall. Brenda Wesseiman. 300 N. Blake Ave. (Just north of Highways 69 and 51 Junction.) (918) 485-5701. New mall with collectibles, furniture, glassware, antiques. Credit cards accepted. Restrooms, handicapped accessible, ample parking. Hours Mon–Sat 10–5, Sun 1–5.

Wagoner Switch Antique Mall. 300 N. Highway 69. ¼ mile north of Highway 51. (918) 485-5701. Lots of furniture, cookie jars, name glassware, Black Americana, quilts. Restrooms, ample parking. Open daily.

WEATHERFORD

Southwestern Antique Mall. 1225 E. Main Street. I-40, exit 82. (405) 772-1535. 14,000 sq ft facility, approximately 60 dealers. Antiques, collectibles, glassware, primitives, toys, quilts, furniture. Hours Mon–Sat 10–6, Sun 1–5.

WEWOKA

Wewoka Switch Mall. 121 S. Wewoka Street. Downtown. (405) 257-2959. Twenty dealers. Antiques, collectibles, furniture, glassware, primitives, pottery, art, Indian items. Good variety and quality of collectibles here. Open Mon–Sat 10–5.

OREGON ❧

BANKS

Old Cannery Antique Co-Op. 42425 NW Banks Road. Variety of quality antiques and collectibles. Furniture, glassware, china, books, advertising items, memorabilia, decorator finds. (503) 324-5800. Open daily.

BEAVERTON
Beaverton Antique Mall. 12905 SW Beaverton Road. (503) 626-3179. Over 70 dealers, furniture, antiques, collectibles, and lots of "unusual" items can be found here. Credit cards accepted. Restrooms, handicapped accessible, ample parking. Open daily.

EUGENE
Oregon Antique Mall. 1215 Willamette Street. (503) 686-2104. Antiques, collectibles, great selection of antique and country furniture. Wide variety and range of items here. Credit cards accepted. Restrooms, handicapped accessible, ample parking. Open daily 11–6.

FLORENCE
Old Town Treasures. 299 Maple Ave. (503) 997-1364. General line of antiques, collectibles, furniture, great selection of collectible toys. Credit cards accepted. Restrooms, handicapped accessible, ample parking.

GRESHAM
Nostalgia Antiques & Collectibles Market. 19 NE Roberts Avenue. (503) 661-0123. Three-story facility with 14,000 sq ft display area and 100 dealers. Furniture, jewelry, glassware, toys, perfume bottles, and a very nice selection of Western memorabilia. Credit cards accepted. Restrooms, handicapped accessible, ample parking. Open Mon–Sat 10–6, Sun 12–5.

HILLSBORO
Hill Theater Antique Mall. 127 NE Third Avenue. (503) 693-1686. Antiques, collectibles, glassware, china, silver, vintage clothing and jewelry, primitives, pottery, advertising, dolls. Credit cards accepted. Restrooms, snack bar, handicapped accessible, ample parking. Open daily 10–6.

LAFAYETTE
Lafayette Schoolhouse Antique Mall. Highway 99W. 97127. (503) 864-2720. A 100+ dealer mall. Walls and shelves in this mall are lined with antiques and collectibles for everyone from the casual shopper to the serious collector. Credit cards accepted. Restrooms, handicapped accessible, ample parking. Open daily 10–5.

MILWAUKIE

Milwaukie Antique Mall. 10875 McLoughlin Blvd. (503) 786-9950. General line of antiques and collectibles. Credit cards accepted. Restrooms, ample parking. Open daily.

MULTNOMAH VILLAGE

Multnomah Antique Gallery. 7784 SW Capitol Highway. Off I-5. (503) 245-3174. Sixty dealers, quality antiques and collectibles, art, jewelry, paper goods, furniture. Credit cards accepted. Restrooms, handicapped accessible. Open daily 10–5.

OREGON CITY

McLoughlin Antique Mall. 502 - 7th Street. Highway 205, exit 9. (503) 655-0393. Sixty-dealer mall. General line of antiques, collectibles, glassware, furniture, kitchen collectibles, and great selection of Vaseline glass. Credit cards accepted. Restrooms, handicapped accessible, ample parking. Open Mon–Sat 10–6, Sundays 12–5.

Carriage House Antique Mall. 712 Main Street. (503) 557-1413. Typical antique mall fare with all kinds of treasures for every taste and budget. Credit cards accepted. Restrooms, ample parking. Open daily.

PORTLAND

Antique Village Mall. 1969 NE 42nd Avenue. (503) 288-1051. 8,000 sq ft. Approximately 50 dealers. New mall. Booths stocked with a wide variety of popular collector lines. Ample parking. Open Mon–Sat 11–6, Sun 12–5.

Antique Alley. 2000 NE 42nd Avenue. (503) 286-9848. Multidealer mall with 70 dealers. Mall has nice selection of Art Deco and reference books along with general line of antiques and collectibles. Credit cards accepted. Restrooms, handicapped accessible, ample parking. Open daily.

Convention Annex Antique Mall. 307 NE Holiday. Oregon Convention Center Max Station. (503) 232-6619. Large multidealer mall with fine antiques and collectibles. Open daily 10–5, free parking.

Stars An Antique Mall. 7030 SE Milwaukie. (503) 239-0346. 20,000 sq ft showroom with 125 dealers. Antiques, collectibles. Lots of extraordinary junque. One of the largest malls in the area. Hours Mon–Sat 11–5, Sun 12–5.

Old Town Antique Market. 32 NW First Avenue. (503) 228-3386. Thirty dealers. Well-stocked booths with glassware, vintage toys, dolls, jewelry, primitives, quilts, linens, Victorian finds. Credit cards accepted. Restrooms, handicapped accessible, ample parking. Open daily 10–6.

New Antique Village Mall. 1969 NE 43rd Avenue. (503) 288-1051. Two-level facility with 60 dealers, antiques and collectibles. Credit cards accepted. Restrooms, handicapped accessible, ample parking. Open daily.

Good & Hansen's Antique Mall & Emporium. 5339 SE Foster Road. (503) 777-9919. Fifty dealers. Antiques, collectibles, furniture, lots of small desirables and great range of collectibles. Espresso and dessert shop. Credit cards accepted. Restrooms, handicapped accessible, ample parking. Open Mon–Sat 11–6, Sun 12–5.

Grand Avenue Antique Mall. 715 SE Grand Avenue. (503) 236-0789. Glassware, books, decorator items, primitives, kitchenware, linens, quilts, vintage jewelry. Credit cards accepted. Restrooms, handicapped accessible, ample parking. Open daily.

Stars Northwest Antique Mall. 305 NW 21st Street. (503) 220-8180. General line of antiques and collectibles. Credit cards accepted. Restrooms, handicapped accessible, ample parking. Open daily.

Stars & Splendid Antique Mall. 7030 SE Milwaukie. (503) 235-5990. General line of antiques and collectibles. Credit cards accepted. Restrooms, handicapped accessible, ample parking. Open daily.

Sellwood Antique Mall. 7875 SE 13th Street. (503) 232-3755. A 100-dealer mall with wide selection of antiques and collectibles. Clean, friendly well-stocked mall. Credit cards accepted. Restrooms, handicapped accessible, ample parking. Open daily 10–6.

Eastside Antique Mall. 2400 SE 834d Street. (503) 774-2844. General line of antiques and collectibles. Credit cards accepted. Restrooms, handicapped accessible, ample parking. Open daily.

Railroad Street Antique Mall. 260 NW Railroad Street. (503)

625-2246. General line of antiques and collectibles. Credit cards accepted. Restrooms, handicapped accessible, ample parking. Open daily.

SANDY
Treasures Antique Mall. 39065 Pioneer Blvd. (503) 668-9042. Two-story facility with 8,000 sq ft showroom. 40 dealers. Antiques and collectibles. Everything from high-buttoned shoes to Disney memorabilia, Aladdin lamps to flow blue. Credit cards accepted. Restrooms, handicapped accessible, ample parking. Open daily 10–6.

SPRINGFIELD
Antique Peddlers I. 448 Main Street. (503) 747-1259. General line of antiques and collectibles, furniture, pottery, paper, jewelry. Credit cards accepted. Restrooms, handicapped accessible, ample parking. Open Mon–Sat 10–5:30. Sun 12–5:30.

Antique Peddlers II. 612 Main Street. (503) 747-1259. General line of antiques and collectibles, furniture, pottery, paper, jewelry. Credit cards accepted. Restrooms, handicapped accessible, ample parking. Open Mon–Sat 10–5:30. Sun 12–5:30.

Paramount Antique Center. 143 N. 21st Street. (503) 747-3881. Antiques, collectibles, primitives, Western items, toys, linens. Credit cards accepted. Restrooms, handicapped accessible, ample parking. Open daily.

Twenty Twenty Antiques. 2020 Main Street. (503) 726-1341. Large, clean, friendly mall with well-stocked and interesting booths of antiques and collectibles. Good variety and interesting shopping here. Credit cards accepted. Restrooms, ample parking, handicapped accessible. Open daily.

PENNSYLVANIA ☙

ADAMSTOWN
Black Angus Antique Mall. Route 222. PA Turnpike, exit 21. Large complex, antique mall, outdoor pavilions, restaurant. Quality antiques and collectibles. This market is a collector's paradise. Market conducts lots of special events. Antique

mall is open daily and has over 250 booths. Flea market is on Sundays with about 100 dealers. This is one of my personal favorites. Great food here, restrooms, ample parking. C/p Carl Barto. Box 880, 19501. (215) 484-4385 or (717) 569-3536. Hours 8–5.

Weaver's Antique Co-Op. One mile North of town. Pa Turnpike, exit 21. Six large rooms of antiques and collectibles, over 90 wall cases. Clean restrooms, snack bar. Mall also conducts special events, call for schedule. Ralph Weaver or Tony Baldassar.(215) 777-8535. Hours Mon–Wed 10–5, Thurs–Sat 9–9, Sun 9–6. Plenty of parking.

ALLENTOWN

Antique Market. 3rd and Hamilton Streets. Phoenix Square. 18105. (610) 437-9022. Open Sat 9–5, Sun 10–5.

ALLENWOOD

Bald Eagle Antique Center. Route 15. I-80, exit 30, 6 miles north. Nine miles south of Williamsport. (717) 538-1886. Over 25 dealers. Antiques, collectibles, china, toys, knives, furniture, glassware, advertising items, books. Open daily 10–5.

BEAVER

Leonard's Gallery of Antiques & Uniques. 723 State Street. 15009. (412) 728-7477. Antiques, collectibles. Hours Mon–Sat 10–5, Sun 12–5, Fri 10–8.

State Street Antiques. 711 State Street. 15009. (412) 774-7255. Antiques, collectibles. Hours Mon–Sat 10–5, Sun 12–5, Fri 10–8.

Leonard's Antiques & Uniques. 652 State Street. 15009. (800) 229-4211 or (412) 728-4211. Thirty dealers, antiques and collectibles. Hours Mon–Sat 10–5, Sun 12–5. Fri 10–8.

BEAVER FALLS

Antique Emporium. Pa Turnpike, Exit 2. Approx 65 dealers, 3 floors. Great selection, quality antiques and collectibles, no crafts. Open Mon–Sat 10–5, Sun 12–5. (412) 847-1919.

BEDFORD

Olde Towne Antique Mall. 244 E. Penn Street. 15522. (814) 623-2637. Antiques, collectibles. Open Mon–Sat 10–5, Sun 12–5.

Graystone Galleria. 203 Pitt Street. 15522. Exit 10, PA Turnpike. (814) 623-1768. 15,000 sq ft in beautiful 3-story building. 64 dealers, packed with quality antiques and collectibles. Many specialty shops and highly specialized professional dealers. Credit cards accepted. Hours Mon–Thurs 10–5, Fri 10–8, Sat 10–5, Sun 12–5.

BURNT CABINS

Burnt Cabins Antique & Flea Market. 17215. PA Turnpike, Exit 13. Four miles north on Route 522. Thirty-five dealers, antiques and collectibles, secondhand and used items and lots of misc. Open Fri–Sun 9–5.

BUTLER

The Store On Main. 108 S. Main Street. 16001. (412) 283-9923. Antiques and collectibles. Hours Mon–Sat 10–5, Fri 10–9.

CANONSBURG

Antique Junction. Route 19. I-79, Exit 10. (412) 746-5119. Thirty dealers. Country, primitive, period, Victorian and oak furniture, paintings, oriental rugs, silver, glassware. Good stop for dealers. Credit cards accepted. Hours 10–5 daily.

Canonsburg Antique Mall #1. 145 Adams Avenue. 15317. (412) 745-1333. Over 30 dealers. Over 500 old stained glass windows, military, jewelry, glassware, toys. Hours 10–5 daily.

Canonsburg Antique Mall #2. Intersection of Weaverton Road and I-79 South. I-79, Exit 10. Fifty dealers, four floors. Loads of smalls and numerous rooms of furniture. Credit cards accepted. Open daily 10–5.

Route 19 Antique Mall. Route 19. I-79, Exit 10. (412) 746-3277. Open 10–5 daily. Credit cards accepted. 23 dealers. Good assortment of antiques and collectibles.

Whiskey Run Southpointe. 849 Washington Road. (Route 19 South). (412) 745-5808 or 745-9999. Open daily 10–5. Credit cards accepted. 40 dealers. 18th and 19th century country and formal furniture and accessories. Expert clock and lamp repair.

CARLISLE

Northgate Antique Malls. 725 and 726 N. Hanover Street.

17013. (717) 243-5802. Two separate malls, across street from each other. Well-stocked malls, good stop for dealers. Open daily 10–5.

CHADDS FORD
Pennsbury-Chadds Ford Antique Mall. 640 E. Baltimore Pike. 19317. (215) 388-1620 or 388-6546. Open daily except Wed 10–5. Mall has two levels. Located in very historic and scenic area. Plenty of parking, air-conditioned.

CHAMBERSBURG
Chambersburg Antiques & Flea Market. 868 Lincoln Way. 17201. (717) 267-0886. Open 9–5 daily.

CLARION
Clarion Antique Mall. Ron and Carol Harris. Route 322. I-80, Exit 8, 3 miles north. 20 dealers. Quality lines, Civil War, Art Moderne, Ming dynasty, Beatles, Indian artifacts, glassware, primitives, crafts, good selection of mechanical banks, oriental rugs, porcelains. Opens at 10 daily. (814) 226-4420.

COLLEGEVILLE
Powerhouse Antiques & Flea Market. 45 First Avenue. 19426. (Highway 29 North). (215) 489-7388. Open Sun 9–5.

DENVER
Lancaster County Antiques & Collectibles Market. 2255 N. Reading Road. 17517. (717) 336-2701. Open Mon–Thurs 9–5, Fri–Sun 9–9.

Covered Bridge Antiques & Collectibles. Route 272. 17517. PA Turnpike Exit 21, 2.5 miles south. (717) 336-4480. Antiques, collectibles, furniture. Credit cards accepted. Open daily, 9–5.

DUNCANNON
Leonard's Co-Op. Huck and Doug Leonard. Junction Highways 11 and 15. 17020. (717) 957-3536. Antiques, nice selection of collectibles. Good selection of furniture, oak, mahogany, walnut. Open daily 9–5.

The Cove Barn Antiques & Flea Market. Pat and Jack Ford. Route 11-15. 1½ miles south of town. (717) 834-4088. Antiques, collectibles, furniture, primitives, books. Open Sun-Thurs 9–5.

ERIE

Folly Antique Mall. 654 W. 26th Street. 16508. (Route 20). Mall is located in an early 1920's movie theater. Antiques, collectibles, furniture, Griswold, pottery. Hours Mon–Fri 9–5, Sat–Sun 12–5.

GRANTVILLE

Black Sheep Antique Center. Junction I-81 and Highway 743. (717) 469-1011. Sixty-dealer antique co-op with quality antiques and collectibles. Thurs–Mon 10–5:30.

GREENSBURG

Antique Treasures. Route 22, east of Route 66. Twenty dealers, antiques, collectibles. Hours 10–5 daily.

HEIDELBERG

Heidelberg Antiques. 1451 and 1550 Collier Avenue. 15106. (800) 860-9222 or (412) 429-9222. Two separate malls with large selection of Victorian and American furniture. Primitives, crocks, glassware, Indian jewelry, pottery. Large selection of Roseville. Credit cards accepted. Restrooms, ample parking, handicapped accessible. Hours daily 10–5.

HERSHEY

Ziegler's Antique Mall. Corner Routes 743 and 322. (717) 533-7990. Sixty-dealer co-op. Open Thurs–Mon 10–5:30.

Ziegler's In The Country. Route 743, 3.5 miles south of Hershey. (717) 533-1662. Ninety-dealer co-op located on a restored 1850's farmstead. This is an experience for the entire family. Open Thurs–Mon 9–5.

INTERCOURSE

The Country Market at Intercourse. 3504 Old Philadelphia Pike. (717) 768-8058. This is a complete old style Amish market featuring traditional Amish goods: quilts, toys, furniture, crafts, foods. This is a most enjoyable shopping experience. Open Mon–Sat. Closed Sundays.

LANCASTER

Antique Marketplace. 2856 Lincoln Highway East. 17601. Five miles east of Lancaster on Route 30. (717) 687-6345. Thirty dealers, antiques, collectibles, and fine furniture. Open 10–5 daily.

LEWISBURG

Brook Park Farm Antique Center. Route 15, One mile west of Route 45. (717) 523-6555. Antiques, collectibles, furniture, quilts, tools, toys, kitchenware, stoneware, glassware. Hours Mon–Sat 10–6, Sun 11–5.

Roller Mills Marketplace. 517 Saint Mary Street. 17837. I-80, Exit 30A South. (717) 524-5723. Large mall with over 300 dealers. New glass showcase area. This is one of the finest and best-stocked malls in the country. Mall is located in an 1883 restored mill. Mall has an excellent restaurant with a country store atmosphere. Open daily 10–5. (717) 524-5733.

LIGONIER

Graham's Antique Mall. Route 30. One mile west of town. (412) 238-8611. 7,000 sq ft building with 40 dealers, antiques, collectibles, nice selection of guns and military items. Hours Wed–Mon 11–5, closed Tuesdays and month of February.

MANSFIELD

Country Trader. Junction Main Street and Route 6. 16933. (717) 662-2309. Thirty-five dealers, antiques and collectibles. Open 10–5 daily.

Mansfield Flea Market & Antiques. 763 S. Main Street. 16933. (717) 662-3624. 5,000 sq ft building with collectibles, used merchandise, secondhand items. Open daily 9–6.

MONONGAHELA

Main Street Antiques. 800 W. Main Street. 15063. (412) 258-3560. Large house, 12 rooms, this is a co-op with nice line of antiques, collectibles, vintage clothing and jewelry. Hours Tues–Sat 10–4, Sun 1–5.

MORGANTOWN

The Mill Property. West Main Street. Highway 23. 19543. (215) 286-8854. Eighty dealers. Antiques, collectibles, lots of country collectibles and furnishings. Open Wed–Mon 10–5:30.

MUNCY

Olde Barn Centre. Highway 220 North. (717) 546-7493. Fifty dealers in 9,000 sq ft 1860's barn. Open daily 10–5.

MYERSTOWN

Union Canal Antique Mall. Route 422 West. 17067. Hours Mon and Thurs 10–5, Fri–Sun 9–5.

NEW OXFORD

Conewago Creek Forks Antique Market. 1255 Oxford Road. 17350. (717) 624-4786. Open Wed–Sat 10–5, Sun 12–5.

New Oxford Antique Mall. 214 W. Golden Lane. 17350. (717) 624-3703. 15,000 sq ft mall with 65 dealers. Antiques, collectibles, oriental rugs, lots of railroad items, art, furniture, dolls, glassware, stoneware, Victoriana. Clean, well-stocked mall where the emphasis is on quality items. Open Mon–Sat 10–5, Sun 12–5.

New Oxford Antique Center. 333 Lincoln Way. 17350. (717) 624-7787. Mall features 40 dealers. Furniture, accessories, quality collectibles. Open daily.

NORTH EAST

Interstate Antique Mall. David Johns. 11019 Sidehill Road. 16428. I-90 exit 11. (814) 725-1603. Antiques, collectibles. Well-stocked mall with many quality items. Lodging and restaurant next door. Hours Mon–Fri 10:30–5. Sat–Sun 12–5.

PENNSDALE

Olde Barn Centre Antiques 'N Such. Highway 220 North. ½ mile east of town. (717) 546-7493. Fifty dealers. Antiques, collectibles, lots of paintings and crafts by locals. Credit cards accepted. Open daily 10–5.

PITTSBURGH

Allegheny City Stalls. 940 Western Avenue. I-279, Three Rivers Stadium exit. (412) 323-8830. Antiques, stained glass, mantels, limited collectibles, lots of Victorian items. Credit cards accepted. Hours 10–5 Tues–Sun.

Canonsburg Antique Mall. I-79, Exit 10. (412) 745-1333. Toys, military items, furniture, lots of stained glass windows. Good mall for dealers. Open daily 10–5.

North Hills Antique Gallery. Junction Routes 19 and 910. Eighteen dealers, good selection of quality antiques, Art Deco, jewelry, neons, memorbilia, glass, furniture, toys. Daily 10–5. (412) 935-9804.

Pittsburgh Antique Mall. 1116 Castle Shannon Blvd. 15234. (412) 561-6331 or 561-9477. Open daily 10–5. Twenty-five shops in two-story building.

South Hills Antique Center. Edna Sluganski. 971 Killarney Drive. (412) 881-4140 or 885-6992. Hours Tues–Sun 10–5. Twenty antique shops here with good and varied selection of furniture, glassware, art gallery, vintage clothing, collectibles, jewelry, and lots of accessories and misc. Credit cards accepted.

REAMSTOWN

Found Treasures Antiques Co-Op. 1543 N. Reading Road. 17567. (Route 272). PA Turnpike, Exit 21, South. (717) 336-6004. Open Sun–Mon 10–5.

DAYS AND TIMES OF OPERATION ARE SUBJECT TO CHANGE!

The Doll Express. Route 272. 17567. (717) 336-2414. A 100-dealer co-op, dolls, bears, and related items. Hours 9–6 Thurs–Tues.

SALISBURY

The Village Theater Antique Mall. Corner of Grant and Union Roads. 15558. (Route 219). (814) 662-2242. I-68, exit 22. PA Turnpike, Exit 10. Antiques and collectibles. Open Mon–Sat 10–5, Sun 12–5, closed Wednesdays.

SCHELSBURG

Route 30 Antiques. Eight miles west of town. Three miles east of Reels Corner. (814) 754-4710. Antiques and collectibles only. Hours Tues–Sun 10–6. Mall has outdoor weekend flea market during the summer.

SHREWSBURY

Shrewsbury Antique Center. 65 N. Highland Drive. 17361. I-83, Exit 1.(717) 236-6637 or 235-5797. Open daily 10–5.

SINKING SPRING

Weaver's Antiques Mall. Route 222. 19608. (215) 777-8535. Over 200 dealers. Antiques, collectibles, nice selection of furniture. Open Thurs–Mon 10–5. Many antique shops adjacent to mall.

STROUDSBURG

Olde Engine Works Market Place. 62 N. 3rd Street. 18360. (717) 421-4340. More than 40 dealers in 10,000 sq ft old machine shop/factory. Antiques, collectibles, crafts, mall has excellent collector's reference section. Open daily 10–5.

Antique Center Mall. #70 Storm Street. I-80 West, Exit 50, 2 quick rights. (717) 421-4441. Multidealer mall with quality antiques and collectibles. Restrooms, ample parking, handicapped accessible. Open daily 10–5.

TROY

Country Sampler Antique Mall. Route 6, 4 miles west of town. (717) 297-2256. Twenty dealers, antiques, collectibles, furniture, glassware, primitives. Open daily 10–5.

TUNKHANNOCK

Village Antique Mall. Junction of U.S. Highway 6 and State Highway 87. Five miles west of town. (717) 836-8713. Twenty-dealer co-op. Antiques, collectibles, glassware, furniture, country primitives, advertising items, tools. Mon–Sat 10–5, Sun 12–5.

WASHINGTON

Downtown Antique Mall. 88 S. Main Street. Twenty dealers. Primitives, collectibles, advertising items, good selection of glassware. Open daily. (412) 222-6800.

WAYNESBURG

Old Pike Antique Center. Donna Bailey. Route 40 and I-79, Laboratory Exit. (412) 228-6006. Mall features quality antiques and has a wholesale barn for dealers only. Open daily 10–5.

WEXFORD

Wexford Antique Mart. 11245 Route 19. 15090. (412) 935-9905. Two-story building with 20 dealers. Antiques, collectibles, primitives, furniture, jewelry, furniture, glassware, toys, dolls. Hours 10–5 daily.

WHITEHALL

Old Dairy Antiques. 105 Franklin Street. 18052. (215) 264-7626. Several individual shops in one building. Antiques, collectibles, wide range of smalls. Credit cards accepted. Restrooms, handicapped accessible, ample parking. Hours Mon–Sat 10–5, Sun 11–5.

WILKES-BARRE

Silk Mill Antique Co-Op. 18 Forrest Street. (717) 823-4433. Thirty-five dealers. General line of antiques and collectibles. Credit cards accepted. Restrooms, ample parking. Open Thurs–Tues 10–5.

YORK

York Antique Mall. 236 N. George Street. 17401. (717) 845-7760. Sixty-dealer mall located in a unique renovated 1887 building. Antiques, collectibles, well-stocked mall. Credit cards accepted. Restrooms, handicapped accessible, ample parking. Open daily 10–5.

SOUTH CAROLINA ✍

ANDERSON

Belinda's Antique Mall & Jewelry. 711 S. Main Street. (803) 224-0938. Open Mon–Sat 10–5:30. Credit cards accepted.

Somewhere in Time Antique, Art Gallery & Mall. I-85, Exit 27. (803) 261-6500. Over 200 dealers. Furniture, glassware, toys, collectibles, advertising signs, quilts, primitives.

BLACKVILLE

Miller's Mini Mall. 326 Main Street. 29817. (803) 294-5000. Open Mon, Wed 10–2, Tue, Thurs, Fri 10–8:30, Sat 9–2.

CLOVER

High Cotton Antique Mall & Southern Folk Art Gallery. 212 S. Main Street. 29710. (803) 222-5045. New mall. 6,000 sq ft building. Antiques, lots of southern decorator items. Edgefield pottery. Local pottery, furniture, Victorian items. Open 10–5 Tues–Sat, Sun 1–5.

COLUMBIA

The Antique Mall. 1215 Pulaski Street. (803) 256-1420. Open Mon–Sat 10–6, Sun 1–6. Fine furniture and accessories.

Attic Fanatic Antique Mall. 4901 Forest Drive. (803) 787-0008. Hours Mon–Sat 10–6, Sun 1–6. One of the area's better malls.

City Market. 701 Gervais Street. (803) 252-1589. Open Mon–Sat 10–5, Sun 1:30–5:30. 50,000 sq ft, 2 buildings, Over 70 dealers. Great selection of furniture.

Keepsakes Antiques & Collectibles Mall. 3143 Forest Drive. (803) 787-0221. Hours Mon–Sat 10–6, Sun 1:30–6. New mall.

Old Mill Antique Mall. 310 State Street. (803) 796-4229. Open Mon–Sat 10–5:30, Sun 1:30–5:30. Seventy-five dealers located in two-story building.

Ole Town Antique Malls. Company has three locations, 8724 Two Notch Road, (803) 736-7575. 2918 Broad River Road, (803) 772-9335, 7748 Garner's Ferry Road, (803) 695-1992. Malls open Mon–Sat 10–6, Sun 1:30–6.

CONWAY
Hidden Attic Antique Mall. 1014 Fourth Avenue. 29526. (803) 248-6262. Open Mon–Sat 10–5.

DARLINGTON
Old Dixie Store & Antique Mall. 2905 Highway 401. 29532. (803) 393-0189. Open Mon–Sat 8–6.

GREENVILLE
The Corner Antique Mall. 700 N. Main Street. Open Mon–Sat 10–6, closed Sun. Credit cards accepted.

Aberdeen Zeppelin. 26 Aberdeen Drive. 29033. (803) 233-9261. Antiques, collectibles, consignments. Open Mon–Fri 10–6, Sat 10–5.

Greenville Mall. 1025 Woodruff Road. 29600. (803) 627-0061. Open daily.

Reedy River Antiques. 220 Howe Street. 29600. (800) 501-0854 or (803) 242-0310. Twenty-five dealers. Antiques, collectibles, lots of English antiques, nice selection of decorator items. Open Tues–Sat 10–4.

GEORGETOWN
Riverfront Antique Mall. 800 Front Street. 29440. (803) 527-6555. Open Mon–Sat.

LANDRUM
Landrum Antique Mall. 221 E. Rutherford Road. 29356. (803) 457-4000. Over 50 dealers. Open Mon–Sat 10–5.

MURRELLS INLET
Legacy Antiques Mall. 3420 S. Highway 17. 29576. (803) 651-0884. Open Mon–Sat 10–5.

SUMMERTON

301 Antique Mall. Main Street. 29148. (803) 485-8714. Open Mon–Sat 10–5.

SUMMERVILLE

The Consignment Gallery. 200 N. Cedar Street 29483. (803) 851-1674. Collectibles, bric-a-brac. Shop is located adjacent to several antique shops.

TAYLORS

Buncombe Antique Mall. Highway 29. I-85, Exit 56 North. (803) 268-4498. Open Mon–Sat 10–5:30, Sun 1–5:30, closed Wed. 17,000 sq ft building with over 100 dealers.

WEST COLUMBIA

Old Mill Antique Mall. 310 State Street. 29169. (803) 796-4229. Open Mon–Sat 10–5:30, Sun 1:30–5:30.

SOUTH DAKOTA 🖋

RAPID CITY

Coachouse Antiques. 2413 S. Highway 79. (605) 399-3838. 5,000 sq ft facility with 42 booths. Lots of country, Western, and farm-related collectibles. Indian artifacts and items. Nice selection of antiques. Restrooms, ample parking, handicapped accessible. Open daily.

ST. JOE

St. Joe Antiques Mall. 615A St. Joe. Downtown. (605) 341-1073. 40 dealers. Credit cards accepted. Restrooms, ample parking, handicapped accessible. Open 9:30–5:30 Mon–Sat.

TEA

I-29 Antiques and Collectibles Mall. 46990 - 271st Street. I-29, exit 73. (605) 368-5810. Antiques, collectibles, Western and Indian items. Restrooms, ample parking, handicapped accessible, food and lodging nearby. Open daily.

INFORMATION IS SUBJECT TO CHANGE—
ALWAYS CALL AHEAD TO AVOID DISSAPOINTMENT!

TENNESSEE ☙

ATHENS

Athens Flea Market Mall. Congress Parkway. C/p Norman Barker, P.O. Box 515, Etowah, 37331. (615) 263-7414. Indoor with outside weekend flea market. Camping avail. New market.

BELL BUCKLE

Bell Buckle & Livery Stable Antique Mall. I-24, exit 97. (615) 389-6174. Ninety dealers. Antiques, collectibles, crafts, used items, gifts. Two separate facilities here, both very interesting. Credit cards accepted. Restrooms, ample parking, handicapped accessible. Open 10–5 Mon–Sat, 1–5 Sun.

CHATTANOOGA

East Town Antique Mall. I-75, Exit #1. Behind Cracker Barrel restaurant. (615) 899-5498. Approx 120 booths. Nice selection of antiques and collectibles. Ample parking, restrooms, handicapped accessible. Open 10–6 daily.

COOKEVILLE

Flea Town Mall. I-40 Exit Burgess Falls Road. 38501. C/p Buddy Franklin, (615) 432-4097. Indoor market with weekend flea market. Market has pony rides, petting zoo, entertainment and train rides. Nice cafe. market conducts auctions on Tuesdays and Thursdays.

FRANKLIN

Franklin Antique Mall. 251 - 2nd Avenue S. (615) 790-8593. A 100-dealer mall located in historic icehouse. General line of antiques and collectibles. Well worth the visit. Credit cards accepted. Restrooms, ample parking. Open Mon–Sat 10–5, Sundays 1–5.

Harpeth Antique Mall of Franklin. 529 Alexander Plaza. I-65 South, Franklin exit #65, Mall located behind McDonalds. (615) 790-7965. Eighty booths in 12,000 sq ft mall. Furniture, fine glass, and collectibles. Credit cards accepted. Restrooms, handicapped accessible, ample parking. Open daily.

GOODLETTSVILLE

The Rare Bird Antique Mall. 212 S. Main Street. I-65, Exit 97, west ¼ mile to Dickerson, south 1 block. Three malls in this town, located 10 minutes north of Opryland. Great little town. Antiques, collectibles. Credit cards accepted. Open daily.

Goodlettsville Antique Mall. 213 N. Main Street. 37072. I-65, exit 97 West. (615) 859-7002. More than 120 dealers. Antiques, collectibles, dealers welcome. Credit cards accepted. Restrooms, handicapped accessible, ample parking. Open daily.

Main Street Antique Mall. 120 N. Main Street. (615) 851-1704.

GREENEVILLE
Greeneville Antique Market. 117 W. Depot Street. (423) 638-2773. Fifty-dealer mall with general line of antiques and collectibles. Credit cards accepted. Open Mon–Sat 10–5, Sun 1–5.

HENDERSONVILLE
Hendersonville Antique Mall. 339 Rockland Road. (615) 824-5850.

HERMITAGE
Hermitage Antique Mall. 4144 Lebanon Road. I-40 East, Exit 221. (615) 883-5789. General line of antiques and col-

SHOPPING SMART—IF YOU HAVE A COLLECTION THAT LACKS PARTICULAR PIECES YOU ARE TRYING TO FIND, MAKE AN INVENTORY LIST OF WHAT YOU ALREADY HAVE. SOME PEOPLE ALSO INCLUDE WHAT THEY PAID FOR AN ITEM IN THEIR INVENTORY. THEN, MOST IMPORTANTLY, TAKE YOUR LIST ALONG ON YOUR NEXT TRIP TO THE ANTIQUE MALL. YOU MIGHT ALSO WANT TO INCLUDE THE TOP PRICE YOU ARE WILLING TO PAY FOR THOSE ITEMS YOU ARE STILL SEARCHING FOR. THAT WAY, IN THE EXCITEMENT OF THE MOMENT, WHEN YOU THINK YOU HAVE FOUND A NEW ADDITION FOR YOUR COLLECTION, YOU WILL BE SURE THAT YOU ARE NOT ACCIDENTALLY DUPLICATING SOMETHING YOU ALREADY HAVE. YOUR LIST MIGHT ALSO PREVENT THE DISAPPOINTMENT OF OVERPAYING FOR AN ITEM.

lectibles. Credit cards accepted. Open Mon–Fri 10:30–5, Sat 10:30–6, Sun 1–5:30.

JACKSON

Old South Antique Mall. 1155 Rushmeade. I-40, Exit 79. Over 100 dealers featuring antiques, collectibles, furniture, toys, primitives, pottery, glassware, military, and sports items. Credit cards accepted. Restrooms, ample parking, handicapped accessible. Open daily.

Yarbo's Antique Mall. I-40, Exit 80A. Hamilton Hills Shopping Center. (901) 664-6600. Antiques, collectibles. Credit cards accepted. Ample parking, restrooms, handicapped accessible. Open Mon–Sat 10–5, Sun 1–5.

JOHNSON CITY

Antique Village. 228 E. Main Street. (615) 926-6996. Hours Mon–Sat 10–6, Sun 1-6. 20,000 sq ft building, three floors. Country items, glass, linens, dolls, militaria, advertising items.

KINGSPORT

Haggle Shop #1. 146 Broad Street. (615) 246-8002. Hours Mon–Sat 10–5, Sun 1–6. Mall has sister mall across street at 143 Broad Street. (615) 246-6588. Same hours. Malls have walnut, oak, and primitive furniture, brass kitchen items, glass, jewelry, books, quilts, collectibles, and good selection of crafts. Good stop for dealers.

The Antique Mall. 9951 Airport Parkway. I-81, Exit 63. (615) 323-2990. Hours Mon–Sat 10–7, Sun 12–6. 15,000 sq ft building. Period furniture, linens, primitives, tools, paper Americana, and collectibles. Lots of showcases of porcelain, art pottery, art glass, and lamps.

KNOXVILLE

Antiques Plus. I-640, Exit 6 to Highway 441, left 1 block. (423) 687-6536. 60+ dealer mall with good variety of antiques and collectibles, lots of country and primitives. Restrooms, ample parking, handicapped accessible. Open daily.

Bearden Antique Mall. 5200 Kingston Pike. 37919. I-40 exit 383. (615) 584-1521. Ninety individual shops. Quality antiques and collectibles.

Kingston Pike Antique Mall. 4612 Kingston Pike. 37919. I-40/75 exit 383 South. (615) 588-2889. Open 10–5:30 Mon–Sat, Sun 1–5:30.

Colonial Antique Mall. 4939 Chapman Highway. Highway 441 South. (615) 573-6660. Forty-four booths, general line of antiques and collectibles. Open Mon–Sat 10–5, Sun 1–5.

LEBANON

Downtown Antique Mall. 112 Public Square. (615) 444-4966. Credit cards accepted. Open Mon–Sat 9–6, Sun 1–5.

LOUDON

Sweet Memories Antique Mall. 930 Mulberry Street (Highway 11). Mall features general line of antiques and collectibles. Credit cards accepted. Ample parking, restrooms, handicapped accessible. Open Mon-Fri 10–5, Sat 11–3.

MADISON

Madison Antique Mall. 320 Gallatin Pike S. (615) 865-4677.

MEMPHIS

Bo-Jo's Antique Mall. 3400 Summer Avenue. 38122. (901) 323-2050. Large 40,000 sq ft building with 170+ dealers. Largest and best-stocked mall in the area. Wide range of quality items here. Credit cards accepted. Restrooms, food, handicapped accessible, ample parking. Hours Mon–Sat 10–5, Sun 1–5.

Antique Mall of Memphis. 3397 Lamar Avenue. 362-7788.

Antique Gallery. 6044 Stage Road. (901) 385-2544. 129 booths, antiques, collectibles, bric-a-brac, gift shop. Mall conducts many retail antique auctions. Credit cards accepted. Tearoom. Restrooms, handicapped accessible, ample parking. Open Mon–Sat 9–6, Sundays 12–5.

MORRISTOWN

Olde Towne Antique Mall. 181 Main Street. Downtown. Building is two floors. Several antique shops nearby. (615) 581-6423.

NASHVILLE

Tennessee Antique Mall. Jim Collins. 654 Wedgewood at I-65. 22,000 sq ft. 150 dealers. General line of antiques, collectibles, furniture, kitchen collectibles, primitives, very interesting and pleasant mall. Credit cards accepted. Restrooms, handicapped accessible, ample parking. Open daily. (615) 259-4077.

Wedgewood Station Antique Mall. 657 Wedgewood Avenue. I-65, Exit 81. (615) 259-0939.

Green Hills Antique Mall. Betty Payne. 4108 Hillsboro Road. (615) 383-4999. Large two-story 20,000 sq ft facility with 150+ dealers. Large and very well-stocked mall. Many quality booths here. Credit cards accepted. Restrooms, handicapped accessible, ample parking. Hours Mon–Sat 10–5, Sun 1–5.

Smorgasbord Antique & Gift Mall. 4144 B. Lebanon Road. I-40 East, exit 221. (615) 883-5789. 7,500 sq ft facility with 44 booths. Antiques, collectibles, gifts, new merchandise. Credit cards accepted. Restrooms, handicapped accessible, ample parking. Hours Mon–Thurs 10:30–5, Fri and Sat 10:30–8.

Whiteway Antique Mall. Carolyn Elam. 1200 Villa Place. Edgehill and Villa Place. (615) 327-1098. Sixty-five dealers, 9,000 sq ft building. Furniture, vintage clothes, rare books, jewelry. Credit cards accepted. Restrooms, handicapped accessible, ample parking. Open Mon–Sat 10–5, Sun 1–5.

Antiques Exchange Mall. 2019 - 8th Avenue S. (615) 269-9638.

Antique Merchants Mall. 2015 - 8th Avenue S. (615) 292-7811. Sterling, crystal, porcelain, old and rare books. Credit cards accepted. Restrooms, handicapped accessible, ample parking. Open daily.

Downtown Antique Mall. 612 - 8th Avenue S. (615) 256-6616. 13,000 sq ft facility in historic warehouse. Credit cards accepted. Restrooms, handicapped accessible, ample parking, use rear entrance. Open daily until 6.

Art Deco Shoppe & Antique Mall. 2110 - 8th Avenue S. (615) 386-9373. Open Mon–Sat 10–5, Sundays 1–5.

Cane Ery Antique Mall. 2112 - 8th Avenue S. (615) 269-4780. Trunks, furniture, hardware, cane, baskets, and wicker supplies and repair.

Antique & Flea Gallery. 4606 Charlotte Avenue. (615) 385-1055.

Cool Springs Antique Mall. 7104 Crossroad Blvd. (615) 661–5435.

Donna Jean's Antique Mall. 7103 Highway 70 S. (615) 646-1825.

Scotts Hollow Antique Mall. 4989 Lebanon Pike. (615) 889-8587.

PARIS

The Treasure Hunt Antique Mall and Flea Market. 415 N. Market Street. 52 dealers with antiques, collectibles, new and used merchandise. Open Mon–Sat 9–5, Sun 1–5.

Market Street Antique Mall and Checkerboard Cafe. 414 N. Market Street. (Highway 641). 38242. (901) 642-6996. Over 60,000 sq ft building with 210+ dealers. Fine antiques, collectibles, quilts, antique dolls, primitives, quality estate merchandise, very nice model train display. Open Mon–Sat 9–5:30, Sun 1–5.

The Grapevine Antique Mall. Courthouse Square, north side. (901) 642-7850. Three-floor building with antiques, collectibles, lots of bric-a-brac and art. Open Mon–Sat 10–5, Sun 1–5.

The Old Depot Antique Mall. 203 N. Fentress Street, downtown in 100-year-old train station. (901) 642-0222. Great selection of quality glassware, Civil War items, Indian relics, railroad items. Ample parking, restrooms, handicapped accessible. Open Mon–Sat 10–5, Sun 1–5.

SEVIERVILLE

Riverside Antique and Collectors Mall. 1442 Winfield Dunn Parkway. I-40, Exit 407, 5 miles. (423) 429-0100. (Near Gatlinburg). A 100+ dealer mall in 35,000 sq ft facility. Over 200 well-stocked showcases. Quality antiques and collectibles, toys, display frames, glassware, large reference book section. Restrooms, snack bar, ample parking, handicapped accessible. Open daily 9–6.

SOUTH CARTHAGE

Gore Antique Mall. 59 Cookeville Highway. 37030. (615) 735-9904. No Al does not work here, he has gone to Washington. General line of antiques, collectibles, primitives, glassware, linens. Credit cards accepted. Restrooms, handicapped accessible, ample parking. Hours Tues–Sat 9–5, Sun 12–5.

TRENTON

Carol's Antique Mall. 148 Davy Crockett Shopping Center, Highway 45 Bypass. (901) 855-0783. Forty-eight-booth antique and collectible mall with antiques, primitives, dolls, china, glassware. Restrooms, ample parking, handicapped accessible. Open Mon–Sat 10–6, Sun 1–5.

TRIBUNE

Tribune Antique Mall & Flea Market. Junction Highways 31 and 41A. (615) 833-5004. Antiques, collectibles, furniture, primitives, quilts, linens, silver, jewelry, kitchen collectibles. Credit cards accepted. Restrooms, handicapped accessible, ample parking. Open daily.

TROY

Troy Antique Mall. 1104 N. Highway 51. (901) 536-4211. Antiques, collectibles, depression glass, kitchen collectibles, primitives, glassware, books. Restrooms, ample parking, handicapped accessible. Open Mon–Sat 9–5, Sun 1–5.

UNION CITY

Stad Avenue Antique Mall. 1318 Stad Avenue. Tom and Marcia Edmundson. (800) 264-4143 or (901) 885-6338. 9,000 sq ft facility on one level. Lots of quality booths and showcases here. Restrooms, ample parking, handicapped accessible. Open Mon–Sat 10–5, Sun 1–5, closed Tuesdays.

TEXAS ❧

ABILENE

Yesterdaze Mall. 2626 E. Highway 80. Exit 290 off of I-20. (915) 676-9030. Mon–Sat 10–5:30. Sun 1–5. Abilene's oldest antique mall.

Poppy's Antique Mall. I-20 at Exit 277. (915) 692-7755. New 20,000 sq ft facility with antiques and collectibles. Restrooms, ample parking, handicapped accessible. Open daily 10–6. Closed Tuesdays.

AMARILLO

6th Street Antique Mall. 2715 W. 6th Street. (806) 374-

0459. 3,000 sq ft building. Glassware, cast iron, furniture, pottery, tools, quilts, china, advertising items, nice selection of reference books. Very pleasant and friendly mall. Credit cards accepted. Open Mon–Sat 10–5:30, Sun 1–5.

Hobbs Street Antique Mall. 3218 Hobbs Street. I-40 West, take Western Street Exit two blocks east. (806) 356-6552. 13,000 sq ft facility. Antiques, collectibles. Restrooms, ample parking, handicapped accessible. Open daily.

ARLINGTON
Antiques & More. 3708 W. Pioneer Parkway. 76013. (At Park Springs Road.) (817) 548-5932. Art, clocks, custom gifts, decorator items, Victorian items, investment quality southwest Indian items, fine furnishings, estate jewelry. Open daily 10–6, Sun 12–6.

Antique Sampler Mall and Tea Room. 1715 E. Lamar. Across from Wet 'n Wild. (817) 861-4747. 250 dealers. Open Mon–Sat 10–7. Sun 12–6.

ATHENS
The General's Store Antique Mall. 400 N. Prairieville Road. 75751. (903) 677-1560. Antiques, glassware, collectibles. Tues–Sat 10–5:30, Sun 1:30–5:30.

AUSTIN
Antique Marketplace. 5350 Burnet Road. 70 dealers. Open Mon–Sat 10–8, Sun 12–6. (512) 452-1000.

Austin Antique Mall. Highway 183 North. 100 dealers. Open daily 10–6. (512) 459-5900.

BEAUMONT
Larry's Antique Mall & Flea Market. 7150 Eastex Parkway. Market comprised of antique and collectible shops. Mall has nice cafe. C/p Larry Tinkle, (409) 892-4000. Market conducts outdoor flea market once a month, usually mid-month.

BAIRD
The Antique Market. 334 Market Street. (915) 854-1997. Antiques and collectibles. Tues–Sat 10–5:30, Sun 12–5.

Antique Memories. 304 Market Street. (915) 854-2021. Antiques and collectibles.

Market Street Mall. 212 Market Street. (915) 854-1408. Tues–Sat 10–5:30, Sun 1:30–5:30.

The Olde Shope. 312 Market Street. (915) 854-1911. Antiques and collectibles. Tues–Sat 9:30–5:30, Sun 1–5:30.

BARTLETT

Bartlett Antique Mall. 110 E. Clark St. P.O. Box 367. 76511. (817) 527-3251. I-35 and Highway 95. Antiques and collectibles. No arts and crafts.

BIG SPRING

Antique Mall of Big Spring. 110 Main Street. (915) 267-2631.

BRECKENRIDGE

Antique Corner & The Corner Tea Room. 201 W. Walker. 76024. (817) 559-6653. Antiques and collectibles. Mon–Sat 9:30–5:30.

BURKBURNETT

Boomtown Indoor/Outdoor Mall. 1003 Sheppard Road. (817) 569-5296. Hours Fri 12–6, Sat 9–6, Sun 10–6.

CARROLLTON

Finishing Touch Antique Mall. 1109 Broadway. (214) 446-3038. Thirty shops here. Open Mon–Fri 10–5, Sat 10–5:30, Sun 1–5.

CLARKSVILLE

The Broadway Emporium. 105 E. Broadway. (903) 427-3044. 5,000 square feet, 25 dealers. Antiques, collectibles, crafts, gifts, baseball cards, books, original works of art. Restrooms, ample parking, handicapped accessible. Credit cards accepted. Open Mon–Sat 10–5.

CLIFTON

Clifton Antique Mall. 206 W. 5th Street (Highway 219). P.O. Box 567. 76634. (817) 675-2300. Mall is located in a beautifully restored limestone building. Open daily Mon–Sat 10–5:30, Sun 1–5.

COLORADO CITY

Good Ole Days Antique Mall. 157 E. 2nd Street. Downtown.

CONROE

The Stock Exchange Antique Mall. 302 N. Frazier Street.

77301. (409) 760-3800. 19,000 square feet. 40 dealers. Furniture, glassware, linens, postcards, silver, jewelry. Credit cards accepted. Open Mon–Sat 10–5, Sun 1–5.

CORSICANA

K. Wolens Marketplace. 227 N. Beaton. 75110. (903) 872-4438. Fax (903) 874-2870. 10,000 square feet. Air-conditioned. Mon–Sat 9:30–5:30, Sun 1–5.

DALHART

Southwest Antique Co-Op. Highway 87 South. (806) 249-4755. 3,500 sq ft building. Furniture, antiques, collectibles. Open Mon–Sat 10–5:30.

DALLAS

Antique Trading Post. 431 Bedford Euless Road. (214) 268-8899. Large well-stocked mall. Great selection of items here. Restrooms, ample parking, handicapped accessible. Open daily.

Inwood Village Antiques. 5560 W. Lovers Lane, #243. Inwood Village. Behind Inwood Theater. (214) 263-8680. Art glass, cut glass, bronzes, silver, chandeliers, furniture. Mon–Sat 9–6.

Knox Street Antique Mall. 3319 Knox Street. (214) 521-8888. One hundred dealers. Estate silver, books, quality antique furniture. Mon–Wed 10–6, Thurs–Sat 10–8, Sun 12–6.

Lone Star Bazaar. 10724 Garland Road. 75218. (214) 324-1484. 30,000 square feet, air-conditioned. 125 dealers. Mall also has flea market. Mall is well-stocked with fine antiques, quality collectibles, a don't miss stop. Mall has Vietnam War Museum open on weekends. Friday 12–6, Sat–Sun 10–6.

Lovers Lane Antique Market. 5001 W. Lovers Lane. (214) 351–5656. Thirty shops here. Antiques, gifts and collectibles. Mon–Sat 10–5, Sun 1–5.

Lower Greenville Antique Mall. (214) 824-4136. Forty-five shops.

McKinney Avenue Antique Market. 2710 McKinney Avenue. 40 shops here. Antiques, gifts, collectibles. Mon–Sat 10–5, Sun 1–5.

New Antique Mall. 910 N. Industrial. (214) 761-1575. Lots of furniture.

Park Cities Antique Mall. 4908 W. Lovers Lane. (214) 497-1703. Open daily.

Unlimited Ltd., "The Antique Mall." 15201 Midway Road, 75244. (One block north of Belt Line). (214) 490-4085. Mall features over 175 antique and collectible shops and 137 showcases. Restrooms, ample parking, handicapped accessible. Mall has excellent restaurant, fine desserts. Open daily 10–6. This mall will take the better part of a day to properly enjoy.

DECATUR

Charles' Antiques. 408 W. Main. (817) 627-2485 or 281-2549. Primitives, French furniture in complete sets, mid Victorian, china, glassware. Mon–Sat 10–5.

Crossroads Antiques Mall. 301 S. Washburn. Junction of Highway 287 and Business Route 380. Hours, Mon–Sat 10–6, Sun 1:30–5.

DUNCANVILLE

Knick Knacks Crafts & Antiques Mall. 215 W. Camp Wisdom Road. 75116. (214) 283-9007. Three hundred booths. Antiques, clothing, jewelry, antique furniture, crafts, wood crafts. Air-conditioned. Largest mall in southern Dallas county.

EL PASO

Westside Antique Mall. 3950 Doniphan Street. Corner Sunland Park and Doniphan. (915) 585-8801. New mall. 7,200 sq ft facility. Antiques, collectibles. Open Mon–Sat 10–5:30, Sun 1–5:30.

Eastside Antique Mall. 7924 Gateway East. I-10 exit at Yarbrough Street. (915) 594-0673. Antiques, collectibles, art, toys, primitives, furniture, glassware, jewelry, linens, quilts, silver. One of the area's largest malls. Hours Mon–Sat 10–5:30, Sun 1–5:30.

ENNIS

On The Corner. Downtown, Dallas Street and Ennis Avenue. (214) 875-8825. 9,000 square feet. Lots of collectibles. Open Mon–Sat 10–5, Thurs 10–7, Sun 1–5.

FAIRFIELD

Fairfield Antique Mall. 221 Commerce Street. Highway 84E, Exit 197 from I-45. (903) 389-5820. Frames, Victorian lamp shades, sports cards, gift items, antiques, art, collectibles. Mall has year-round Christmas shop. Open Tues–Sat 10–5, Sun 1–5.

FORNEY

Antiques East. Highway 80 at County Road. Large collection/complex of over 200 antique shops. Furniture, glassware, primitives, collectibles, a vast amount of fine quality items here. (214) 564-1229 or 564-1331. Open daily.

GAINESVILLE

Town & Country Mall. Sue McCutchen, 2235 N. I-35. Exit #496. (817) 665-5974. 4,000 sq ft building. Antiques, collectibles, glassware, primitives, kitchen collectibles, vintage clothing, lots of Southwestern and Indian items. Mall has a pawnshop. Hours Mon–Sat 9–5, Sun 1–5.

Carousel Antique Mall. 112 S. Dixon Street. 76240. East side of downtown square. (817) 665-6444. This building houses 64 different antique shops. Fine antiques, collectibles, sandwich shop, tearoom. Mon–Sat 10–6, Sun 1–5.

Gainesville Antique Mall. 1808 N. I-35. Junction 82 and I-35. (817) 668-7798. Antiques, crafts, collectibles. Mon–Sat 10–6, Sun 1–5.

GARLAND

Grandpa's Trunk Antiques & Collectibles Mall. 906 S. Jupiter. 75042. (214) 276-1751. Lots of antique shops in this town.

Olde Garland Antique Mall. 108 N. 6th Street. (214) 494-0295. Lots of fine one-of-a-kind antique furniture. Collectibles, good selection of victorian and vintage costume jewelry. Mon–Sat 10–5.

GRAPEVINE

Collectors Exchange & Grapevine Antique Mall. 415 E. Northwest Highway. First stoplight east of Main on NW Highway. (817) 329-6946. Arts, antiques, collectibles. Credit cards accepted. Mon–Sat 10–6, Sun 12–6.

GROESBECK

Groesbeck Antiques Mall. 105 N. Ellis Street. (Highway 14).

76642. (817) 729-3443. Lots of furniture. Primitives, kitchenware, glass, linens, jewelry, lots of small items. Open Mon–Sat 10–5, Sun 1–5.

HOUSTON

Almeda Antique Mall. 9837 Almeda Genos. (713) 941-7744. Over 60 dealers. Nice selection of antiques, collectibles and gift items. Restrooms, ample parking. Open Wed–Sat 10–6, Sun 1–7.

Country Home Co-Op. 14916 Stuebner Airline. (Veterans Memorial Parkway). 77069. (713) 440-1186. Twenty-seven dealers. American and European furniture, glass, pottery, silver, quilts, art, books, primitives, collectibles. Open Mon–Sat 10–4:30, Sun 12–5.

Old Katy Road Antiques. 9198-B Old Katy Road. Between Campbell and Blalock. 77055. (713) 461-8124. Twenty-one dealers. Open Mon–Sat 10–5, Sun 12–5.

HUBBARD

Hubbard Antique Mall. 204 NE 4th Street. (Highway 31E). Russ and Dot Carlisle. (817) 576-2926. Antiques, gifts, collectibles. Restrooms, ample parking, handicapped accessible. Open daily 9–7.

HURST

Antique Homestead. 750 W. Pipeline. 76053. (817) 268-1527. Fifty shops, antiques, collectibles, lots of dolls, glassware, Victorian, linens, American country and oak furniture, quilts, advertising, collectible bears, 1920 carousel horses, estate jewelry. Credit cards accepted. Mon–Sat 10–6, Sun 12–6.

Antique Trading Post. 431 Bedford-Euless Road. 76053. (817) 268-8899. One hundred dealers. Open daily.

HUNTSVILLE

Bluebonnet Square Antique Mall. 1110 - 11th Street. 77340. (409) 291-2800. Twenty dealers. Mall occupies two floors in historic 1800's building. It is not recommended that you stay overnight in Huntsville.

Sam Houston Antique Mall. 1210 Sam Houston. 77340. (409) 295-7716. Collectibles, country crafts, primitives, antiques, country store.

IRVING

Irving Antiques Shops, Inc. 129 W. Irving Blvd, #102. (214) 254-0339. Antiques, collectibles, glassware. Hours, Mon–Sat 10–6, Sun 12–5.

LEWISVILLE

Lewisville Antiques and Crafters Mall. 201 Mill Street. One block south of Main Street. (214) 219-1335. Antiques, furniture, collectibles, handcrafted items. Lots of individual antique shops in the area.

Antiques, Etc. Mall. 180 Lewisville Center. (214) 436-5904. Sixty dealers. One of the oldest malls in the Dallas area.

LUBBOCK

Antique Mall of Lubbock. 7907 W. 19th Street. (806) 796-2166. 24,000 sq ft building. Fifty dealers. antiques, collectibles, furniture, toys, dolls, quilts, juke-boxes and nickelodeons, advertising items, old store items. Open daily 10–6.

MADISONVILLE

Madison Street Mall. 105 S. Madison. Exit 142 from I-45. (409) 348-9119. Antiques, collectibles, crafts. Open Mon–Sat 10–5, Sun 1–5.

MALAKOFF

The Lindy Antiques Mall. Highway 31 east of town. (903) 489-1967. 10,000 square feet. Lots of glassware and crystal, furniture, antiques, collectibles. Very beautifully decorated mall. Open Mon–Sat 10–5, Sun 1–5.

MCGREGOR

A Sunday Afternoon Antique Mall. 320 S. Main Street. 76657. (817) 840-4410 or 840-3406. Antiques, collectibles, gifts.

MCKINNEY

Remember This Antique Mall. 210 N. Tennessee. 75069. (214) 542-8011. Antiques, collectibles. New mall. Mon–Fri 10–6, Sat 10–8, Sun 1–5.

MEMPHIS

Crafts & Collectibles. 315 Highway 287. (806) 259-3817. Consignment shop, antiques, collectibles, glassware, primitives, nice gemstone jewelry, local crafts. Hours Mon–Sat 10–5:30.

MINERAL WELLS

Wynnwood Antique Mall. 2502 E. Hubbard. 76067. (817) 325-9791. Country, primitive, European, Victorian, early American, glassware, jewelry, quilts, tea leafs, Indian artifacts, original art. Credit cards accepted. Mon–Sat 10–6, Sun 1–6.

NEW BRAUNFELS

Palace Heights Antique Mall. 1175 Highway 81E. I-35, Exit 189. Open daily. (210) 625-0612.

> ### SHOPPING SMART—
>
> IF YOUR VEHICLE IS LARGE ENOUGH TO ACCOMMODATE FURNITURE AND YOU THINK YOU MIGHT BE BUYING A PIECE, OR, IF YOU ARE SHOPPING FOR A PICTURE, A MIRROR, OR SOME OTHER LARGE OBJECT FOR YOUR HOME OR OFFICE. TUCK IN A TAPE MEASURE AND A NOTEBOOK.

Gruene Antique Company. 1607 Hunter Road. Gruene Historic District. 30 dealers. Open daily. (210) 629-7781.

PALESTINE

Shelton Gin Antiques. 310 E. Crawford. (903) 729-7530. Country primitives, quilts, Coca-Cola and railroad memorabilia, china, furniture, lots of Civil War items here. Metal toys and collectibles. Excellent restaurant on premises.

PARIS

Paris Antique Mall. Junction Highways 19 and 245. 75460. (903) 785-0872. Furniture, glass, collectibles, primitives. Open Mon–Sat 10–5, Sun 1–5.

Pratt's Antique and Craft Mall. 301 Bonham. (903) 785-3658. Antiques, collectibles, and handcrafted items. Crafts and antiques are displayed in separate areas. Open Mon–Sat 9–5, Sun 1–5 pm.

PEARLAND

Cole's Co-Op Antique Village & Flea Market. 1020 N. Main. 77581. Two miles south of Hobby on Alvin Highway 35. (713) 485-2277 or 485-8317. Antiques, collectibles, crafts, new and used merchandise. Mall open daily, flea market on weekends. One of the largest malls in the Houston area.

PLANO

Cobwebs Antiques Mall. 1400 Avenue J. Between 14th and 15th Streets, Downtown. (214) 423-8697. Antiques, collectibles, vintage clothing, furniture, lots of Civil War items here.

RICHARDSON

Memories Antique Mall. #25 Richardson Heights Village. SW Corner Highway 75 and Beltline Road. (214) 669-8277. Furniture, glassware, silver, collectibles, books, pottery, china, jewelry, and showcase gallery. Mall features a complete clock shop. Open Mon–Sat 10–6, Sun 1–5.

Main Street Antiques. 107 E. Main Street. 75081. Downtown. (214) 644-1558. Antiques, gifts, collectibles. Tearoom serves lunch. Mon–Sat 10–6.

ROSENBERG

Old town Antiques. 828 - 3rd Street. Fourteen dealers. Open Thurs-Sun 10–6. (713) 232-2125.

SALADO

Salado Antique Mall. 550 Main Street. P.O. Box 1050. 76571. Exit 285 on I-35 then south on Main Street. Approx ¼ mile on right just past post office. (817) 947-1010. Fine antiques and collectibles. No arts and crafts. Wed–Sat 10–6, Sun 12–6.

SAN ANTONIO

Antique Center. 5525 Blanco Road. 7,500 sq ft building. Good selection of merchandise, furniture, jukeboxes, slot machines, glass, jewelry. Mon–Sat 10–6, Sun 12–6. (512) 344-4131.

SHERMAN

Memory Lane Antique Emporium. 1205 S. Sam Rayburn Freeway. (903) 893-8894. East side of U.S. Highway 75 South, take Park Street exit. Fifty-five dealers. Antiques, collectibles, memorabilia, toys, jewelry, art pottery and glass, primitives, kitchen collectibles, oak and English furniture, quilts, lots of quality smalls here. Open Mon–Sat 10–5, Sun 1–5.

Pratt's Antique & Craft Mall. 1727 Texoma Parkway. (903) 870-7030. Antiques, collectibles, handcrafted items. Crafts and antiques are displayed separately. Open Mon–Sat 9–5, Sun 1–5.

SPRING

Spring Antique Mall. 1426 Spring Cypress Road. (713) 355-1110. Twenty dealers. Furniture, glass, carnival, silver, jewelry, toys, primitives, dolls. Open Tues-Fri 10–5, Sat 10–6, Sun 1–6. Dealers welcome.

TYLER

Antiques on Broadway Mall. 320 S. Broadway. Mon–Sat 10–5, Sun 1–5.

Front Street Antiques. 202 W. Front Street. (Highway 31). 9,000 sq ft. Air-conditioned. Open daily.

Pratt's Antique and Craft Mall. 1827 Troup Highway. (903) 531-9558. Antiques, collectibles, handcrafted items. Crafts and antiques are displayed separately. Open Mon–Sat 9–5, Sun 1–5.

Tyler Square Antiques. 117 S. Broadway, downtown. (903) 593-6888. 25,000 sq ft. 50 dealers located on three floors. Tearoom. Air-conditioned.

V J's Antique Mall. 236 S. Broadway. Antiques, collectibles, jewelry, tools, furniture, glassware, unusual items here. Mon–Sat 10–5, Sun 1–5, closed Tuesdays.

VALLEY MILLS

Bosque Valley Mall. Highway 6. Downtown. P.O. Box 932. 76689. (817) 932-6868 or 932-6584.

WACO

Antiquibles Mall. 1-35 N. Exit 345 N. P.O. Box 155244. 76715. (817) 829-1921. Over 50 dealers. Antiques, collectibles, furniture, prints, glass, Western toys, vintage watches. Credit cards accepted. Restrooms, ample parking, handicapped accessible. Open daily 10–6.

WAXAHACHIE

Gingerbread Town Antique Mall. 319 S. College. Downtown. (214) 937-0968. Forty-two dealers. Furniture with lots of European furniture here, lots of cut glass, flow blue, crystal, collectibles. Credit cards accepted. Mon–Sat 10–5:30. Sun 12–6.

Jefferson Street Antiques and Tearoom. Downtown. One block south of courthouse. Large well-stocked mall with many fine antiques and collectibles. Mall is located in a historic restored building erected in 1913. Open daily.

WEATHERFORD

Main Street Mall. 311 N. Main Street. (817) 596-0902. Tues–Sat 10–5, Sun 1–5.

On The Level Antique Mall. 1716 Blair Drive. Off Highway 80, 2 miles east of courthouse. (817) 594-8991. Open daily 10–6.

WICHITA FALLS

Kemp Street Antique Mall. 2201 Kemp Street. (817) 723-9222. Antiques, collectibles, lots of handmade crafts. Tues–Fri 10–5:30. Sat 10–4, Sun 1:30–5:30.

Monroe Street Antique Mall. 1523 Monroe Street. (817) 761-4151. Antiques and collectibles. Wed–Sat 10–5:30, Sun 1–5.

Village Antique Mall. 1516 Monroe Street. (817) 322-MALL. Lamp parts, shades, chimneys, antiques, collectibles. Wed–Sat 10–5:30, Sun 1–5.

WORTHAM

Wortham Antique Mall. Highway 14 and Main Street. 76693. (817) 765-3773. Furniture, quilts, linens, dolls, books, jewelry, glass, and lots of Fiesta. Open Tues–Sat 10–5, Sun 1:30–5.

UTAH ✍

SANDY

Sandy Antique Mall. 8672 S. State Street. 20 dealers. Small mall with nice selection of antiques and collectibles. Glassware, china, silver, jewelry, primitives, clocks, lamps, furniture. (801) 568-9840.

VERMONT ✍

BURLINGTON

Burlington Center for Antiques. 1966 Shelburne Road. Furniture, china, toys, glassware, two floors. Open daily 10–5. Credit cards accepted. (802) 985-4911.

CONCORD

T-n-B Country Barn. Route. 2. (802) 695-4641. Antiques, glassware, used furniture, flea market items. Ample parking, restroom. Open Tues–Sun 10–4.

EAST BARRE

East Barre Antique Mall. #33 Mill Street. Junction of Route 302 E and Route 110. Right at fire station. (802) 479-5190. 12,000 sq ft facility with one of the area's largest selections of antique furniture. Antiques, collectibles, great selection of country collectibles. Credit cards accepted. Restroom, ample parking, handicapped accessible. Open Tues–Sun 10–5.

ELY

Conval Antique Mall & Auction House. Route 5. I-91, Exit 15, 2 miles south. Nice mall with approximately 30 exhibitors. Good selection antiques, collectibles, vintage clothing, books, and country crafts. Some new and used furniture. C/p Martin or Kitty Diggins, Box 37. Ely, VT 05044. (802) 333-9971. Hours daily, 10–5.

VIRGINIA 🐚

ALEXANDRIA

Thieves Market Antiques. 8101 Richmond Highway. (703) 360-4200. Quality antiques and collectibles. Primitives, RR items, dolls, toys, a bit of everything from the turn-of-the-century to baby boom nostalgia. Open Mon–Fri 10–5, Sat 10–6, Sun 12–5.

AMELIA

Amelia Antique Mall. Church Street, next to post office. Lots of oak and walnut furniture, dolls, quilts, primitives, and collectibles. Open Mon–Sat 9–5, Sun 1–5. (804) 561-2511.

ANNANDALE

Showcase Antiques. 7120 Little River Turnpike. (703) 941-0130. Thirty dealers and 25+ individual shops. Wide range of stock here, some very nice quality collectibles and antiques. Open Wed–Sun 11–6.

ARLINGTON

Laws Antique World. 2900 Clarendon Blvd. (703) 525-8300. Open daily 11–6, Sat 10–6, closed Tues and Wed. 50 stores on 2 floors. Antiques, furniture, home furnishings from the 1800's and 1900's. Plenty of parking.

BEDFORD

Bedford Antique Mall. 109 S. Bridge Street. (703) 587-9322. Hours Mon–Sat 10–4:30, Sun 1–5. Victorian collectibles, furniture, arts and crafts, jewelry, Christmas shop.

Things Past & Pleasant. 122 S. Bridge Street. (703) 586-6694. Hours Mon–Sat 10–5. Sun 2–5. Twelve dealers. Good assortment of quality antiques and collectibles.

CHARLOTTESVILLE

Charlottesville Antique and Lighting Gallery. Route 29 North. American, English, and continental formal and country furnishings. Accessories, collectibles, jewelry, books. Open Mon–Sat 10–5, Sun 12–5. (804) 978-3784.

Tiquer's Mall. Route 29 North. Across from the Sheraton Hotel. (804) 973-3478. Open Mon–Sat 10–5, Sun 12–5. Eighty dealers, 20,000 sq ft. High-quality items, wide variety. From period furniture to hat pins and a bit of everything in between. A collector's haven.

CHRISTIANSBURG

A-1 Flea Market Antique Emporium. 940 Radford Street. I-81, Exit 114. (703) 382-9811. Twenty dealers. Antiques, collectibles, and lots of misc. Mall has a remote-controlled racetrack. There are also over 40 individual shops located here. Open daily.

CULPEPER

Minute Man Mini Mall. 746 Germanna Highway. (Route 3). (703) 825-3133. Open Mon–Sat 9–6, Sun 12–5. Over 200 dealers. Trains, books, furniture, glassware, and collections of original carnival glass. Civil War items, coins, radios and collectibles.

DUMFRIES

The Antique Station. 110 Possum Point Road. Four miles south of Potomac Mills. (703) 221-7534. Open Mon–Sat 10–6, Sun 12–6. Credit cards accepted. 20,000 sq ft building, 75+ dealers. Quality antiques, collectibles, limited editions, quilts, tools, sports cards, autographs.

FALLS CHURCH

Falls Church Antique Co. 250 W. Broad Street. (703) 241-7074. Two separate buildings with 20 dealers in one building, with a general line of antiques, collectibles, toys, jewelry, primitives and decorator items. Ten dealers in the other building, with fine British and American antiques, collectibles. Open daily.

FOREST

The Peddler. Route 854, between Routes 811 and 221. (804) 525-6030. Open Mon–Sat 11–4, Sun 1–4. More than 20 dealers, quality antiques and collectibles in charming old schoolhouse setting. Large inventory here. Numerous antique shops in the local area.

FT. CHISWELL

Snoopers Antique and Craft Mall. I-81 and I-77, Exit 77 or 80. (703) 637-6441. Open daily 10–6. Credit cards accepted. Over 100 shops in 20,000 sq ft building. Good variety of merchandise, very clean mall.

HAMPTON

Free City Traders. 22 Mellen Street. (804) 722-3899. Open Tues–Sat 10:30–4:30. Twenty-four dealers in two-story building with furniture, glass, jewelry, primitives, militaria, books, clocks, and unusual items.

HARRISONBURG

Valley View Antiques & Collectibles. Route 33, 2.5 miles east of Valley Mall. (703) 434-7261 or 433-0899. Hours Thurs–Mon 10–5.

MADISON

Madison Antiques Center. Intersection of U.S. Highway 29 and 230 West. (703) 948-3428. Hours Mon–Sat 10–5, Sun 12–5. Closed Wednesday. Fine selection of furniture from all periods. Wide range of lines here with many quality items and complete collections.

MANASSAS

Laws Antique Complex. 7208 Centreville Road. (Route 28). (703) 361-3148. Open daily 10:30–5, closed Tues and Wed. Very large complex. Two antique malls consisting of eight buildings and specialty shops. Plan a long stop here if you want to see everything.

MARTINSVILLE

West Piedmont Regional Antique Mall. 26 Fayette Street. (703) 638-3044. Hours Mon 10–5, Wed–Sat 10–6, Sun 1–6. 20,000 sq ft building, 50+ dealers. Quality antiques and collectibles.

MECHANICSVILLE

Mechanicsville Antique Mall. 6206 Mechanicsville Turnpike. Old Safeway Shopping Center. New mall, 90 booths. Open daily 10–6. (804) 730-5091.

Mechanicsville Flea Market & Trade Center. 5500 Mechanicsville Turnpike. 30 shops. Antiques, collectibles, furniture, advertising signs, antique radios, glassware, oriental style rugs. A good place to browse. (804) 746-4248. Open Thursday through Monday.

NELLYSFORD

Tuckahoe Antique Mall. Route 151. (804) 361-2121. Open Thurs–Sun 10–5. 10,000 sq ft building. Air-conditioned, large parking area. Credit cards accepted.

NORFOLK

Norfolk Antique Company. 537 W. 21st Street. (804) 627-6199. Wide variety of quality antiques and decorative accessories. The Norfolk area has many fine antique shops. Give yourself time to see it all.

PULASKI

Pulaski Antique Center. 80 W. Main Street. (703) 980-5049. Antiques, collectibles, glassware, furniture, gift items.

PURCELLVILLE

Antiques Group. 118 W. Main Street. 22132. (703) 338-2725. Twenty-eight dealers with wide range of antiques, collectibles, smalls, and decorator items. Open Tues–Sat 10–5, Sun 12–5.

RADFORD

New River Valley Antiques Mall. I-81 and Exit 109. (703) 639-0397. Open Mon–Sat 9–5, Sun 1–5.

RICHMOND

Antique Village. U.S. Highway 301 North. Four miles north of I-295. 10,000 sq ft building. African arts gallery, jewelry shop, old paper shop, furniture, jewelry, art, paintings. Open

Mon–Sat 10–6. Sun 12–6, Closed Wednesday. (804) 746-8914.

Antique Gallery. 3140 W. Cary Street. Cary Court Shopping Center. 60 dealers. Quality mall, monthly auctions. Open Mon–Sat 10–6, Sun 1–5. (804) 358-0500. Fax (804) 359-0149.

Billy's Dodge City Antiques. U.S. Highway 1, 6.5 miles north of Richmond. 11 shops under one roof. Wide range of collectible items here. (804) 798-9414. Open Thurs–Sat 10–5, Sun 12:30–5.

Rabbit Hill Antiques Gallery. 3318 W. Cary Street. (804) 358-4661. Open Mon–Sat 10–6. Antique co-op. American glass, chandeliers, flatware, quality walnut furniture, fine linens.

Richmond Antique Center. Corner Hull Street and Belt Blvd. (804) 231-6261. Open Fri–Sun 10–7.

West End Antiques Mall. 6504 Horsepen Road. (804) 285-1916. Open Mon–Sat 10–6, Sun 12–6. High-quality mall with glassware, furniture, decorating items, lots of fine Japanese antiques and collectibles, and many fine quality American and traditional lines. Over 80 dealers, 20,000 sq ft building.

ROANOKE

Roanoke Antique Mall. 2944 Orange Avenue NE. (703) 344-0264. Antiques, collectibles. Mall has an outside flea market on weekends during the summer. Open Tues–Fri 10–6, Sat–Sun 9–5.

RUCKERSVILLE

Country Store Antique Mall. Corner of Routes 33 and 29. Twenty shops here. Open Mon–Fri 11–4, Sat–Sun 10–5. (804) 985-3649.

The 48 Green House Shops. Corner Routes 29, 7, 33. 15,000 sq ft building. Antiques, collectibles, crafts, and specialty shops. Open Mon–Sat 10:30–5:30, Sun 12–5. (804) 985-6053.

SALEM

House of Collectibles. 27 W. Main St. (703) 389-2484. Hours Mon–Sat 11–5, Sun 12–5. Credit cards accepted. Over 50 dealers with several individual shops featuring a wide variety of antiques and collectibles. Good stop for dealers. Reasonably priced merchandise.

Green Market Antique Mall. #8 E. Main Street. (703) 387-3879. Hours Mon–Sat 10–6, Sun 12–6. 16,000 sq ft building, fine antiques and collectibles. Credit cards accepted.

Olde Curiosity Shoppe. 27/29 E. Main Street. (703) 387-2004. 16,000 sq ft antique mall. Hours Mon–Sat 10–6, Sun 12–6. Credit cards accepted.

SPERRYVILLE

Sperryville Antique Market. Highway 211. (703) 986-8050. 20,000 sq ft building, antiques and collectibles, consignments.

STRASBURG

The Strasburg Emporium. 110 N. Massanutten Street. I-66 and I-81S, Exit 298. (703) 465-3711. 65,000 sq ft building. 100 dealers. One of the premier malls in the country. This is a large, clean, well-stocked, and well-managed mall with high-quality and many fine investment/museum quality pieces. This is an all-day stop. If you are a collector or antiquer, you will think that you have found your way to heaven at this mall. Open daily.

TROUTVILLE

Troutville Antique Mart. Two miles north of Exit 150-B off I-81. (703) 992-4249. Open Fri, Sat, and Mon 10–5, Sun 12–6. Multipledealer mall featuring quality antiques and collectibles in an old schoolhouse setting.

VERNONE

Pat's Antique Mall. Route 11, I-81, Exit 227. (703) 248-PATS. A collection of shops at this location with a very friendly atmosphere. Fine jewelry, formal and country furniture, dolls, toys, coins, books. Open 9–5 Thurs–Sun.

VIRGINIA BEACH

Colonial Cottage Antiques Mall. 3900 Bonney Road. Grande Junquetion Center. (804) 498-0600. Open Tues–Sat 10–6, Sun 1–6. 9,000 sq ft building. 18th and 19th century furniture, jewelry, porcelain, fine glassware, and collectibles. Many antique shops located in neighboring area.

WEYERS CAVE

Rocky's Antique Mall. I-81 and Exit 60. Approximately 150

dealers, 40,000 sq ft building. Average daily attendance 1,000. Air-conditioned, food, clean restrooms. Camping available. Mall conducts outdoor flea market Thurs–Sun.

WINCHESTER

Antique Mini Mall. 1000 Valley Avenue. 25 dealers. A good selection of antiques and collector items. Glassware, pottery, primitives, Victorian era items. Open daily 10–5.

WOODBRIDGE

Mom's Memories Antique Mall. Thom and Janet Houk. 13636 Jeff Davis Highway. Potomac Shopping Center. I-95, Woodbridge exit, 1 mile south on Highway #1. (703) 491-0244. Antiques, collectibles, lots of police and military memorabilia. Mall also has regularly scheduled auctions. Open Mon, Wed–Sat 10–7, Sun 12–5, closed Tuesdays.

WYTHEVILLE

Old Fort Emporium. I-77 and I-81, exit 80. Five miles east of town. (703) 228-4438. Over 80 dealers. Antiques, collectibles. This is the kind of place where you can sometimes find a treasure. Open daily 10–7.

YORKTOWN

The Galeria. 7628 George Washington Memorial Highway. 23690. (Route 17). Ninety dealers, bi-weekly auctions. Antiques and collectibles of all kinds for every taste and budget. Repair and refinishing on premises. Open daily 10am–6pm.

WASHINGTON ✒

ABERDEEN

Clevenger's Antique Mall. Broadway and Wishkah Streets. (360) 533-1631. Small mall with 27 dealers. Great collection of quality antiques and collectibles here. Mall has probably the area's highest quality merchandise. Restroom, ample parking, handicapped accessible. Open daily.

APPLETON

Fox River Antique Mall. 1074 S. Van Dyke Road. (Highway 41 Frontage Road). 20,000 sq ft one-level facility. More than 165 dealers. Large, well-stocked mall with wide variety of antiques and collectibles. Restrooms, ample parking, handi-capped accessible. Open daily 10–6.

BREMERTON

Perry Mall. 2901 Perry Avenue. General line of antiques and collectibles. Restroom, ample parking, handicapped accessible. Open daily.

CENTRALIA

Centralia Square Antique Mall. 201 S. Pearl Street. Downtown. I-5, Exit 82. (360) 736-6406. Eighty individual shops here. Lots of fine antiques and collectibles provide shoppers with a chance to turn back time for a short while as they poke through the booths in this interesting mall. Credit cards accepted. Restrooms, handicapped accessible, ample parking. Open daily 10–5.

EDMONDS

Waterfront Antique Mall. 190 Sunset Avenue. (206) 670-0770. 20,000 sq ft facility with 150+ dealers. A bit of everything, from the unique to the time-worn classic, in antiques and collectibles. Open daily.

Edmonds Antique Mall. 5th Avenue S. and Maple Streets. Parking level, Old Milltown Mall. Downtown. (206) 771-9466. Seventy-five dealers. Hours Mon–Sat 10–6, Sun 12–5.

Aurora Antique Pavilion. 24111 Highway 99. (206) 744-0566. Large 30,000 sq ft showroom with 200+ dealers displaying a general line of antiques and collectibles. Nice cafe on premises.

GRAHAM

A & C Mini Mall. 9409 Kapowsin Highway. (206) 847-2286.

GREENWOOD

Great Dolphin Antique Mall. 8560 Greenwood N. Fine antiques and plenty of popular collectibles fill the booths in this mall. Glassware, china, books, lamps, bottles, linens, quilts, furniture, plenty of small desirables. (206) 794-9940.

ISSAQUAH

Gilman Antique Gallery. 625 NW Gilman Blvd. (206) 391-6640. 150+ dealer mall featuring furniture, glassware, jewelry, silver, orientals, prints. Credit cards accepted. Restrooms, handicapped accessible, ample parking. Open daily.

KENT

Robins Antique Mall. 201 First Avenue S. Downtown. (206) 854-6543. Mall features a wide variety of nice collectibles and has a large refinished American furniture department. Credit cards accepted. Restrooms, handicapped accessible, ample parking. Hours Mon–Sat 10–5:30, Sun 11–5.

MOUNTLAKE TERRACE

Mountlake Terrace Antique Mall. Downtown. Antique furniture, glassware, vintage clothing, jewelry, toys, dolls, kitchen collectibles, collector items in all categories at reasonable prices. (206) 744-0533.

PORT ORCHARD

Olde Central Antique Mall. 801 Bay Street. (206) 895-1902. Seventy individual antique and specialty shops. Great selection of quality items here. Credit cards accepted. Restrooms, food, handicapped accessible, ample parking. Open daily.

PUYALLUP

Puyallup Antique Mall. Downtown. (206) 848-9488. Antiques, collectibles, country and primitives. Restrooms, handicapped accessible. Open daily.

Carnaby Antique Mall. 8424 River Road, East. (206) 840-3844. Forty dealers. Large selection of antique furniture, jewelry, kitchen items, prints. Credit cards accepted. Restrooms, handicapped accessible, ample parking. Mon–Sat 10–6, Sun 11–4.

Brandy Rose Antique Mall. 316 E. Pioneer Avenue. (206) 845-5772. Mall specializes in Western items. Also glassware, pottery, art glass, toys, dolls, jewelry, miniatures, linens, country primitives, and Victorian items.

ROY

Red Barn Antique Mall. 34011 SR #507. Antiques, jewelry, furniture, lots of crafts, pottery, and books. (206) 458-2870.

SEATTLE

Antique Plaza. 9530 Aurora Venue North. 15,000 sq ft building. (206) 524-9626. 18th and 19th Century European furniture, antiques, collectibles, fine art and paintings. Open daily.

Pioneer Square Mall. 602 First Street. I-5, exit James Street. (206) 624-1164. Eighty-five-dealer mall, with booths of antiques and collectibles in all lines. Credit cards accepted. Restrooms, handicapped accessible, ample parking. Open daily.

222 Westlake Antique Mall. 222 Westlake N. Downtown. (206) 628-3117. Multidealer mall with 60+ dealers. Mall features a great selection of antique, estate and fine jewelry. Open daily.

Downtown Antique Market. 2218 Western Avenue. (206) 448-6307. Sixty dealers. Hours Mon–Sat 10–6, Sun 12–5.

Lyons Antique Mall. 4516 California SW. (206) 935-9774. Fifty-dealer mall. Hours Mon–Sat 10–7, Sun 12–5.

Fremont Antique Mall. 3419 Fremont Place N. 98103. (206) 548-9140. Clothing, jewelry, prints, primitives, art pottery. Mid-century modern furnishings. Credit cards accepted. Open daily 10–6.

Country Crafts Mall. Corner Baker and Railroad Streets. (208) 886-2663.

Market Street Antique Mall. 2026 NW Market Street. (206) 782-1125. Forty-five-dealer mall with general line of antiques and collectibles. Credit cards accepted. Restrooms, handi-

---

SHOPPING SMART—AVOID TAKING VERY YOUNG CHILDREN AND BABY STROLLERS TO ANTIQUE MALLS IF AT ALL POSSIBLE. THE AISLES CAN BE VERY NARROW AND THE BOOTHS CROWDED WITH EXPENSIVE MEMORABILIA. AND, WHETHER YOU ARE A PARENT OR GRANDPARENT, HAVE YOU EVER NOTICED HOW FAR A LITTLE ONE'S ARMS CAN REACH. IF YOU DON'T WANT TO HAVE TO PAY FOR AN ACCIDENTALLY BROKEN PIECE OF LIMOGES OR ANY OTHER OF THE THOUSANDS OF FRAGILE ITEMS THAT ARE ON DISPLAY IN AN ANTIQUE MALL, LEAVE THE YOUNGSTERS AND STROLLERS AT HOME.

capped accessible, ample parking. Open Mon–Sat 10–7, Sundays 12–5.

SMOHOMISH

Star Center Antique Mall. 829 Second Street. (206) 568-2131. One hundred sixty-five shops under one roof. Great variety of quality items here. Credit cards accepted. Restrooms, handicapped accessible. Open daily 10–5, Sat until 8.

SPOKANE

Collectors & Showcase Antique Mall. N5201 Market Street. (509) 482-7112. Quality booths here with fine antiques and collectibles and great showcases. Credit cards accepted. Restrooms, handicapped accessible, ample parking. Open daily.

The Antique Gallery. N620 Monroe Street. (509) 325-3864. Mall is located in a restored turn-of-the-century building. 30 dealers. Quality oriented mall with fine antiques and collectibles. Restrooms, ample parking, handicapped accessible. Open daily.

Monroe Bridge Antique Market. N604 Monroe Street. (509) 327-6398. Fifty-four dealers in a 9,000 sq ft facility. General line of antiques and collectibles. Credit cards accepted. Restrooms, handicapped accessible, ample parking. Open daily.

Schade Brewery Antique Mall. E528 Trent Street. (509) 624-0272. Twenty-four vendors. Lots of primitive country furniture, orientals and Victorian items. Credit cards accepted. Restrooms, handicapped accessible, ample parking. Open Mon–Sat 10–6.

Spokane Antique Mall. W12 Sprague Street. Downtown. (509) 747-1466.

Spokane Valley Antique Mall. 523 Pines Road. (509) 928-9648. Twenty-five individual shops here. Great selection of furniture, Victorian and country. Primitives, antiques, collectibles. Credit cards accepted. Restrooms, handicapped accessible. Ample parking. Open daily.

Vintage Rabbit Antique Mall. N2317 Monroe Street. (509) 326-1884. Antiques, collectibles, linens, pottery, furniture, children's items. Credit cards accepted. Restrooms, handicapped accessible, ample parking. Open daily.

TACOMA

Pacific Rim Antique Mall. 10228 Pacific Avenue. (206) 539-0117. Large well-stocked mall with 100+ dealers featuring a general line of antiques and collectibles. Credit cards accepted. Restrooms, food, handicapped accessible, ample parking. Open Mon–Sat 10–6, Sun 11–5.

Katy's Antique & Collectibles Mall. 602 E. 25th Street. (206) 305-0203. 3,000 sq ft facility with general line of antiques and collectibles. Open daily.

VANCOUVER

Vancouver Antique Mall. 2000 Main Street. Downtown. Antiques and collectibles. Furniture, books, advertising and paper items, jewelry, primitives. Mon–Sat 10–5. (206) 695-5574.

WEST VIRGINIA 🦢

BERKELEY SPRINGS

Berkeley Springs Antique Mall. 100 Fairfax Street. (304) 258-5678. Thirty dealers. Antiques, collectibles. No crafts. Open 10–5 daily, closed Wednesdays.

BLUEFIELD

Landmark Antique Mall. 200 Federal Street. 25801. (304) 327-9686. Large 20,000 sq ft building completely full of quality antiques and collectibles. Lot of railroad items here, depression glass, furniture, toys, primitives. Open Mon–Fri 8–4, Sat 8–5, Sun 12–5.

BRUCETON MILLS

Bruceton Antiques Mall. Route 26 North. I-68, exit 23. Over 40 dealers. Antiques and collectibles. Mon–Sat 10–5, Sun 12–5.

BUCKHANNON

Buckhannon Antique Mall. Route 20. Three miles north of town. 20+ dealer mall. Antiques and collectibles. (304) 472-9605. Tues–Sat 10–4, Sun 12–5.

BUNKER HILL

Bunker Hill Antiques Associates. I-81, Exit 5. South on Route 11 to Bunker Hill. Mall is located in a restored 19th century woolen mill. Open daily. (304) 229-0709. Two-story building with 30,000 sq ft. Ample parking. Deli restaurant. Quilts, Roseville, clocks, oak and Victorian furniture, primitives, slot machines.

CHARLESTON

Hale Street Antique & Collectibles Mall. 213 Hale Street. (304) 345-6040. Well-stocked mall with good selection of quality antiques and collectibles. Open Tues–Sun 11–5.

Mink Shoals Antique Mall. Route 119 South. I-79, exit 1. Collector items of all kinds, glassware, pottery, vintage clothing and jewelry. (304) 343-7941. Open Tues–Sat 10–5, Sun 1–5.

South Charleston Antique Mall. 4800 McCorkle Avenue. This mall might actually have it all. A wide variety of antiques and collectibles in every category. (800) 999-MALL or (304) 766-6761. Open Wed–Sun 10–6.

CLARKSBURG

West End Antiques. #97 Milford Street. Multidealer shop featuring early furniture, oak, antiques, and collectibles. No crafts. Credit cards accepted. Ample parking, restrooms. Open daily 10–5, closed Mondays.

HUNTINGTON

Adams Avenue Antique Mall. 1460 Adams Avenue. Well-stocked booths with plenty of reasonably priced antiques and collectibles. (304) 523-7231. Open Mon–Sat 10–5.

Antique Center, Inc. 610 - 14th Street, West. Antiques, collectibles, Art Deco, Victorian, country primitives, oriental. Furniture and many smalls. (304) 523-7887. Open Mon–Sat 9–5.

Collectors Store Antiques Mall. 1660 Adams Avenue. Glassware, china, pottery, silver, postcards and paper collectibles, vintage clothing and jewelry, books. (304) 429-3900. Open Mon–Sat 10:30–6, Sun 12:30–4.

ALWAYS CALL AHEAD BEFORE TRAVELING LONG DISTANCES
TO VERIFY MARKET INFORMATION.

MILTON

Somewhere in Time Antique Mall. Milton Plaza. I-64, Exit 28. Everything here to interest the newest collector or serious investor. Many quality antiques and collector items. Open daily. (304) 743-1708.

ST. MARY'S

Rusty Nails Antique Mall. 305 Second Street. 26170. (304) 684-3109. Antiques, collectibles. Quality oriented mall with many fine items. Credit cards accepted. Open Mon–Sat 10–6, Sun 12–6.

WELLSBURG

Watzman's Old Place. 709 Charles Street. (614) 282-2138 or (304) 737-0711. Antique co-op. Antiques, collectibles, gifts, furniture, decorator items, china, vintage clothing. Open Mon–Sat 10–5.

WHEELING

Antiques On The Market. 2265 Market Street. (304) 232-1665. Three-story building with a large variety of individual shops. Great selection of merchandise here. Open Mon–Sat 10–5, Sun 12–4.

Downtown Wheeling Antiques. 1120 Main Street. (304) 232-8951. Twelve-dealer mall with quality antiques, collectibles, jewelry, furniture, clocks, etc. No reproductions or crafts. Open Mon–Fri 10–5, Sat 10–6, Sun 12–4.

WILLIAMSTOWN

Williamstown Antique Mall. 439 Highland Avenue. I-77, Williamstown Exit. Variety and quality are hallmarks of this mall. Glassware, linens, china, silver, pottery, art, wicker and wood, books and paper collectibles. Open Mon–Sat 10–6, Sun 12–6.

WISCONSIN ✦

APPLETON

Memories Antique Mall. 1074 S. Van Dyke Road. Highway 41 and BB Exit. (414) 731-9699. Large 20,000 sq ft one-level facility. Clean, well-managed mall featuring 165+ dealers displaying quality line of antiques, collectibles, and a great selection of furniture. Credit cards accepted. Ample parking, restrooms, handicapped accessible. Open daily 10–6.

Fox River Antique Mall. 1074 S. Van Dyke Road. 20,000 sq ft building. 130+ dealers. New mall. Large selection of antiques and collectibles. Credit cards accepted. Restrooms, ample parking, handicapped accessible. Open daily 10–6. (414) 731-9699.

BEAVER DAM

General Store Antique Mall. Highway 33 and Business 151. (414) 887-1116. Sixty dealers with great buys in quality antiques and popular collectibles. Advertising items, country primitives, Victorian, Art Deco, oriental items, glassware, books. Open 10–5. Credit cards accepted. Restrooms, ample parking, handicapped accessible.

BELOIT

Riverfront Antiques Mall. 306 State Street. (608) 362-7368. Antiques, furniture, lamps, glassware, jewelry, primitives. Hours Mon-Sat 10–5, Sun 12–4.

Elegant Chicken Antique Mall. 412 Prospect. (608) 364-4791. Country accessories and gifts. Also, plenty of fine antiques and collector items for every taste and budget. Hours Mon–Sat 10–4.

BONDUEL

Hearthside Antique Mall. 129 N. Cecil Street. (715) 758-6200. Quality antiques, furniture, glassware, collectibles. Restroom, ample parking, handicapped accessible. Open daily 10–5.

CAMBRIDGE

Cambridge Antique Mall. 109 N. Spring Street. Two-story facility. Quality line of antiques and collectibles. No new, reproduction, or secondhand items. Ample parking. Open daily 10–5.

CLINTON

Nana's House of Antiques. 244 Allen Street. 53525. (608) 676-5535. One mile south of Highway 43. Approximately 50 dealers. Open daily, Mon–Sat 10–4, Sun 11–4.

COLUMBUS

Columbus Antique Mall & Museum. (414) 623-1992. Large 65,000 sq ft mall with 150 dealers and 300 booths. Well-stocked with excellent quality items. Museum is devoted to

Christopher Columbus and things relating to his voyages and life. Includes many Columbian Exposition items. $1 admission charge. Mall is open daily 8:30–4.

CUBA CITY

Tin Lantern Antiques Mall. 118 S. Main Street. General line of antiques and collectibles. Credit cards accepted. Ample parking, restroom, handicapped accessible. Open daily.

DELAFIELD

Delafield Antiques Center. 803 Genesee Street. I-94, Exit 285. Twenty-five miles west of Milwaukee. (414) 646-2747. Seventy-five-dealer mall. Nice selection of 18th and 19th century furniture, accessories, and art. Large reference book section. Restrooms, ample parking, handicapped accessible. Open Mon–Sat 1–6, Sundays 12–6.

EAU CLAIRE

Antique Emporium. 306 Main Street, downtown. 20 dealers. Lots of American and Victorian furniture. Glassware and plenty of small collectibles. Mon–Sat 10–5:30. (715) 832-2494.

FOUNTAIN CITY

Antique Market. 27 N. Shore Drive. 54629. (608) 687-7600. Six dealers, collectibles, secondhand and bric-a-brac. Open daily.

GERMANTOWN

Pilgrim Antique Mall. W156 N11500 Pilgrim Road. (414) 250-0260. Twenty-dealer mall in 5,000 sq ft facility. Very quality oriented mall with many fine pieces here. Great place to find unique and investment quality items. Restrooms, handicapped accessible, ample parking. Open daily.

GRAFTON

Grafton Antique Mall. 994 Ulao Road. I-43 and Highway 60. Exit 92, east one block. (414) 376-0036. Antiques, collectibles, pottery, oak, Victorian, china, hunting and fishing items, books, coins, toys. Credit cards accepted. Ample parking, restrooms, handicapped accessible. Open daily 10–5.

KEWASKUM

General Store Antique Mall. 1277 Fond du Lac Avenue. Junction Highways 45 and 28. (414) 626-2885. Seventy-five dealers. A bit of everything for both new and serious collectors. Credit cards accepted. Restrooms, handicapped accessible, ample parking. Open 10–5 daily.

LA CROSSE

Antique Center of La Crosse. 110 S. Third. Downtown. 75 booths, 3 floors. Antique furniture, china, silver, coins, vintage jewelry, lamps, linen, quilts, primitives. Credit cards accepted. Mon–Sat 9–5:30, Sun 11–4.

LAKE GENEVA

Lake Geneva Antique Mall. 829 Williams Street. (Highway 120). (414) 248-6345. 10,000 sq ft facility featuring quality antiques and collectibles. Credit cards accepted. Ample parking, restrooms, handicapped accessible. Open daily 10–5, Fridays until 8.

MADISON

Antiques Mall of Madison. 4748 Cottage Grove Road. Behind Pizza Hut. ¼ mile east of Highway 51. (608) 222-2049. Seventy-dealer mall. General line of antiques and collectibles. Restroom, ample parking, handicapped accessible. Open daily.

Mapletree Antique Mall. 1293 N. Sherman Street. (608) 241-2599. 20,000 sq ft facility with a general line of antiques and collectibles. Separate craft section. Open daily.

MILTON

Campus Antique Mall. 609 Campus Street. 18,000 sq ft facility which is the gym of the former Milton College. Antiques and collectibles of all descriptions. Credit cards accepted. Ample parking, restrooms, handicapped accessible. Mon–Sat 10–5, Sun 12–5. (608) 888-3324.

MILWAUKEE

Water Street Antiques. 318 N. Water Street. (414) 278-7008. A 100+ dealer mall in three-story building. Restrooms, handicapped accessible. Open daily.

Milwaukee Antiques Center. 341 N. Milwaukee Street. 75 dealers displaying three floors full of great antiques and collectibles. Give yourself plenty of time to poke around in this mall. (414) 276-0605.

Pastime Antiques. 7637 W. Beloit Road. Westwood Center. (414) 321-1398. 6,000 sq ft facility. Restrooms, ample parking. Open daily.

MONTELLO

Granite City Antique Mall and Flea Market. 145 Clay Street. Indoor market with approximately 50 dealers. Market has outdoor flea market on weekends. Snack bar, camping available. (608) 297-7925.

MT. HOREB

Hoff Mall Antiques. 101 E. Main Street. (608) 437-4580. Open daily.

OSHKOSH

Original's Mall of Antiques. 1475 S. Washburn. 54901. (Highway 41 West Frontage Road) at 9th Street. (414) 235-0495. Approximately 80 booths of quality antiques and collectibles. Restrooms, ample parking, handicapped accessible. Open 10–6 daily.

PHELPS

Rainy Day Antique Mall & Flea Market. Antique mall open daily May through October. Even though it operates on a relatively short schedule, this mall has many nice antiques and collector items. (715) 547-3114.

PLYMOUTH

Hub City Antique Mall. Business Highway 23. (414) 893-9719. General line of antiques and collectibles. Credit cards accepted. Ample parking, restrooms, handicapped accessible. Open Mon–Sat 9–5, Sundays 12–5.

Timekeepers Clocks & Antique Mall. #11 Stafford Street. (414) 892-TIME. Antiques, collectibles, large selection of clocks. Restrooms, ample parking, handicapped accessible. Open daily.

PORTAGE

Antiques Mall. 114 W. Cook Street. Glassware, kitchen collectibles, boudoir items, china, glassware, collector finds of all kinds. Open daily. (608) 742-1640.

REEDSBURG

Big Store Plaza Antique Malls. 195 Main Street. Highways 23/33. 53959. (608) 524-4141. Downtown. Three antique malls here with a nice restaurant. Malls total 80 dealers with quality antiques, collectibles. Lots of smalls and unusual items. A colorful, quirky, and interesting stop.

RICHLAND CENTER

Valley Antique Mall. 178 S. Central Avenue. 20 dealers. Antiques and collector items for everyone from the newest to most seasoned collector. Restroom, ample parking, handicapped accessible. Open daily. (608) 647-3793.

STURTEVANT

School Days Mall. 9500 Durand Avenue. Highway 11. Two miles east of I-94. (414) 886-1069. 12,000 sq ft facility, 50 dealers, 7 specialty shops under one roof. Hours Tues–Sat 10-8, Sun 12–5.

TOMAH

Antique Mall of Tomah. P.O. Box 721. 54660. (608) 372-7853. I-94 and Highway 21E, Exit #143. Forty dealers with quality antique furniture, primitives, collectibles, jewelry, coins. Mall welcomes dealers. Open April–January, daily 9am–5pm.

UNION GROVE

Storm Hall Antique Mall. Highway 45, Five miles west of I-94. Quality antiques and collectibles. (414) 878-1644.

WALKERS POINT

Antique Center. 1134 S. First Street. (414) 383-0655. Forty-eight-dealer mall in three-story facility. General line of antiques and collectibles. Restrooms, ample parking. Open daily 10–5. Closed Tuesdays.

WALWORTH

On The Square Antique Mall. Junction Routes 14 and 67. 55184. (414) 275-9858. Over 85 dealers. Quality antiques and collectibles. Open daily 10–5.

WATERFORD

Freddy Bears Antique Mall. 2819 Beck Drive. Highway 20W. (414) 534-BEAR. 8,000 sq ft facility with 45 dealers featuring a general line of antiques and collectibles. Credit cards accepted. Ample parking, restrooms, handicapped accessible. Open daily 9:30–5.

Heavenly Haven Antique Mall and Divine Shoppes. 318 W. Main Street. 35 dealer mall. Restroom, ample parking. Open daily 9:30–5.

WAUKESHA

A Dickens of a Place Antique Center. 521 Wisconsin Avenue. 53186. (414) 542-0702. Thirty-five dealers. Quality furniture, jewelry, collectibles, primitives, glassware, vintage clothing, and general line of antiques. Credit cards accepted. Restrooms, ample parking, handicapped accessible. Open 10–5 Mon–Sat, Sun 12–5.

WEST BEND

Half Mile Antique Fair Mall. 7003 Highway 144 North. (414) 338-6282. Nice antiques and quality collectibles. Glassware, books, collectibles, china, vintage jewelry, paper and advertising memorabilia, linens, quilts, boudoir items.

WYOMING ✤

CASPER

Tuckway's Flea Market. 4040 Sam Howell Road. (307) 234-0756. Used merchandise, collectibles, bric-a-brac of all kinds, Western items. Credit cards accepted. Restrooms, snack bar, handicapped accessible, ample parking. Open daily.

CHEYENNE

Tee Pee Flea Market. 3208 S. Greeley Highway. (307) 778-8312. Indoor market with approximately 30 permanent booths. Collectibles, small antiques, some furniture. Some new and used merchandise. Credit cards accepted. Restrooms, snack bar, handicapped accessible, ample parking. Open daily 10–7.

Bargain Barn Flea Market. 2112 Snyder Avenue. (307) 635-2844. Indoor market with approximately 25 permanent booths. Collectibles, crafts, furniture, new and used merchandise. Credit cards accepted. Restrooms, handicapped accessible, ample parking. Open Mon–Sat 10–6, Sundays 12–5.

Frontier Wholesale Flea Market. 1515 Carey Avenue. (307) 634-4004. Indoor market. Collectibles, glassware, crafts, new and used merchandise. Credit cards accepted. Restrooms, handicapped accessible, ample parking. Open daily 10–6.

Downtown Flea Market. 312 W. 17th Street. (307) 638-3751. Antiques, furniture, Western collectibles, secondhand items including great home furnishings and decorator items. Restrooms, ample parking. Open daily.

Odds 'N Ends Flea Market. 1408 Greeley Highway. (307) 635-3126. Collectibles, souvenirs, glassware, Western items, used merchandise. Home furnishings, nice selection of new and secondhand furniture. Restrooms, handicapped accessible, ample parking. Open daily.

CANADA

BRITISH COLUMBIA ☙

ABBOTSFORD
The Attic Antique Mall. 101–2485 W. Railway Street. (604) 859-1664. General line of antiques and collectibles. Restrooms, ample parking. Open daily.

FT. LANGLEY
Village Antiques & Craft Mall. 23331 Mavis Street. (604) 888-3700. One block from the fort. 45 dealers, antiques, collectibles, crafts. Coffee shop. Credit cards accepted. Restrooms, ample parking, handicapped accessible. Open Tues–Sun 10–5.

Gasoline Alley Antique Mall. 9203A Glover. (604) 888-1772. Twenty-five-dealer mall. Antiques, collectibles, bric-a-brac. Restroom, ample parking. Open daily.

VANCOUVER
Bennett's Antique Mall. #1 Alexander Street. (604) 682-2803. Antiques, collectibles, and lots of antique weapons and guns. Restrooms, ample parking. Open daily 12–5.

Shaughnessy Antique Gallery. 3025 Granville. (604) 739-8413. Two-story facility with 45 dealers with a general line of antiques and collectibles. Restrooms, ample parking. Hours Mon–Sat 10:30–6, Sun 12–5.

Ledner Harbour Antique Village. 4917 Delta Lad. (604) 940-8700. Forty dealers, collectibles, furnishings, nostalgia. Credit cards accepted. Restrooms, ample parking. Open daily 10–6.

ONTARIO ☙

ALTON

Alton Antique Affair & Crafts. Doug Wheeler. Millrun Inn. Off Highway 136 N. (416) 423-9425. Approx 30 dealers. Indoor space. Market has snack bar, tearoom, and deli. Open daily.

CEDAR SPRINGS

Ken's Antiques/Cedar Springs Sales Yard. Ken Lucio. Water St. Open 9–6. (519) 676-8185. Auction on Thursdays. Approx 30 dealers. Market has cafeteria and picnic area. Indoor and outdoor space avail. Open daily 9–6.

NIAGARA FALLS

Olde Country Antique & Flea Market. Rudy or Betty Tychynski. 4604 Erie Blvd. (416) 356-5523. Approx 20 dealers. Indoor market. General line of antiques and collectibles, lots of interesting smalls and new souvenirs. Restrooms, ample parking. Open daily 10:30–4:30. Closed Wednesdays.

ONTARIO

Newmarket Flea Market. Newmarket Plaza. (416) 745-3532. Open May–Sept. Approx 100 dealers, market has been open approx four years. Secondhand items, new and used furniture, farm items, collectibles. Restrooms, ample parking. Open daily.

ORILLIA

Second Time Around Market. 37 Mississauga Street W. Diane Dicks. (416) 325-0280. Indoor market. Collectibles, secondhand items, furniture, bric-a-brac. Restrooms, ample parking. Open daily.

OTTAWA

Ottawa By Ward Market. P. H. J. Powell. (613) 564-1521. 55 By Ward. Market Square. Approx 250 vendors. Antiques, furniture, collectibles, farm items, bric-a-brac. Restrooms, ample parking. Open daily.

SHOPPING SMART—STAY AWAY FROM ANTIQUES THAT HAVE BEEN OBVIOUSLY REPAIRED, ARE OVERLY RUSTED OR IN VERY "ROUGH" CONDITION. CONDITION DIRECTLY AFFECTS AN ITEM'S VALUE. NO MATTER HOW RARE A FIND YOU THINK YOU MIGHT HAVE STUMBLED UPON, IF YOUR DISCOVERY IS IN SHODDY SHAPE, PASS IT BY. IT WILL NOT MAGICALLY MEND ITSELF AT HOME ON YOUR SHELF. IT IS ALSO HIGHLY UNLIKELY THAT SUCH AN ITEM WILL EVER INCREASE IN VALUE OR EVER BE WORTH ANY MORE THAN YOU PAID FOR IT.

SUDBURY

69 Antique Market. 16 km South of Sudbury on Highway 69. J. Johnson, (705) 682-2186. Restrooms, ample parking. Open Thurs–Mon.

SUNDRIDGE

Sundridge Flea Market. Highway 11. Joseph Bogensberger. (705) 384-7059. Inside and outside market. Open all year. Restrooms, ample parking. Open daily.

TORONTO

Harbour Front Antique Market. 390 Queens Quay West. Suzanne Pope. (416) 869-8444. Approx 200 dealers. 60 mini shops. Market has snack bar. This is Canada's largest and finest antique market. During the summer months this is a vacation itself. Open May–Oct, Tues–Sat 11–6, Sundays 8–6.

Showcase Antique Mall. Downtown. (416) 730-6255. Large well-stocked 25,000 sq ft building with quality line of antiques and collectibles. 300+ dealers. Overall standard of booths here is very high. Many high-quality items. Restrooms, ample parking, handicapped accessible. Hours daily 10–6.

WINDSOR

Windsor Public Market. J. L. Boyer. 195 McDougal Street. (519) 255-6301. Approx 325 vendors, market is more a traditional farmer's market. Credit cards accepted. Restrooms, food available, handicapped accessible, ample parking. Open daily.

Reference Section

ASSOCIATIONS, ORGANIZATIONS, CLUBS

(NOTE: When requesting information from any of the following groups, please include a large SASE. These groups for the most part are operated by volunteer collectors and postage is very expensive.)

Abingdon Pottery Collectors Club, Elaine Westover, 210 Knox Highway, #5. Abingdon, IL 61410. (309) 462-3267.

Akro Agate Collectors Club, Roger Hardy, #10 Bailey Street, Clarksburg, WV 26301. (304) 624-4523. Group publishes a quarterly newsletter.

Aluminum Collectors Society, Dannie Woodard, P.O. Box 1347, Weatherford, TX 76086. (817) 594-4680.

American Antique Deck Collectors Club, Ray Hartz, P.O. Box 1002, Westerville, OH 43081. (614) 891-6296. Group publishes quarterly newsletter dealing with antique playing cards.

American Barb Wire Collectors Society, John Mantz, 1023 Baldwin Road, Bakersfield, CA.(805) 397-9572.

American Bell Association, Dorothy Malone, P.O. Box 19443, Indianapolis, IN 46219.

American Game Collectors Association, Joe Angiolillo, 4628 Barlow Drive, Bartlesville, OK 74006.

Antique Bottle Club, P.O. Box 571, Lake Geneva, WI 53417.

Antique Mall Owners Association, Antoinette Kopp, P.O. Box 219, Western Springs, IL 60558. (708) 246-4990.

Antique & Art Glass Salt Shaker Collector's Society, 2832 Rapidan Trail, Maitland, FL 32751.

Antique Radio Club of America, 81 Steeplechase Roade, Devon, PA 19333.

Antique Scale Collectors Association, Bob Stein, 176 W. Adams, #1706, Chicago, IL 60603. (312) 263-7500. Group publishes newsletter and holds annual convention.

Antique Stove Association, Clifford Boram, 417 N. Main Street, Monticello, IN 47960.

Antique Wireless Association, Ormiston Road, Breesport, NY 14816.

Appraisers Information Exchange, International Society of Appraisers, P.O. Box 726, Hoffman Estates, IL 60195. (708) 882-0706.

Appraisers National Association, 120 S. Bradford Avenue, Placentia, CA 92670. (714) 579-1082.

Arkansas Pottery Collectors Society, P.O. Box 7617, Little Rock, AR 72217

Association of Coffee Mill Enthusiasts, John White, 5941 Wilkerson Road, Rex, GA 30273.

Autographs of America, Tim Anderson, P.O. Box 461, Provo, UT 84603.

Big Little Book Collectors Club, Larry Lowery, P.O. Box 1242. Danville, CA 94526. (415) 837-2086.

Boyd's Art Glass Collectors Guild, P.O. Box 52, Hatbor, PA 19040.

Buttonhook Collectors Society, Box 287, White Marsh, MD 21162. Group publishes monthly newsletter.

Candy Container Collectors of America, P.O. Box 1088, Washington, PA 15301.

Carousel Shopper Resource Catalog, Box 47, Millwood, NY 10546.

Cat Collectors Club, 33161 Wendy Drive, Sterling Heights, MI 48310.

Central Florida Insulators Collectors Club, 557 Nicklaus Drive, Titusville, FL 32780.

Ceramic Arts Studio Collectors Association, P.O. Box 46, Madison, WI 53701. (608) 241-9138. Group publishes newsletter.

Chase Collectors Society, Barry Van Hook, 2149 W. Jibsail Loop, Mesa, AZ 85202. (602) 838-6971.

Coca-Cola Collectors Club, P.O. Box 49166, Atlanta, GA 30359.

The Cola Clan, Alice Fisher, 2084 Continental Drive NE, Atlanta, GA 30345.

Compact Collectors Association. Roselyn Gerson, P.O. Box S, Lynbrook, NY 11563. Group publishes newsletter.

Cookie Cutters Collectors Club, Ruth Capper, 1167 Teal Road SW, Delroy, OH. (216) 735-2839.

Dedham Pottery Collectors Society, Jim Kaufman. 248 Highland Street, Dedham, MA 02026, (508) 283-8070. Group publishes newsletter.

Depression Era Glass Society, Edith Putanko, Route 88 & Broughton Road, Bethel Park, PA 15102. (412) 831-2702.

Doorstop Collectors of America, Jeanie Bertoia, 2413 Madison Avenue, Vineland, NJ 08630. (609) 692-4092. Group publishes newsletter.

Early American Industries Association, J. Watson, P.O. Box 2128, Empire State Plaza Station, Albany, NY 12220. Information on early tools and trades.

Ephemera Society of America, P.O. Box 37, Schoharie, NY 12157.
(518) 295-7978.

Ertl Collectors Club, Mike Meyer, Highways 136 & 20,
Dyersville, IA 52040. (319) 875-2000.

Fenton Glass Collectors of America, Williamstown, WV 26187.

Figural Bottle Opener Collectors Club, Donna Kitzmiller, 117
Basin Hill Road, Duncannon, PA 17020.

Findlay Glass Collectors, P.O. Box 256, Findlay, OH 45840.
Group publishes quarterly newsletter.

Fostoria Glass Society of America, P.O. Box 826, Moundsville,
WV 26041.

Frankoma Collectors Association. Nancy Littrell, P.O. Box 32751,
Oklahoma City, OK 73123. Group publishes quarterly
newsletter and has annual convention.

Glass Knife Collectors Club, Wilber Peterson, 711 Kelly Drive,
Lebanon, TN 37087.

H. C. Fry Society, P.O. Box 41, Beaver, PA 15009. Group publishes quarterly newsletter dealing only with Fry glass.

Hatpin & Hatpin Holders Collectors Club, Lillian Baker, 15237
Chanera Avenue, Gardena, CA 90249. (213) 329-2619. Group
publishes monthly newsletter.

Haviland Collectors International, Jean Kendall. Iowa Memorial
Union, University of Iowa, Iowa City, IA 52242. (319) 335-
3513.

Heisey Collectors of America, National Heisey Glass Museum,
169 W. Church Street, Newark, OH 43055. (614) 345-2932.

Indiana Historical Radio Society, 245 N. Oakland Avenue, Indianapolis, IN 46201.

International Association of Calculator Collectors, Guy Ball,
14561 Livingston Street, Tustin, CA 92680. Group publishes
quarterly newsletter.

International Carnival Glass Association, Lee Markley, Rt. 1, Box
14, Mentone, IN 46539. (219) 353-7678.

International Rose O'Neill Club, Karen Steward, P.O. Box 668,
Branson, MO 65616.

Marble Collectors Society of America, Claire Block, P.O. Box 222,
Trumbull, CT 06611. Group publishes newsletter.

Midwest Antique Fruit Jar and Bottle Club, P.O. Box 38, Flat
Rock, IN 47234.

Morgantown Collectors of America, Jerry Gallagher, 420 First
Avenue NW, Plainview, MN 55964. Group publishes newsletter and catalog dealing only with Morgantown glass.

Mt. Washington Art Glass Society, P.O. Box 24094, Ft. Worth, TX
76124. Group publishes newsletter and holds annual convention.

Mouse Club East, P.O. Box 3195, Wakefield, MA 01880. Club
for Disney collectors.

Mystic Lights of the Aladdin Knights, J. W. Courter, Rt. 1, Simpson, IL 62985. (618) 949-3884. Association and newsletter for collectors of Aladdin lamps.

National Association of Avon Collectors, Connie Clark, 6100 Walnut, Kansas City, MO 64113.

National Association of Breweriana Advertising, John Murray, 475 Old Surrey Road, Hinsdale, IL 60521.

National Association of Milk Bottle Collectors, Thomas Gallagher, #4 Ox Bow Road, Westport, CT 06880. (203) 277-5244.

National Association of Miniature Enthusiasts, P.O. Box 2621, Anaheim, CA 92804.

National Association of Paper and Advertising Collectors, P.O. Box 500, Mt. Joy, PA 17552. (717) 653-4300.

National Association of Watch and Clock Collectors, Thomas Bartels, 514 Poplar Street, Columbia, PA 17512. (717) 684-8621.

National Autumn Leaf Collectors Club, Gwynne Harrison, P.O. Box 1, Mira Loma, CA 91752. (909) 685-5434.

National Bit, Spur and Saddle Collectors Association, P.O. Box 3098, Colorado Springs, CO 80934.

National Cambridge Collectors, P.O. Box 416, Cambridge, OH 43725.

National Depression Glass Association, Anita Wood, P.O. Box 69843, Odessa, TX 79769. (915) 337-1297.

National Early American Glass Club, P.O. Box 8489, Silver Spring, MD 20907.

National Fantasy Fan Club, P.O. Box 19212, Irvine, CA 92713. Club for Disney collectors.

National Graniteware Society, P.O. Box 10013, Cedar Rapids, IA 52410.

National Greentown Glass Association, 1807 W. Madison, Kokomo, IN 46901.

National Imperial Glass Collectors Society, P.O. Box 534, Bellarie, OH 43906. Group publishes quarterly newsletter and holds an annual convention.

National Insulator Association, 1315 Old Mill Path, Broadview Heights, OH 44147.

National Milk Glass Collectors Society, Helen Storey, 46 Almond Drive, Cocoa Townes, Hershey, PA 17033.

National Reamer Association, Larry Branstad, Rt. 3, Box 67, Frederic, WI 54837.

National Scouting Collectors Society, 806 E. Scott Street, Tuscola, IL 61953.

National Toothpick Holders Collectors Society, Joyce Ender, P.O. Box 246. Sawyer, MI 49125. Group publishes newsletter and holds annual convention.

National Valentine Collectors Association, Evalene Pulati, P.O. Box 1404, Santa Ana, CA 92702. (714) 547-1355.

New England Society of Open Salt Collectors, Mimi Waible, P.O. Box 177, Sudberry, MA.

Newspaper Collectors Society of America. Rick Brown, P.O. Box 19134, Lansing, MI. 48901. (517) 887-1255.

Nippon Collectors Club, Phil Fernkes, 112 Oak Avenue N., Owatonna, MN 55060. Group publishes newsletter and holds an annual convention.

North American Torqual Society, Jerry Kline, 604 Orchard View Drive, Maumee, OH 43537. Group publishes quarterly newsletter.

North American Trap Collectors Association, Tom Parr, P.O. Box 94, Galloway, OH 43119. Group publishes bimonthly newsletter.

Novelty Salt & Pepper Club, Irene Thornburg, 581 Joy Road, Battle Creek, MI 49017.

The Occupied Japan Club, Florence Archambault, 29 Freeborn Street, Newport, RI 02840. Group publishes bimonthly newsletter.

Open Salt Collectors, Le Anne Gommer, 56 Northview Drive, Lancaster, PA 17601.

Paperweight Collectors Association, P.O. Box 1059, Easthampton, MA 01027. (413) 527-2598.

Peanuts Collector Club, Andrea Podley, P.O. Box 94, North Hollywood, CA 91603.

Pen Collectors of America, P.O. Box 821449, Houston, TX 77282. (713) 496-2290. Group publishes quarterly newsletter.

Pen Fanciers Club, 1169 Overcash Drive, Dunedin, FL 34698. Publishes bimonthly newsletter.

Perfume & Scent Bottle Collectors, Jeane Parris, 2022 E. Charleston Blvd, Las Vegas, NV 89104. (702) 385-6059.

Phoenix & Consolidated Glass Collectors Club, Jack Wilson, P.O. Box 81974, Chicago, IL 60681. (312) 282-9553.

Pie Birds Unlimited, Lilliam Cole, 14 Harmony School Road, Flemington, NJ 08822.

Planters Peanuts Collectors Club, 804 Hickory Grade Road, Bridgeville, PA 15017. (412) 221-7599.

The Political Gallery, Thomas Slater, 1325 W. 86th Street, Indianapolis, IN 46260. (317) 257-0863. Group specializes in political memorabilia.

Postcard History Society, John McClintock, P.O. Box 1765, Manassas, VA 22110. (703) 368-2757.

Red Wing Collectors Society, Doug Podpeskar, 624 Jones Street, Eveleth, MN 55734. (218) 744-4854.

Roy Rogers-Dale Evans Collectors Association, Nancy Horsley, P.O. Box 1166, Portsmouth, OH 45662.

Salt & Pepper Novelty Shakers Club, Irene Thornburg, 581 Joy Road, Battle Creek, MI 49017. (616) 963-7953. Group publishes quarterly newsletter and holds an annual convention.

Shawnee Pottery Collectors Club, P.O. Box 713, New Smyrna Beach, FL 32170.

Shelley National China Club, LaDonna Douglass, P.O. Box 5802, Chokoloskee, FL 33925. Group publishes quarterly newsletter and holds an annual convention.

The Shot Glass Club of America, Mark Pickvet, P.O. Box 90404, Flint, MI 48509.

The Smurf Collectors Club, 24 Cabot Road, W. Massapequa, NY 11758.

Society of Inkwell Collectors, Vince McGraw, 5136 Thomas Ave. S., Minneapolis, MN 55410. (612) 922-2792.

Statue of Liberty Collectors Club, Iris November, P.O. Box 535, Chautauqua, NY 14722.

Steiff Collectors Club, Beth Savino, 7856 Hill Avenue, Holland, OH 43528. (419) 865-3899.

Table Toppers Collectors Club, 1340 W. Irving Park Road, P.O. Box 161. Chicago, IL 60613. (312) 769-3184. Group publishes bimonthly newsletter dealing with tabletop collectibles.

Tea Leaf Club International, 222 Powderhorn Drive, Houghton Lake, MI 48629.

Thermometer Collectors Club of America, Richard Porter, 6130 Rampart Drive, Carmichael, CA 95608.

Thimble Collectors International, 6411 Montego Road, Louisville, KY 40228.

Tiffin Glass Collectors Club, P.O. Box 554, Tiffin, OH 44883.

Tin Container Collectors Association, Clark Secrest, P.O. Box 4555, Denver, CO 80204.

Uhl Collectors Society, Dale Blann, #4 Appaloosa Drive, Vincennes, IN 47591. (812) 886-5895.

Vintage Fashion & Costume Jewelry Club, P.O. Box 265, Glen Oaks, NY 11004. (718) 969-2320.

Vintage Fashion Sourcebook, Kristina Harris, 904 N. 65th Street, Springfield, OR 97478.

Westmoreland Glass Society, Jim Fisher, 513 Fifth Avenue, Coralville, IA 52241. (319) 354-5011.

The Whinsey Club, Christopher Davis, 522 Woodhill, Newark, NY 14513. Group publishes quarterly newsletter.

The White Ironstone China Association, Rt. 1, Box 23, Howes Cave, NY 12092. Group publishes newsletter.

Worlds Fair Collectors Society, Michael Pender, P.O. Box 20806, Sarasota, FL 34238.

Zane Grey's West Society, Carolyn Timmerman, 708 Warwick Avenue, Ft. Wayne, IN 46825. (219) 484-2904.

NEWSPAPERS, NEWSLETTERS

Action Toys Newsletter, P.O. Box 31551, Billings, MT 59107. (406) 248-4121.

American Carnival Glass News, Dennis Runk, P.O. Box 235, Littlestown, PA 17340. (717) 359-7205.

American Ceramic Journal, P.O. Box 1495, Grand Central Station, New York, NY 10163.

American Lock Collectors Newsletter, Charles Chandler, 36076 Grennada, Livonia, MI 48154. (313) 522-0920.

American Pottery Journal, P.O. Box 14255, Parkville, MO 64152. (816) 587-9179.

American Quilter Magazine, P.O. Box 3290, Paducah, KY 42002.

American West Archives, Anderson Warren, P.O. Box 100, Cedar City, UT 84721. (801) 586-9497. Company issues 26-page catalogs six times a year covering auction offerings of early Western documents and other ephemera.

American Willow Report, Lisa Kay Henze, P.O. Box 900, Oakridge, OR 97463.

Antique & Collectible News, P.O. Box 529, Anna, IL 62906. Monthly.

Antique & Collectors Reproduction News, Mark Cherenka, P.O. Box 71174, Des Moines, IA 50325. (800) 227-5531.

Antique & Collectors Reproduction News, Lorna Bambrook, P.O. Box 71174, Des Moines, IA 50325. (515) 270-8994.

Antique Gazette, 6949 Charlotte Pike, #106, Nashville, TN 37209. Monthly.

Antique Monthly, Stephen Croft, 2100 Powers Ferry Road, Atlanta, GA 30339. (404) 955-5656.

Antique Press of Florida, 12403 N. Florida Avenue, Tampa, FL 33612.

Antique Souvenir Collector's News, Gary Leveille, P.O. Box 562, Great Barrington, MA 01230.

Antique Trader, P.O. Box 1050, Dubuque, IA 52004. Considered by many to be the nation's leading newspaper on antiques, collecting, auctions, and events. Weekly.

Antique Week, Tom Hoepf, P.O. Box 90, Knightstown, IN 46148. (800) 876-5133. Excellent newspaper for antiques, collecting, auctions, and events. Company publishes two separate editions Eastern and Central. Weekly.

Antiques and Collecting, 1006 S. Michigan Avenue, Chicago, IL 60605. Monthly.

Art Deco Reflections, Barry Van Hook, 2149 W. Jibsail Loop, Mesa, AZ 85202. (602) 838-6971.

Arts & Crafts Quarterly, P.O. Box 3592, Trenton, NJ 08629. (800) 541-5787.

Arts & Crafts Quarterly, #9 S. Main Street, Lambertville, NJ 08530. (609) 397-9374.

Ashtray Journal, Chuck Thompson, P.O. Box 11652, Houston, TX 77293. Bimonthly newsletter devoted to ashtrays.

Auction Block Newspaper, P.O. Box 337, Iola, WI 54945. (715) 445-5000.

Avon Times, Dwight Young, P.O. Box 273, Effort, PA 18330.

Barbie Bazaar Newsletter, 5617 Sixth Avenue, Kenosha, WI 53140. (414) 658-1004.

The Baum Bugle, Fred Meyer, 220 N. 11th Street, Escanaba, MI 49829. Newsletter for Wizard of Oz collectors.

Beam Around the World, Shirley Sumbles, 5013 Chase Avenue, Downers Grove, Il 60515. (708) 963-8980. Newsletter for Jim Beam collectors.

Beer Can Collectors News, Don Hicks, 747 Merus Court, Fenton, MO 63026. (314) 343-6486.

Beer Stein Journal, Gary Kirsner, P.O. Box 8807, Coral Springs, FL 33075. (305) 344-9856.

Bulletin, 14 Chestnut Road, Westford, MA 01886. (617) 692-8392. Magazine for doll collectors.

California Pottery Newsletter, Verlangieri Gallery, 816 Main Street, W. Cambria, CA 93428. (800) 292-2153.

The Cane Collectors Chronicle, Linda Beeman, #15 Second Street NE, Washington, DC 20002.

Chicagoland Antique Amusements Slot Machine & Jukebox Gazette, Ken Durham, P.O. Box 2426, Rockville, MD 20852. Group also publishes the *Coin-Op Newsletter*.

Collecting Tips Newsletter, Meredith Williams, P.O. Box 633, Joplin, MO 64802. (417) 781-3855. Magazine for fast food collectibles.

The Carousel News & Trader, 87 Parke Avenue W. #206. Mansfield, OH 44902. Newsletter for carousel collectors. Monthly.

The Cookie Jar Collectors News, Louise Daking, 595 Cross River Road. Katonah, NY 10563. (914) 232-0383.

The Courier, 2503 Delaware Avenue, Buffalo, NY 14216. (716) 873-2594. Newsletter for Civil War collectors. Bimonthly.

The Cutting Edge, Adrienne Escoe, P.O. Box 342, Los Alamitos, CA 90720. Newsletter for glass knife collectors. Quarterly.

Currier & Ives Quarterly Newsletter, Patti Street, P.O. Box 504, Riverton, KS 66770. (316) 848-3529.

Depression Glass Daze, Teri Steel, P.O. Box 57, Otisville, MI 48463. Newsletter for glass, china, and pottery.

Dept. 56 Collectors, Roger Bain, 1625 Myott Avenue, Rockford, IL 61103.

Eggcup Collector's Corner, Joan George, #67 Stevens Avenue, Old Bridge, NJ 08857.

Elegance of Old Ivory, P.O. Box 1004, Wilsonville, OR 97070.

Farm Antique News, Gary Van Hoozer, 812 N. Third Street, Tarkio, MO 64491. (816) 736-4528.

The Fenton Flyer, P.O. Box 4008, Marietta, OH 45750. Newsletter for collectors of Fenton glassware.

Fiesta Collector's Quarterly, China Specialties Inc., 19238 Dorchester Circle, Strongville, OH 44136.

Flea Marketeer, P.O. Box 686, Southfield, MI 48037. (313) 351-9910.

Golf Club Collectors Newsletter, Dick Moore, 640 E. Liberty Street. Girard, OH 44420.

Gonder Pottery Collectors Newsletter, John McCormick, P.O. Box 3174, Shawnee, KS 66226.

Gone With the Wind Collectors Newsletter, 8105 Woodview Road, Ellicott City, MD 21043. (301) 465-4632.

Hall China Collectors Newsletter, P.O. Box 36-488, Cleveland, OH 44136.

The Heisey News, 169 W. Church Street, Newark, OH 43055. (612) 345-2932.

Hobby News, P.O. Box 258, Ozone Park, NY 11416.

Hopalong Cassidy Newsletter, P.O. Box 1361, Boyes Hot Springs, CA 95416.

The Illustrator Collectors News, Dennis Jackson, P.O. Box 1958, Sequim, WA 98382.

Inside Antiques, Robert Reed, P.O. Box 204, Knightstown, IN 46148. Newspaper dealing with antiques and collectibles. Monthly.

Kitchen Antiques & Collectibles Newsletter, Dana DeMore, 4645 Laurel Ridge Drive, Harrisburg, PA 17110. (717) 545-7320.

The Lady's Gallery, (800) 622-5676, Fashion, decorative arts, and collectibles magazine.

The Lighter Side, Judith Sanders, 136 Circle Drive, Quitman, TX 75783. (903) 763-2795. Bimonthly newsletter dealing with cigarette lighters.

Madame Alexander Newsletter, Earl Meisinger, 11 S. 767 Book Road, Naperville, IL 60564.

Maine Antique Digest, Sam Pennington, P.O. Box 645, Waldoboro, ME 04572. (207) 832-7534.

Majolica Newsletter, Michael Strawser, 1275 First Ave, #103, New York, NY 10021.

Marble Mania, Stanley Block, P.O. Box 222, Trumbull, CT 06611. (203) 261-3223.

Master Collector, Fun Publications, 12513 Birchfalls Drive, Raleigh, NC 27614. (800) 772-6673. Excellent newspaper for doll, bear, and toy collectors. Weekly.

McDonald's Collector Newsletter, Tenna Greenberg, 5400 Waterbury Road, Des Moines, IA 50312. (515) 279-0741.

The Melting Pot, P.O. Box 256, Findlay, OH 45840. Newsletter for Findlay Glass collectors. Quarterly.

Mid-Atlantic Antiques Magazine, Lydia Tucker, P.O. Box 908, Henderson, NC 27536. (919) 492-4001. East Coast magazine covering antiques, shops, collecting, auctions, and events. Monthly.

Model and Toy Collector Magazine, 137 Casterton Ave., Akron, OH 44303. (216) 836-0668.

Movie Advertising Collector Magazine, George Reed, P.O. Box 28587, Philadelphia, PA 19149.

News and Views, Anita Wood, P.O. Box 69843, Odessa, TX 79769. (915) 337-1297. Newsletter for collectors of depression glass.

Olympic Collectors Newsletter, Bill Nelson, P.O. Box 41630, Tucson, AZ 85717.

Our McCoy Matters, Kathy Lynch, McCoy Publications, P.O. Box 14255, Parkville, MO 64152. (816) 587-9179.

Paper Pile, Ada Fitzimmons, P.O. Box 337, San Anselmo, CA 94979. (619) 322-3525. Quarterly magazine dealing with paper collectors.

Pepsi-Cola Collectors Newsletter, Bob Stoddard, P.O. Box 1275, Covina, CA 91722. (714) 593-8750.

Pottery Lovers Newsletter, Pat Sallaz, 4969 Hudson Drive, Stow, OH 44224.

Powder Puff, P.O. Box 40, Lynbrook, NY 11563. (516) 593-8746. Newsletter dealing with compact collectors.

Precious Collectibles, Rosie Wells, Rt. 1, Canton, IL 61520. Magazine for Precious Moments collectors.

Purinton Pastimes, P.O. Box 9394, Arlington, VA 22219. Newsletter devoted to Purinton pottery.

Quint News, P.O. Box 2527, Woburn, MA 01888. (617) 933-2219. Newsletter for Dionne Quint collectors.

Red Wing Collectors Newsletter, David Newkirk, Rt. 3, Box 146, Monticello, MN 55362.

Roseville's of the Past Newsletter, Jack Bomm, P.O. Box 681117, Orlando, FL 32868.

Royal Doulton International Collectors Club Newsletter, Royal Doulton, P.O. Box 1815, Somerset, NJ 08873. (908) 356-7929.

The Shirley Temple Collectors News, Rita Dubas, 8811 Colonial Road, Brooklyn, NY 11209.

Singing Wires, George Howard, 19 N. Cherry Drive, Oswego, IL 60543. (708) 554-8154.

Spoonville News, Margaret Alves, 84 Oak Avenue, Shelton, CT 06484. (203) 924-4768. Newsletter devoted to spoon collecting.

Stanley Tool Collector News, 208 Front Street, Marietta, OH 45750.

Tobacco Jar Newsletter, Charlotte Tarses, 3011 Falstaff Road, #307. Baltimore, MD 21209.

Toy Gun Collectors of America Newsletter, Jim Buskirk, 312 Starling Way. Anaheim, CA 92807. (714) 998-9615.

Toys and Prices Magazine, 700 E. State Street, Iola, WI 54990. (715) 445-2214. Monthly.

The Trade Card Journal, Kit Barry, 109 Main Street, Brattleboro, VT 05301. (802) 254-3634.

Trainmaster Newsletter, P.O. Box 1499, Gainesville, FL 32602. (904) 377-7439.

Vaseline Glass Newsletter, Jerry Chambers, 2163 Pomona Place, Fairfield, CA 94533. (707) 425-6166.

Vernon Views, P.O. Box 945, Scottsdale, AZ 85252. Newsletter devoted to Vernon Kilns collectors.

Vintage Clothing Newsletter, Terry McCormick, P.O. Box 1422, Corvallis, OR 97339. (503) 752-7456.

Vintage Fashion and Costume Jewelry Newsletter, David Baron. P.O. Box 265, Glen Oaks, NY 11004. (718) 969-2320.

Walking Stick News, Cecil Curtis, 4051 E. Olive Road, Pensacola, FL 32514.

Watt's News, P.O. Box 184, Galesburg, IL 61402. Newsletter for Watt collectors published by the Watt Collectors Association.

The Willow Word, Mary Berndt, P.O. Box 13382, Arlington, TX 76094.

REFERENCE BOOKS

I highly recommend the following reference books. They are available at most bookstores. The prices listed are the suggested retail price. A good reference book is a necessity for serious collecting. It not only establishes a ball park value for items, but it will also keep you from overpaying on items and help you in making sure that you are buying authentic items and not reproductions. Whatever your specialty and no matter the level of your expertise, Buy the book, it's worth the money!

The following list is only a sampling of the many fine books on the market today.

American Militaria Sourcebook. Terry Hannon, P.O. Box 245, Lyon Station, PA 19536. (800) 446-0909.

American Premium Guide to Pocket Knives and Razors. Jim Sargent. $22.95.

An Illustrated Guide to Cookie Jars. Ermagene Westfall. $9.95.

An Illustrated Value Guide to Cookie Jars. Ermagene Westfall. $19.95.

Antique Tools. Our American Heritage. Kathryn McNerney. $9.95.

Avon Bottle Collectibles Encyclopedia. Bud Hastin. $19.95.

Book of Country. Don and Carol Raycraft. $19.95.

Black Memorabilia Catalog, Judy Posner, Rt. 1, Box 273, Effort, PA 18330. (717) 629-6583.

Bottle Pricing Guide. Hugh Cleveland. $7.95.

Cambridge Glass, 1930–1934. $14.95

Cambridge Glass, 1949–1953. $14.95.

Character Collectibles Catalog. Judy Posner, Rt. 1, Box 273, Effort, PA 18330. (717) 629-6583.

Collectible Glassware of the 40's, 50's, 60's. Gene Florence. $19.95.

Collecting Toys. A Collector's Identification & Value Guide. Richard O'Brien. $29.95.

Collector's Encyclopedia of American Art Glass. John Shuman. $29.95.

Collector's Encyclopedia of American Furniture. Robert and Harriet Swedberg. 2 editions, each $24.95.

Collector's Encyclopedia of Cookie Jars. Fred and Joyce Roerig. $24.95.

Collector's Encyclopedia of Depression Glass. Gene Florence. $19.95

Collector's Encyclopedia of Disneyana. David Longest and Michael Stern. $24.95.

Collector's Encyclopedia of Fiesta. Sharon and Bob Huxford. $19.95.

Collector's Encyclopedia of Heisey Glass. Neila Bredehoft. $24.95.

Collector's Encyclopedia of Occupied Japan. Gene Florence.

Collector's Encyclopedia of RS Prussia. Mary Frank Gaston. $24.95.

Collector's Encyclopedia of Roseville Pottery. Sharon and Bob Huxford. 2 editions, $19.95 each and $9.95 for the price guide.

Collector's Guide of Shawnee Pottery. Don and Carol Raycraft. $11.95.

Collector's Guide to Hull Pottery. Barbara Burke. $16.95.

Fostoria. Ann Kerr. $24.95.

Furniture of the Depression Era. Robert and Harriett Swedberg. $19.95.

Imperial Glass Identification & Value Guide. $14.95.

Kitchen Glassware of the Depression Years. Gene Florence. $19.95.

Keen Kutter Collectibles. Jerry and Elaine Heuring. $14.95.

Kovel's Antiques & Collectibles Price List. Ralph and Terry Kovel. $13.

North American Indian Artifacts. Lar Hothem. $22.95

Salt & Pepper Shakers. Helene Guarnaccia. Four volumes priced from $9.95 to $18.95.

Schroeder's Antiques Price Guide. $12.95.

Standard Carnival Glass Price Guide. Bill Edwards. $9.95.

Standard Knife Collectors Guide. Roy Ritchie & Ron Stewart. $12.95.

100 Years of Collectible Jewelry. Lillian Baker. $9.95.

ANTIQUE MALL READER'S POLL

VOTE HERE FOR YOUR FAVORITE MALL!!!

Take part in our reader's poll and cast your vote today. See how your favorite mall stacks up against all the other malls around the country. The results will be published in the next edition of the National Mall Directory.

NAME OF MALL:_____

LOCATION:_____

STREET:_____

CITY:_____STATE_____
ZIP_____

TELEPHONE:(   )_____

COMMENTS:_____
_____
_____
_____
_____
_____
_____

Please mail your completed form to:

> Jim Goodridge
> National Mall Directory
> Alliance Publishing
> P.O. Box 080377
> Brooklyn, NY 11208